GRAPHIC DESIGN AS COMMUNICATION

What is the point of graphic design? Is it advertising or is it art? What purpose does it serve in our society and culture? In this companion volume to *Fashion as Communication*, Malcolm Barnard explores how meaning and identity are at the core of every graphic design project and argues that the role and function of graphic design is, and always has been, communication.

Examining a range of theoretical approaches, including those of Shannon and Weaver, Lasswell, Barthes, Derrida and Foucault, the author argues that graphic design should be approached logically and treated as a language rather than as an art form. He analyses how meaning is constructed and communicated, and explains how graphic design relates to this construction and reproduction of meaning.

Taking examples from advertising, magazines, illustration, website design, comics, greetings cards and packaging, *Graphic Design as Communication* looks at the ways in which graphic design contributes to the formation of social and cultural identities, discussing the ways in which racial/ethnic, age and gender groups are represented in graphic design, as well as how images and texts communicate with different cultural groups.

Finally, the author explores how graphic design relates to both European and American modernism, and its relevance to postmodernism and globalisation in the twenty-first century and asks why, when graphic design is so much an integral part of our society and culture, it is not better studied, acknowledged and understood.

Malcolm Barnard is Senior Lecturer in the history and theory of art and design at the University of Derby. His previous publications include *Fashion as Communication* (second edition, 2002), *Art, Design and Visual Culture* (1998) and *Approaches to Understanding Visual Culture* (2001).

GRAPHIC DESIGN AS COMMUNICATION

Malcolm Barnard

LEARNING RESOURCES
CENTRE

Havering College
of Further and Higher Education

Routledge
Taylor & Francis Group

LONDON AND NEW YORK

First published 2005
by Routledge
2 Park Square, Milton Park, Abingdon, Oxon OX14 4RN

Simultaneously published in the USA and Canada
by Routledge
270 Madison Ave, New York, NY 10016

Routledge is an imprint of the Taylor & Francis Group

© 2005 Malcolm Barnard

Typeset in Times by Book Now Ltd
Printed and bound in Great Britain by
MPG Books, Bodmin, Cornwall

British Library Cataloguing in Publication Data
A catalogue record for this book is available from the British Library

Library of Congress Cataloging in Publication Data
Barnard, Malcolm, 1958–
Graphic design as communication/Malcolm Barnard.
p. cm.
Includes bibliographical references.
1. Graphic arts. 2. Communication in art. 3. Symbolism in art. I. Title.
NC997.B28 2005
741.6–dc22   2004014488

ISBN 0–415–27812–0 (hbk)
ISBN 0–415–27813–9 (pbk)

TO MY STUDENTS

AUT DISCE

AUT DISCEDE

CONTENTS

CONTENTS

ILLUSTRATIONS

ACKNOWLEDGEMENTS

I'd like to thank Rebecca Barden, Mark Durden, Helen Faulkner, Rob Harland, Gus Hunnybun, Matt Jones, Rob Kettell, Helen Neil, Zora Payne, Richard Tyler, Josie Walter and Julia Welbourne, for variously making/ helping me teach this stuff, recommending reading or examples, providing illustrations, rubbishing my arguments and other welcome advice. Heather Watkins and the staff in the Learning Resource Centre at the University of Derby helped with Inter-Library Loans and Inter-Site Favours.

Thanks are due to all of the copyright-holders who granted permission for the illustrations. Thanks to Calum Laird, Parker's Seeds, The Pistachio Information Service and D.C. Thomson for permission to use material from *The People's Friend* and *My Weekly*. And to the Research Group in the School of Arts, Design and Technology at the University of Derby for supporting a semester out of teaching. Every effort has been made to trace all the copyright-holders, but if any have been inadvertently overlooked, the publishers will be pleased to make the necessary arrangements at the first opportunity.

1

INTRODUCTION

INTRODUCTION

Most people see more examples of graphic design before they get to work than they see examples of art in a year. Before they are even fully awake, most people will see the numbers and letters on the faces of alarm clocks, the colours, shapes and lettering on tubes of toothpaste, the letters and symbols on taps and showers, the signs for 'On' and 'Off' on the kettle, the packaging of their tea or coffee, the station idents on morning television and the print, photography and layout of the newspaper. This is before they climb into cars (with front and rear badges and logos, and a dashboard full of tiny pictures, symbols and numbers) or onto buses and trains (encrusted with corporate identities, advertising and more badges and corporate logos), and make it along the road (adorned with advertising, bus-stops, shop-fronts and other signs giving warnings, instructions, information and directions), to work (where yet more graphic design informs them of the location of 'Reception', lavatory, lift and, in some cases, library). Graphic design is everywhere. Yet it is often taken for granted, passing unnoticed and unremarked as it blends in with the visual culture of everyday life.

Graphic design is even unnoticed by those unacknowledged legislators of the lexical world, the compilers of dictionaries. It may come as something of a surprise to learn that 'graphic design' and 'graphic designer' are included in neither *Chambers English Dictionary* (1988) nor *The Shorter Oxford English Dictionary* (1990 imprint). Writing in 1993, Alina Wheeler (1997: 84–5) noted that no American dictionary included these phrases either. Moreover, assuming that anyone who has got this far already has an inkling of what graphic design is (why pick up the book otherwise?), the fact that entire cultures have a blind spot to something that is so obvious, that literally stares people in the face every time they turn on a tap, glance at a newspaper, open a pack of gum or click on a website, will be as inexplicable as it is surprising. As Wheeler points out, these dictionaries pride themselves on being up to date: they encourage members of the public to inform them of new words and they employ teams of specialist experts who are constantly alert to the spoken and written appearance of novel words. How did they miss graphic design/er? There are even quite respectable universities with departments of graphic design, who churn out thousands of eminently employable graphic designers every year. How is it that the words denoting them and the work they produce are not included in dictionaries?

One explanation may begin with the idea that graphic design passes unnoticed. Newspapers, gum-wrappers and websites are read for their content, not for their layout, choice of typeface or use of colour. Most people don't even know they are reading the letters or words on their bathroom taps; they study the newspaper headline for the politics or the sports results and they pick up the gum with the blue wrapper and white writing. What most people do not do is admire the sans serif in the bathroom, nor do they marvel at the clarity of Helvetica on the page or appreciate the way the nutritional information has been incorporated into the overall design of the wrapper. The graphic work is invisible in that sense and the hitherto insupportable claim of lazy and irresponsible designers everywhere, that they are merely providing a vehicle with which to communicate someone else's message, suddenly finds a prop. If most graphic design passes most people by most of the time, then it is no wonder that the language of most people, as it is reported by dictionaries, does not include the words 'graphic design'.

However, maybe it is not so clear that all graphic design passes unnoticed. It may be argued that some graphic design attracts a great deal of notice, and that its power is held to be all but irresistible. In 2001, for example, the British television company Channel 4 got into serious trouble with the Advertising Standards Authority (ASA) over a poster it had produced to advertise one of its programmes (see Figure 1.1). The programme concerned the sport known as 'base-jumping' (jumping, with a parachute, from tall buildings) and the poster depicts a person standing at the edge of a roof on a tall building. The text of the poster reads 'Go on. Jump.' Among the complaints was one from the Samaritans, who said that 'the force of the caption and image could have led to copycat action' (Wells 2001). In its judgement, the ASA agreed with the Samaritans, saying that 'the prominence

Figure 1.1 Poster, 'Go on. Jump.', Chanel 4 (2001). Courtesy of Channel 4

of the text: "Go on. Jump", with the image of a person standing on the edge of a high-rise building could have encouraged members of the public to commit suicide' (Wells 2001). A poster, a piece of graphic design containing a single image and three words of text, is deemed by the ASA to be powerful enough to encourage members of the public to kill themselves.

One problem here is that the example is a piece of advertising and is presented and understood as such. Most people are familiar with advertising; they know it when they see it and they are more or less happy to be entertained, offended and persuaded by it. As William Dwiggins – whom Margolin credits with coining the phrase 'graphic design' (Margolin 1994: 236) – pointed out in 1922, 'advertising design is the only form of graphic design that gets home to everybody' (quoted in Jobling and Crowley 1996: 6). The word 'advertising' is, consequently, defined in every dictionary. Now, while advertising is one of the functions performed by graphic design, it is not the only function. There are other things that graphics does. There is more to graphic design than advertising. Despite the references to text and image, neither the Samaritans nor the ASA engage with the poster as a poster, as a piece of graphic design. No mention is made of the typeface that is used, why it is used or of the point size it is used in. No mention is made of the way in which the image is constructed, or cropped, its style or even whether it is in colour or black-and-white. No mention is made of the style or function of the Channel 4 logo which is included in the poster. And no mention is made of the layout, of how the text is positioned with relation to the image. These features of the advert, which are common if not peculiar to graphic design, pass apparently unnoticed, as do those of the newspaper and gum-wrapper mentioned earlier.

Wheeler (1997) suggests that another explanation for the failure of English dictionaries to define graphic design/er may be cultural. Japanese dictionaries, she says, are perfectly happy and able to define 'graphic designer' as the term is 'in the mainstream of Japanese life'. That Japanese culture assigns much greater importance to graphic design than the western cultures mentioned so far may be seen in Taiga Uranaka's (2001) article in *Japan Times Online*. Uranaka goes into immense detail about the problems associated with designing pictograms for the 2002 World Cup, explaining the communication problems that arise if the picures are too abstract, or too stylised, or too iconic (http://www.japantimes.co.jp/cgi-bin/getarticle. pl5?sw20010924a1.htm). Wheeler seems to be correct to suggest that a more sophisticated appreciation of graphic design is found in Japanese culture and that the term is therefore deemed worthy of inclusion and definition in dictionaries. However, since the early 1990s there have been signs that the cultural profile of graphic design in western cultures is beginning to be recognised. This may be partly on the back of a growing interest in the image generally which, as the blurbs on the backs of such books as Aumont's (1997) *The Image* and Mitchell's (1994) *Picture Theory* testify, has been seen to signify that a 'pictorial turn' has taken place in the humanities since the early 1980s. There is now a distinct market for critical texts which analyse and explain the workings of what is called graphic design, as well as for more impressionistic, anecdotal or journalistic texts. The former is represented by such texts as Kress and van Leeuwen's (1996) *Reading Images: The Grammar of Visual Design* and Jobling and Crowley's (1996) *Graphic Design: Reproduction and Representation since 1800* which bring sophisticated semiological, political and social concepts to bear on graphic design. And the latter is epitomised by the *Looking Closer* series of books, each of which contains a plethora of essays, from a variety of sources, including practising graphic designers, teachers, historians and design journalists (Bierut et al. 1994, 1997, 1999, 2002).

Another component or symptom of this growing interest in graphic design is to be found in the increasing numbers of books and exhibitions that are either by or about prominent designers. Lewis Blackwell's (1995) *The End of Print: The Graphic Design of David Carson* and Carson's (2004) *Trek*, Jon Wozencroft's (1988, 1994) *The Graphic Language of Neville Brody* and the work of such publishers as Laurence King, Booth Clibborn Editions, Allworth Press and Gingko Press have done much to bring graphic design to the attention of the general public. This growing interest in graphic designers may be a belated response to the so-called 'designer decade' of the 1980s, in which fashion designers, product designers and furniture designers (along with architects) were lionised and championed in the popular press, but it is no less welcome for that. However, while the cultural profile of graphic design is slowly becoming more noticeable, and the academic study of it is slowly becoming more sophisticated, the dictionaries are still slow to adapt. The *New Shorter Oxford English Dictionary* (1993) defines 'graphic' as a 'product' of the graphic arts or graphic design, which is a start, at least. Unfortunately, it then goes on to define graphic design in terms of 'decoration' or 'pictures accompanying text', which is not a definition that many practitioners or students of graphic design would either recognise or welcome.

Interest in the nature, role and function of graphic design is increasing on both sides of the Atlantic. The central ideas of Naomi Klein's (2000) *No Logo*, brands and branding, are understood in terms of the 'image' and meaning of those brands (Klein 2000: 4) and in relation to graphic design and advertising. Branding is also understood as a level or type of meaning and as a form of communication. Brands are said to be the 'core meaning' of corporations and those 'meaning brokers' who are in charge of creating such brands are described as 'meaning seeking' (Klein 2000: 21, 36). Meaning, identity and communication are thus at the core of every graphic design project and there is much interest in how they work. This book not only is a response to the market for critical texts dealing with graphic design, but also intends to contribute to the development of graphic design as a subject that is worthy of serious critical and analytical attention. Drawing from the full spectrum of graphic production, it seeks to provide an introduction to graphic design as a form of communication. And it seeks to contribute to these apparently urgent debates on the present role and function of graphics by arguing that the role and function of graphics is, as it always was, communication.

WHO IS THIS BOOK FOR?

This book has in mind students of graphic design, communication arts, communication design, illustration and visual communication. It also has in mind students of photography, communication studies, media studies and cultural studies. And, given the ways in which art and design tend to run into each other, in the realms of print-making and advertising, for example, it does not ignore students of art (see Chapter 8, on Graphic Design and Art). It is written for anyone who encounters or works with mass-produced communication media and who wishes, or is obliged, to explain and analyse such design. Most of the book will be of interest to degree and pre-degree students of all the above disciplines. Some of it will also be of interest to graduate-level students. However, given that there is almost nobody who does not encounter mass-produced communicative design (few people will never see a newspaper, a piece of packaging or a logo on a piece of clothing, after all), there is a case for arguing that the book will be, or even should be, of interest to everyone. Of course, there is also a case for arguing that, while everyone may have experience of such graphics, not everyone will wish, or be obliged, to understand, analyse or explain it.

This latter argument, however, begs the question. It presupposes that people do not understand, analyse and explain their experience of graphics all the time, whether they choose to or not and whether they are obliged to or not. Nobody selects the first birthday card they see to send to their friend or their mother, for example. Everybody selects one that they think is appropriate. To that extent, they have interpreted and understood the meaning and decided that it does or does not communicate the 'right' message (see the section on Gender in Chapter 5). It is more difficult to argue that, in so far as someone understands a piece of graphic production (a logo, a wrapper, a newspaper layout), they have already analysed and explained it. But the decision or judgement that is involved in the selection of the 'right' card for one's friend or mother indicates that some form of analysis has taken place, even if it is unconscious. People may find themselves in the position of Molière's bourgeois gentleman, also occupied by my newsagent who, having sold newspapers, magazines, paperbacks, greetings cards, packs of cigarettes, bottles of drinks and stationery for twenty years, was astonished to learn that he had had a shop full of graphic design without knowing it. They may find that they have more experience

5

and understanding of graphic design than they knew, even if that experience and understanding is unexamined.

WHAT IS THIS BOOK ABOUT?

This book is proposed as a contribution to the explanation and critical analysis of graphic design. The definition of graphic design used here is intended to be very broad and inclusive: graphic design is considered as communication. Expressed in terms of functions, or the tasks that graphics performs, the definition covers magical, illustrative, persuasive and informative graphics. (These functions, or tasks, are themselves explained in detail in Chapter 2.) Expressed in terms of what might be called graphic disciplines, or specialisms, the definition includes illustration, typography, photography, layout, packaging design, book design, newspaper and magazine design, corporate design and website design. Examples of all of these will be found throughout the book.

A few words about 'explanation' and 'critical analysis' may also help to give an idea of what this book is about. Explanation might be thought of as providing answers to the question 'Why does this piece of graphic design look the way it does?' Explanation here looks for the reasons why a layout, a newspaper design or a birthday card is as it is. Why does this text run illegibly up the side of the page? Why does my birthday card have Purple Ronnie on it? Why is my newspaper arranged in six orderly, regimented columns? Explanations may be sought in the function or task the piece of design is intended to perform, or in the people it is communicating with, for example. This text runs illegibly up the side of the page because it is in an achingly trendy surfing magazine, communicating with a subculture of achingly trendy young people and intended to construct and reinforce a sense of belonging. My newspaper contains orderly columns because it is intended to communicate clearly in five-point type and needs to accommodate rectangular photographs in the page.

Similarly, critical analysis seeks to account for what makes up a typographic design, a book cover or a flyer for your local 'Nite-Spot' and for what makes that design, cover or flyer possible. What are the elements of this flyer, and what has made it possible? The flyer may be analysed into its elements (the choice of type, image, layout, paper and so on), and what makes it up may be accounted for. How it is made possible could be explained in terms of available print or reproductive technologies, the market or audience it is aimed at, the existence of social and cultural institutions such as leisure, clubbing, the music industry and so on. Were there no cheap, fast presses or photocopiers, for example, the flyer might not exist at all: if nightly entertainment were prohibited, or if there were no sub-cultural groups interested in sex, drugs and loud music, then, similarly, the flyer would probably not have been produced.

So, this is not a 'How to Do It' book: it will not explain how to do website design and you will not find any intentional advice on how to produce better advertisements or typestyles, for example. Nor is it a 'Book of Crits': 'critical' does not mean fault-finding or judgemental here and you will find neither detritus nor compliment heaped upon the heads of those responsible for the Lycos homepage or the opening titles of *Friends*, for example. It is about what meaning is, how meaning is constructed and communicated and how graphic design relates to the construction and reproduction of meaning.

CHAPTER OUTLINES

Chapter 2 introduces graphic design and communication. Both are defined and explained. The various functions of graphic design are enumerated and untangled. And two schools of thought as to what sort of thing communication is are outlined. The first, communication theory, is shown to be inadequate to explain either graphic design, or graphic design as communication. The second, semiology, is proposed as a more useful way of conceiving what graphic design is and how it goes about communicating.

Chapter 3 develops these introductory explanations. Having said in chapter two that communication is about constructing and reproducing meaning, chapter three explains two different types or levels of meaning. In addition to showing how images are meaningful, it also outlines how layouts, the arrangements of image and text on a page, are significant. The role of words in graphic design is explained, as are some of the problems concerning the relation of words and images. Rhetoric, the art of persuasive image-making, is introduced by looking at three central figures and showing how graphic design can use them.

Chapter 4 takes issue with the contexts in which graphic design is found. No graphic design has ever been produced outside of a society, a culture or an economy and this chapter explains the way in which graphic production relates to society, culture and economy. It also charts the jobs that graphic design does in these contexts and argues basically that, were it not for graphic design, there would be no societies, cultures and economies, at least in the forms with which we are familiar with them. So, the construction of social and cultural groups (such as ethnic groups and gender groups) and the relation to economics (via consumption) are explained here.

In Chapter 5, what are commonly referred to as the markets, or the audiences, with which graphic design communicates are introduced. The problems involved in using terms such as 'target markets' will be explained before investigating the ways in which racial/ethnic groups, age groups and gender groups are represented in graphic design. Advertisements, magazines and illustration are among the examples of graphic design that will be used here to show how images and texts communicate with different cultural groups.

The theme of communication is approached from a more historical perspective in Chapters 6 and 7. Chapter 6 will consider modernism and graphic design. It will explain what is the difference between modernity and modernism and show what it is that makes modern graphic design modern. A selection of modernist highlights (the Bauhaus, Swiss design and American corporate design) will be used to illustrate how modernism manifested itself in graphics and how European modernist graphics differed from American modernist graphics.

Postmodernism and graphic communication is the topic of Chapter 7. The central ideas of postmodernism will be explained and the ways in which some of the graphic design since the mid-1970s or so is postmodern will be illustrated. Globalisation, which some commentators say is a key feature of postmodernity, will also be dealt with in this chapter. First the idea of globalisation itself will be explained and then the ways in which the idea has affected graphic design will be investigated.

Chapter 8 considers a problem that many artists and graphic designers seem unable to leave alone, whether graphic design is art, or not. This chapter will consider six arguments which appear to show that graphic design is different from art, but which are, in fact, invalid. These six arguments concern things like expression, problem-solving, creativity, the cultural significance of art and design and the nature of the activities that artists and designers get up to. The chapter will then present one argument which, it is claimed, really does show that graphic design is different from art.

2

GRAPHIC DESIGN AND COMMUNICATION

INTRODUCTION

This chapter will present different definitions of graphic design, drawing ideas from practitioners and theorists in the history and theory of graphic design. It will describe the functions of graphic design, and it will introduce and explain the idea of communication. There are various everyday or commonsense definitions of graphic design and they must be illuminated and addressed. The chapter will first consider the most prevalent and popular view of graphic design. This view is sometimes held by students of graphic design, as well as by the general consuming public (see Crafton Smith 1994: 300). This is the idea of graphic design as an innocent or transparent medium, or vehicle, for the communication of messages and information. It is often found where there is talk of graphic designers sending messages to receivers (see Meggs 1992: 3 for example), or of designers using 'effective media' for the 'transmitting' of messages or 'information' to 'target audiences' (see Cronan 2001: 216). There are various problems involved in this conception of graphic design and they will be explained here.

This chapter will also explain various models of how communication works and it will assess how well each describes the business of graphic design. It will consider classic theories of communication proposed by Shannon and Weaver, Lasswell and others. It will also introduce some of the basic ideas of a semiological model of communication, based on the work of Saussure and Barthes, for example. The principal concepts and methods of these models, along with their strengths and weaknesses, will be clearly enumerated in this chapter. The main technical terms of communication theory, and the ways in which they may be used to account for graphic design, will also be explained here. Certain recent critiques of certain models of communication and of graphic design's implied role in that communication must also be dealt with here.

9

WHAT IS GRAPHIC DESIGN?

Satisfactory definitions and explanations of what graphic design is are hard to find. As noted in Chapter 1, some English dictionaries do not even include the words 'graphic design/er' and, when they do, the definitions are often less than helpful. As ever, etymology can help us to understand where words have come from, what ancient associations they arrive with, as well as what they have come to mean now.

The word 'graphic' in graphic design derives from the ancient Greek word *graphein*, which meant 'mark-making' and which covers written and drawn marks. The word 'design' entered English from the Renaissance French word *dessiner* and the later Italian word *disegno*, which meant drawing, planning, sketching and designing. The root is the Latin *signum*, meaning 'a mark'. There is evidently some overlap between 'graphic' and 'design': drawn marks are common to the definitions of both words, for example. There is also some repetition, or tautology, within the definition of 'design'. And there is evidence that graphic design involves more than mere mark-making; the presence of 'planning' and 'designing' should alert us to the fact that thought and reflection are already included in the process of producing written and drawn marks. These definitions generate a very wide range of activities that might be called graphic design and this is why, in Chapter 1, it was said that this book is intended for students of graphic design, communication arts, communication design, illustration and visual communication. The range of activities referenced by graphics and graphic design in this book includes all of the preceding. Given the involvement of such value-laden and cultural activities as reflection and thought, it also intends to be relevant to students of communication studies, media studies and cultural studies. And, given the definition of graphics in terms of mark-making, and the ways in which art and design tend to run into each other (in the realms of print-making and advertising, for example), it also raises questions pertinent to artists. In order to discover what, if anything, all these activities have in common, what it is that makes them graphic design, the following paragraphs will consider two practitioner's explanations of what graphic design is.

Tibor Kalman proposes a very broad definition of graphic design. He says it is 'a medium . . . a means of communication' consisting in 'the use of words and images on more or less everything, more or less everywhere' (Kalman 1991: 51). Such a broad definition generates a wide variety of examples that may be called graphic design and Kalman includes fourteenth-century Japanese erotic engravings as well as twentieth-century 'publications like *Hooters* and *Wild Vixens*', Hallmark cards as well as Esprit and the design of cheap paperback books as well as of expensive hardbacks (Kalman 1991). Kalman's selection is clearly intended to make the point that graphic design is not limited to high culture or low culture and to that extent may be applauded. This definition, however, does not exclude art: the production of a single image, painted in oils on a canvas, would count as graphic design on Kalman's definition. Not everyone would be happy with the idea that images such as the *Mona Lisa*, *Guernica* and *Sunflowers* are unproblematic- ally graphic design. Therefore, it should perhaps be made explicit, as Kalman does not, that the products of graphic design are always at least potentially reproducible and it is worth noting in his defence that all of his examples exist as multiple reproductions.

In his *Graphic Design: A Concise History*, Richard Hollis (1994) suggests that graphic design is a form of 'visual communication'. More precisely, it is 'the business of making or choosing marks and arranging them on a surface to convey an idea' (Hollis 1994: 7). Like Kalman, Hollis presents graphic design as a form of visual communication; it is there to 'convey' ideas. And, like Kalman's, his definition does not explicitly exclude the 'artistic' production of imagery; Monet's oil paintings or Matisse's collages are examples of making, choosing and arranging marks on a surface in order to convey an idea. Only later does Hollis insist that, 'unlike the artist, the designer plans for mechanical reproduction' (Hollis 1994: 8). Again, it is the point concerning actual or potential reproduction of the work that differen- tiates graphic design from art; artistic production exists in unique 'one-offs' and graphic design is mass produced.

An alternative to these positions, from a more historical and theoretical background, is to be found in Paul Jobling and David Crowley (1996). Most importantly, they say that graphic design is a form of visual culture. It is a form of culture. This is important because this is how graphic design will be understood in this book. The cultural functions of graphic design will be enumerated in more detail in Chapter 4. In order to determine what constitutes graphic design, they propose three 'interdependent factors' (Jobling and Crowley 1996: 1, 3). The first is that graphic design is mass reproduced. The second is that it is 'affordable and/or made accessible to a wide audience'. And the third is that it conveys ideas through a combin- ation of words and image (Jobling and Crowley 1996: 3). Clearly, there can be no problem with the first of their factors. The mass production or reproduction of graphic design is necessary in order to distinguish it from art (see Chapter 8 for more on this). However, the second and third factors are acceptable up to a point, yet stand in need of some qualification. The shapes and styles of the numbers and letters on the face of a Rolex watch are undoubtedly the products of graphic design, yet few would claim that Rolex watches are affordable or accessible to a wide audience in the sense that many people can easily purchase them. The numbers and lettering are, however, accessible in the sense that they are easily understood by a wide range of people. Similarly, the logo on a Brooks Brothers' Polo shirt is a product of graphic design and relatively affordable. But a sheep hanging from a bit of rope is inaccessible in the sense that few people will understand it as signifying that particular company and even fewer will understand its reference to the medieval dukes of Burgundy. The third factor is perhaps the least defensible. If graphic design is the 'juxtaposition or integration of word and image' (Jobling and Crowley 1996: 3), then most logos, all typefaces, all text-only graphics and all image-only graphics are not graphic design. The possibility of graphic production which is not a juxtaposition or integration of word and image must be allowed.

While the question of how graphics relates to art will be dealt with in more detail in Chapter 8, it is worth introducing some of the issues involved here, especially as some people are keen to distinguish graphic design from art precisely as a means of defining the former. One matter which exercises many theorists is the 'purity' or otherwise of graphic design. In his essay, 'Is There a Fine Art to Illustration?', Marshall Arisman (2000) places art, illustration, graphic design and advertising in a scale of 'purity':

1 Fine Art is pure.
2 Illustration is the beginning of selling out.
3 Graphic Design is commercial art.
4 Advertising is selling – period.

(Arisman 2000: 3)

David Bland (1962) also distinguishes art from illustration in terms of 'purity': because illustration often has to do with words and letters, it is not as 'pure' as fine art, which deals in images alone (Bland 1962: 13). Although Arisman differentiates graphic design from art in terms of commerce and Bland differentiates illustration from art in terms of the image–text relation, both are concerned with 'purity' and both conclude that their respective disciplines are somehow 'impure'. The notion of 'purity' is an odd one with which to distinguish practices of visual culture from each other and one which does not really stand much scrutiny. Art inhabits an economic 'context', just as much as graphic design and illustration. And fine art paintings are given titles, even if the words do not always appear in the actual image, thus establishing a relation to words. Fine art cannot be distinguished from graphic design on the basis of 'purity'; each is as 'pure', or 'impure' as the other and the notion is of no use in the definition of graphic design.

However, as a working definition of graphic design, 'the mass-production or reproduction of image or text' that may be gleaned from the preceding accounts will suffice only if it is supplemented by stressing the economic role, or commercial nature, of graphic design. Hollis (1994: 8), for example, refers to the client who is paying for the graphic designer's work: the idea that graphic design is usually commissioned, bought and paid for by someone who is not a designer must be stressed here. Although it is not to suggest that fine art is not commissioned, bought and sold, it is to insist on the commercial aspect of graphic design.

THE FUNCTIONS OF GRAPHIC DESIGN

The functions of graphic design may be approached from two directions. There are the social, cultural and economic functions of graphic design 'as a whole'. And there are the functions of individual examples of graphic design. The following sections will address the latter and Chapter 4 will consider the former. Richard Hollis (1994: 9) proposes three basic functions of examples of graphic design which, he says, have changed little over many centuries. The first is 'identification': the role of graphics here is 'to say what something is, or where it came from' (Hollis 1994: 10). Examples of graphics performing this function include inn signs, heraldry, company logos and labels on packaging. Hollis's second function concerns 'information and instruction' and the job of graphics here is to 'indicate the relationship of one thing to another in direction, position and scale'. Maps, diagrams and direction signs are proposed as examples of graphics performing these tasks. And the third function is that of 'presentation and promotion' (Hollis 1994: 10). Posters and advertisements which aim to catch a spectator's eye and make the message 'memorable' are the examples that Hollis supplies here.

Jacques Aumont also suggests there are three functions that graphic images perform and that they are very old. He explains these functions as the 'symbolic', the 'epistemic' and the 'aesthetic' (Aumont 1997: 54–5). In symbolic images the image stands for, or represents, something else. The something else might be a god, an idea or a cultural value and according to Aumont (1997: 55), there is a 'virtually endless' number of such images. These images may be religious or secular, but where they are religious they are often believed to grant direct access to the realm of the sacred. Such images may also be representational or abstract and they may be figurative or non-figurative; images or personifications of Liberty, Charity, Christ, Zeus or Buddha as well as abstract representations in the form of Christian crosses, Hindu or Nazi swastikas and ancient Egyptian ankhs are therefore understood to be symbolic in this sense. Epistemic images (from the ancient Greek word for knowledge) are those which convey information about the world and its contents. Such images may also be religious or secular; in both stained glass windows and botanical illustrations, knowledge is communicated. The nature of the information communicated by an epistemic image can vary enormously and Aumont (1997) includes road maps, landscapes, portraits and playing cards among his examples. Aesthetic images are those 'intended to please the spectator [or] to produce in the spectator specific sensations' (Aumont 1997: 55) and Aumont suggests that this function has become inseparable from the idea of art; that an image 'aiming to produce some aesthetic effect' is taken automatically to be 'art'. Ironically enough, Aumont's example of this phenomenon is advertising, a graphic product, which he says strongly confuses the 'artistic' with the 'aesthetic'.

Unfortunately, neither of these accounts of the function of graphics is satisfactory: both are incomplete and Hollis's is verging on the tautological. There is little room in either account for a rhetorical function, for example. Hollis mentions the word 'promotion' but explains posters and advertisements only in terms of being 'eye-catching' and 'memorable': there is no mention of persuasion or of altering the behaviour of the person whose eye is caught. Aumont also finds no place for rhetorical images: he mentions advertising, but only to explain it entirely in terms of a confusion between the 'artistic' and the 'aesthetic'. In describing the functions as 'identification', 'information' and 'presentation', Hollis's account comes close to saying the same thing three times. In 'identification' the first function he identifies, an image 'says what something is' (Hollis 1994: 10). To say what something is sounds like providing information about that thing, which is supposedly the second, different, function. To provide information about that thing sounds suspiciously like a 'presentation', which is offered as the third function. There is simply not enough difference between these things that images do to constitute three different functions; as Hollis explains them, they all perform the 'informative' function.

Consequently, these accounts must be supplemented and made more logical. The four functions that will be described below were outlined in an unpublished lecture given by Richard Tyler at what was then Leeds Polytechnic. The source was given as being 'based on St Thomas Aquinas', but in nearly twenty years I have not found that source. Some of these four functions will be only marginally different from Hollis's and Aumont's, others will be entirely different from them, but between them, they will account for all graphic production.

Information

The first function is the informative function. The role of graphics here is to impart (by definition new) knowledge, or intelligence. Clearly, this is much the same as Aumont's 'epistemic' function and covers everything described by Hollis. Pub signs, shop-fronts, coats of arms, company logos and packaging are all examples of graphics where one of the roles performed is that of providing information. The information provided may be very basic, that this place is a shop or a pub and not a private house, for example. It may also be more sophisticated, telling us that these two families have combined through marriage to form a new social unit, or that this company is caring and efficient. Signage, in our towns and cities, on our highways and motorways, along with maps, diagrams, portraits, landscapes and much illustrative work are also providing information. Again, the type of information may be very basic or it may be more complex. Some road or street signs merely say that the public conveniences, or Birmingham, are this way. Others distinguish motorways from minor roads, or tourist attractions, by means of different background colours. In the United Kingdom, motorway signs use a blue ground, minor roads a white ground and tourist attractions are indicated by a brown background. And advertising has an informative function; as described by Hollis (1994), one of the jobs an advert is there to do is to inform the spectator that a certain product exists. Although it is clearly not the whole story, one of the things that advertising undoubtedly does is to inform the public.

Persuasion

The second function is the persuasive, or rhetorical function. Here the job of graphics is to persuade, to convince or merely affect a change in thought or behaviour. Again, this bears obvious resemblances to Aumont's (1997) description of the rhetorical image. It may be argued that all graphic production has a rhetorical function, that it all exists in order to change people's thought or behaviour in some way or other. What, it may be argued, is the point of a graphic sign that has no effect on anyone? Why would a designer produce a sign intended to have no effect on its viewers? Is such a sign even possible? The logo mentioned above informs of the identity of the company but also and at the same time seeks to persuade us that that company is caring and efficient. The rhetorical function takes many forms. Advertising is only the most conspicuous example and may be located on a spectrum of graphic production ranging from political propaganda and electoral publicity to illustration and documentary.

Decoration

The third function is the decorative or aesthetic function. It should be surprising that a graphic design historian such as Hollis (1994) does not countenance the idea that graphic design might have a decorative function, that it might be fun, or that it could be entertaining, ornamental and the source of enjoyment and pleasure. Aumont (1997) begins to approach this function when he describes aesthetic images as being intended to please the spectator, but, like Hollis, his account stops short of explaining graphic production as decorative.

Magic

The fourth function is the magical function. This is probably the least obvious function of graphic production. However, it attempts to analyse and explain two things that graphic design does. The first thing is hinted at in Aumont's (1997: 55) account when he suggests that symbolic images somehow grant 'access to the sphere of the sacred' (compare Benjamin 1992: 218). The second thing is alluded to by Tibor Kalman (1991), when he says that what most graphic design is about is 'making something different from what it truly is' (quoted in McCarron 2001: 113). The first thing they do is to make absent or distant people or places 'present' to us, the spectator. When Aumont says that symbolic images give access to the realm of the divine, he is describing the process by which the gods are made present, or made to appear to humans, but there is clearly a secular version of the function. If this were not true, then we would not keep pictures or photographs of our loved ones in our wallets or on our desks and walls. Nor would we feel distinctly uncomfortable at the prospect of sticking a needle in the photograph of our mother, right in the eye. The second thing that images do, and which concerns Kalman, is to transform one thing into another thing. Thirty graphics students asked to draw a garden will produce thirty different gardens, thus transforming one thing into another thing. It is also well known that a garden painted by Monet is altogether a different kind of place from a garden painted by Van Gogh. Ignoring for the moment the question of whether we can have access to 'what really is', making things appear and turning one thing into another thing are exactly what magicians do and that is exactly why graphics may be said to have a magical function, however residual, or primitive it may sound.

Metalinguistic and phatic functions

In his chapter 'Drawing, Design and Semiotics', Clive Ashwin proposes six functions for graphic design. His 'referential' function covers the ground covered by 'Information', and his emotive and conative (to do with the desire to perform an action) functions correspond to 'Persuasion'. Ashwin's account of the poetic or aesthetic function makes the point that a designer's work may be pleasurable to an interpreter, but that pleasure is not any image's only function (Ashwin 1989: 207). Ashwin is useful here because he adds 'metalinguistic' and 'phatic' functions to the account of graphic design. An example of phatic communication in speech would be someone saying 'Hi there . . .', 'I see . . .', 'you know', 'uh huh' or 'anyway' in the course of a conversation. Such phrases are conventional and predictable; they are what is known as 'redundant' in communication studies, and their purpose is to initiate, continue or conclude a conversation. Ashwin (1989: 208) suggests that comics are 'rich in phatic devices and signs'. The ways in which drawings are framed, whether as grid-based squares or rectangles or as chaotic and overlapping, can indicate the relation between those frames and suggest where one is to go next. Arrows, changes of viewpoint or of perspective and moving from close-up to landscape are also phatic. The framing, or the move from close-up to landscape, may have nothing to do with the narrative, but it keeps the story going, it tells the reader where to look next.

A 'metalanguage' is a language that is used to talk about some other language. A metalinguistic communication, therefore, is a communication that comments on, explains, clarifies or qualifies another piece of communication (Ashwin 1989: 208). Quotation marks around a word or a piece of text in this book, for example, indicate that someone else has written it, that it is a concept that needs to be 'handled with care', or that it is singled out for some other sort of special attention. Ashwin suggests that the 'Key' on a map performs a metalinguistic function; it explains what shapes, lines or colours used in the map mean. The metalinguistic function is therefore connected to codes. Fiske (1990: 36) explains that, in order to understand a word or an image, one needs to be clear which code is being used. Frames are a good example: a frame around an image may indicate that it is to be understood as a work of art, or that it is the next image in a comic, depending on the frame and the code that is being used.

It should be stressed that these functions are treated analytically here. What this means is that the functions have been identified, separated and explained in order to make them clearer. It is not the case that they can always be separated in one's experience of graphic design. One does not first experience the 'entertaining' function and then, later, get persuaded by the rhetorical function of an advertisement, for example. When one looks at an advertisement, the pleasure of the image, its entertainment value, is experienced at the same time as its persuasive function. Indeed, some would argue that the pleasure engendered is an integral part of its rhetorical power. Nor is it the case that an example of graphic design will perform only one of these functions. There can be no piece of graphic design that is only decorative, or only informative. It is the case that any and all examples of graphic design will perform more than one of these functions. Two testing examples will be discussed to show how these ideas work.

'The Rhetoric of Neutrality', by Robin Kinross (1989), can be read as demonstrating how an example of graphic design which might be thought of as performing only one function in fact performs another function as well. He takes a railway timetable, an example that Gui Bonsiepe calls an 'extreme case', which might reasonably be thought to be purely informative, 'innocent of all taint of rhetoric' (Bonsiepe, quoted by Kinross 1989: 131–2). Kinross shows that the timetable also operates rhetorically, using eloquence to persuade or influence others. He concentrates on the use of typeface to make his point and reproduces three timetables, one from 1928 (which uses a nineteenth-century serif), one from after 1928 (which uses Gill Sans) and one from 1974 (using Gill Sans again, but employing more lower-case letters). The 'major' change which has taken place is the different typeface, but Kinross also identifies changes of 'detail', substituting dashes for dots in alternate rows, for example (Kinross 1989: 132). In the 'sober' context of the timetable, he says, even this tiny typographic detail represents the exercise of 'eloquence'. The change of typeface is more obviously rhetorical. The move from a serif to a sans serif gives the impression of being 'stripped for action' (Kinross 1989: 136). Clearly, the sense of an impediment-free, efficient and active train service is one that a railway company will want to foster and if the typeface and layout can communicate this, then they will use it. Kinross goes on to consider the use of colour, and the typographical challenge to Gill Sans that was represented by Univers. He concludes that the timetables do not only perform an informative function, but also persuade and influence, using typeface, layout and colour to connote modernity, efficiency and even cultural identity.

A slightly less extreme, but no less illustrative, example, may be found in many of Toulouse Lautrec's posters. The 1891 poster for La Goulue at the Moulin Rouge will be used here. It is almost the opposite of Kinross's example in that, where his example takes an example that appears to do only one thing and shows that it in fact does another thing as well, this one represents a piece of graphic design that performs all four of the main functions identified earlier. The poster informs the viewer of the place and times at which La Goulue will be dancing – every night at the Moulin Rouge. It persuades the viewer to attend by presenting the location as a popular, exciting and lively 'night-spot'. The magical function may be said to be performed in that something of the atmosphere, the energy, darkness and sexuality of the place, is made present. And the decorative, aesthetic function is performed by the use of colour, silhouette and composition: many of these posters, of course, are reproduced in order to be hung on people's walls as decoration today.

WHAT IS COMMUNICATION?

All of the accounts of what graphic design is that have been noted so far have insisted that graphic design is a means of communication. Kalman says that graphics is a 'means of communication' (1991: 51). Hollis implies that it is a kind of 'visual communication' (1994: 7). Although Jobling and Crowley appear to eschew the word entirely, it is clear that 'a means of conveying ideas' (1996: 3) indicates communication. So, this section must consider the idea of communication. It will do this first by examining the way communication is described by practitioners and theorists of graphic design. It will look at the metaphors used to describe and explain communication. Second, it will look at the various models of communication that have been proposed as descriptions of the transmission of messages or information.

However, as Kalman, Hollis and Jobling and Crowley all agree that graphic design is communication, so they all agree that communication is a 'conveying'. They all use this metaphor of transporting or carrying something from one place to another to explain communication. For these practitioners and theorists, graphic design is the medium or vehicle by means of which something is transported from one place to another. The something that is thus transported or communicated is customarily referred to as a message, and may be further specified as an idea or a meaning. The 'places' between which messages are conveyed are commonly described as 'senders' and 'receivers'; communication is therefore understood as the conveying of a message from sender to receiver.

This conception of communication is what lies at the root of the common understanding of graphic design as an innocent, transparent medium, or a neutral transporter of messages. This understanding emphasises the idea that graphics is transparent in the sense that it adds nothing and takes nothing away from the message; that it has no message of its own and does not constitute a message in or by itself. A transparent medium is one that distorts nothing that passes through it and graphics is often presented as such a medium. The idea of the neutral vehicle is also popular. This is the idea that, like a train or a bus, graphics does not affect its cargo: messages are taken on at one end, taken off at the other end and remain unmodified by either the vehicle itself or the journey. Some graphic designers believe that this is the ideal to be achieved by graphic communication. Katherine McCoy, for example, recalls her time working at the American design company, Unimark International, a company dedicated to the idea of the 'rationally objective professional' graphic designer. She says that the stated goal of the graphic designer at that company was to be the 'neutral transmitter of the client's messages' (McCoy 1997: 213).

These are fecund metaphors and may be multiplied almost at will. However, they are metaphors and, although they cannot be eliminated or avoided, they cannot pass uninspected. They must be inspected because they predispose the people who use them to favour a specific model of communication, which contains ideas that may be misleading or inaccurate. Specifically, these metaphors predispose people to the model of communication that is used in communication theory, which will be investigated in the following section. These problems are compounded because, as Derrida points out, communication can only be described metaphorically (as transporting or conveying), but metaphor is itself a kind of transporting, to the extent that using 'is' here is problematic (Derrida 1978a: 6–7). Metaphor is itself always already metaphorical in that its Greek derivation suggests a carrying over from one place to another, a communication: 'meta' means over or beyond and 'phero' means transfer or convey. So, communication is commonly explained in terms of a metaphor of carrying over, a conveying from one place to another. But metaphor itself is already a form of communication (a carrying over), which is what we are trying to explain 'in the first place'.

These reflections are clearly complex and difficult. Their consequences are more complex and more difficult (see Derrida 1982a: 307–330; 1982b, for example). However, they at least alert us to the problems involved in certain models of communication. One of the consequences is that there can be no neutral, objective conveying of a message, if by neutral and objective is meant non-transforming or non-rhetorical. (Transforming

19

should be understood as referring only to the information or the message, not to the receiver of the message. Information that does not transform the receiver is not information (Wildbur and Burke 1998: 6)). Metaphor is a rhetorical trope and it is transforming (it is describing one thing in terms of another thing): if there is no non-metaphorical communication, then there can be no non-transforming, non-rhetorical communication. The impossibility of a neutral, information-only communication was shown by the reading of Kinross (1989). The neutral, objective communication of information by the railway timetable was seen to be impossible and was always accompanied by, or transformed by, a rhetorical element. With these problems in mind, the next section will investigate the models of communication that are found in communication theory.

COMMUNICATION THEORY

In *Type and Image*, Meggs (1992) begins his account of communication in graphic design from the perspective of communication theory. Following Shannon and Weaver (1949), he explains communication as the 'transfer of information between people' and he defines information as 'knowledge about facts and events' (Meggs 1992: 3). Meggs' graphic depiction of this theory makes its linear process quite clear (see diagram below).

Information source	>	Transmitter (encoder)	>	Signal (in channel)	>	Receiver (decoder)	>	Recipient (destination)

$$\wedge$$

Noise
source

First, the 'information source' produces the 'raw information' to be transmitted and the transmitter (encoder) transforms the information into a signal that is appropriate for the channel of communication. Then, the receiver (decoder) translates the signal back into 'the original message' and the recipient receives the message. All the while, the signal is subject to potential 'noise', which is a 'distortion' of, or an 'interference' with, that signal (Meggs 1992). Despite Shannon and Weaver's claim that this model will apply to all human communications (Fiske 1990: 6), the origins of this theory in their work in telecommunications engineering are quite clear.

It is significant that Meggs makes no further use of this model in *Type and Image*. He says that, although this theory 'addresses the method of communication', it does not deal with the 'content' or 'purpose' of communication and is therefore 'inadequate to explain communicative art forms including . . . graphic design' (Meggs 1992: 3). In fact, there are many things that this theory does not deal with and there are a few things concerning the 'method' that are not entirely convincing. Even with electronic media, which is where Shannon and Weaver (1949) start from, the identity of transmitters and receivers is relatively unclear. Is the graphic designer the 'information source' on this account, or the 'transmitter (encoder)'? Is the client, perhaps, the 'source'? The client will contract a designer for a specific task, after all. In turn, the graphic designer will select the shapes, lines, colours, typefaces and layouts that make up a website design, for example: does that make him or her the 'information source'? Similarly, is a program such as Dreamweaver the information source or the transmitter (encoder)? Or is the server the transmitter? Graphic designers also interpret subjects and topics on behalf of clients and turn those subjects and topics into visuals: does that make them the 'encoder'? If not, why not? More seriously, the theory does not account for the fact that a graphic designer will know who the 'recipient' is (either the market or audience, or the client), and tailor the image/text and layout to suit: to this extent, the 'recipient' has something like a 'causal effect' on the 'transmitter' and the linear sequence is simply inaccurate. Similarly, with regard to the 'receiver (decoder)' and the 'recipient': is the young black guy who interprets an advertisement or magazine cover the 'decoder' or the 'recipient' or is the white middle-class female client in some sense the 'recipient'?

The nature of 'noise' is not clear in a graphic design context: the fact that 'snow' on a television screen might make the designer's wizzy animated title sequence difficult to see is true, but it is surely a trivial engineering problem that need not detain graphic designers *qua* graphic designers. A more interesting version of noise might be the plethora of pop-ups on a website, which obscure part of the page one is trying to look at but, again, this might also be a trivial engineering or programming problem. The idea of noise (defined as 'any signal received that was not transmitted by the source': Fiske 1990: 8) raises a number of problems for this theory of communication. The definition of noise as provided by Fiske seems to require that the source knows what was and was not transmitted, that they are thus in in full control of their message and signal. The source or sender must know exactly what was transmitted in order to recognise that which was not transmitted and therefore identify it as noise. How, then, are we to explain the offence caused by 'obscene' advertisements? In 2003, some people complained that one of the advertisements produced by the charity Barnardo's were offensive as it showed a cockroach emerging from a baby's mouth. If the sender knows what was transmitted (as they must do, in order to tell noise from non-noise), then the offence is not noise and the offence must have been intentionally 'transmitted' by the sender. Few graphic designers and fewer advertisers, however, will admit to intentionally broadcasting offensive material. If, however, the offence is noise, then the sender cannot be in control of the signal and they cannot be said to know what they are transmitting. However, there are not many graphic designers who will admit to not being in control of their work and to communicating unintended meanings.

Of course, it may be argued that 'offensiveness' is not a 'signal' on this account, or that 'offensiveness' is a cultural variable and not part of the process of communication. In this case, one would have to reply that a theory which is unable to explain how 'messages' are found offensive by people is clearly no theory of graphic communication. It is at this point that Meggs' objections to the theory become pertinent. He is clearly correct regarding the content, or meaning, of the message: a satisfactory explanation of communication would have to account for the content of that communication. Similarly with 'purpose'; an explanation of a piece of communication would need to refer to the function the text/image was to perform. As it is, Shannon and Weaver's model explains neither content nor purpose. Nor is it concerned with the social and cultural locations of communication. The class, gender, nationality and cultural identity of the people involved in communication, which have tremendous impact on graphic communication, are no part of this model. To that extent, the model fails to account for communication.

There are more sophisticated versions of this basic model of communication. One, which Fiske suggests has been followed by 'most mass-communication research', is that provided by Lasswell (Fiske 1990: 30–1). Lasswell's version argues that communication can be explained as:

Who, says what, in which channel, to whom, with what effect.

(Fiske 1990: 30)

That this is a reproduction of Shannon and Weaver's linear model is clear. The element that has been added is the notion of 'effect'. 'Effect' is some change or alteration that is produced in the receiver (the 'whom'), by what is said. Lasswell's model assumes that there is an effect, and that it is clearly identifiable. If an 'effect' cannot be identified, how is one to know that there has been an effect? The first problem here is the passivity of the receiver. The audience of the message, the recipient, is said to be affected by the message. The message acts upon the receiver and the receiver is passively changed by it. However, the social and cultural contexts of these messages is not included in the account. In the case of graphic design, the 'who' is unclear: is the client the 'who', or the designer, or an as yet unspecified combination of the two? To that extent, it is incomplete. The ways in which the (culturally and socially located) receiver itself has an effect on the sender are not included. To that extent, it is inaccurate.

Theodore Newcomb's model of communication represents an attempt to locate the role of communication in a social context. The role, or function, as described by Fiske (1990: 31), is to maintain equilibrium within the social system. Rather than a simple linear process, Newcomb proposes a triangular structure, where A is the sender, B is the receiver and X is a part of the social environment (see diagram on facing page).

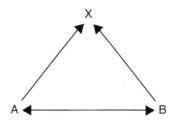

A change in any one of these elements will effect a change in the others. Fiske uses two examples to illustrate the changing 'equilibrium' between these elements. In the first example, A is a Labour government, B represents the trade unions and X is pay policy. He says that A and B, who in theory 'like each other', will be under pressure to communicate frequently in order to reach an agreement on X. In the second example, A is a Conservative government, B is the trade unions and X is pay policy. In this case, there will be less pressure on A and B to communicate about X as they do not 'like each other' and are thus free to disagree on the matter. As Fiske (1990: 32) says, in both cases the system is 'in equilibrium'. While the attempt to account for the social position of communication is welcome, this model is not without its problems. The emphasis on the function of communication as 'maintaining equilibrium' within the social system sounds conservative. What of communication where either A, or A and B, are critical of the X? In the case where both A and B are determined to change X, Newcomb's model has little to say. Like the two accounts already discussed, Newcomb's model cannot account for meaning. The identity of the sender is also unclear. Is it the designer, the client, or the client's marketing department. Given Fiske's example, might it be what have become known in political circles as 'spin doctors'?

A more general and more serious problem affecting all versions of this model of communication concerns the conception of meaning that they presuppose. Meaning is not mentioned in Shannon and Weaver's, or Newcomb's account and it only appears as the 'what' of the communication in Lasswell's. A conception of meaning is, however, presupposed by all these theories. The central metaphor discussed above gives that preconception away. In that metaphor the meaning arrives at its destination unaffected by the vehicle in which, or the journey by which, it is conveyed. Meaning on these accounts is conceived as already formed, or as preceding communication. This is where the notion of 'target audiences' (see Bielenberg 1997: 183) comes from. Meaning is thought of as being like an arrow, or a bullet (or a passenger on a bus), which exists before the communication takes place and which does not change as it is transported to its 'target', or destination. There is no room for the active consumer or interpreter in these theories and alternative interpretations of the 'message' can only be seen as 'missing the target'.

Another of the underlying assumptions of the theory is that the aim of communication is 'efficiency'. This assumption comes from the theory's origins in telecommunications and may be connected to the way in which graphic designers are sometimes characterised as visual 'engineers' (see Bielenberg 1997: 183). Efficiency here means that the message arriving at the receiver is or should be identical to the one transmitted. Any different message that is received is seen as a 'failure' or a 'breakdown' in communication. Such an assumption cannot deal with or explain differences in the interpretation of meaning. Where one 'receiver' interprets a typestyle as conservative and another sees it as a little racy, where one 'receiver' will not buy a packet of tea because the colours and layout used are 'vulgar' and another sees them as 'classy', and where a 'receiver' objects to the depiction of women in an advertisement as 'degrading' but another sees it as 'a bit of fun', these theories would see only a 'breakdown' or a 'failure' in communication. The idea that different people, from differing social and cultural backgrounds, can actively interpret graphic designs in different ways cannot be accounted for except as a failure. This is not a strength of the theory. As Fiske says, the engineering and mathematical backgrounds of the theories unfit them for dealing with different, more complex, forms of communication (Fiske 1990: 6).

Finally, Raymond Williams (1980) argues in his *Problems in Materialism and Culture* that the 'means of communication are themselves means of production' (1980: 50). This is the idea that the notions of 'senders', 'receivers', 'information' and 'messages', used in communication theory, ideologically reduce the idea that graphic design, for example, is a means of social production. None of these ideas refers to anything 'outside' of the linear process of communication. The social, cultural and economic locations, or identities, of the people producing and interpreting graphic design are detached or ignored in the talk of 'sender', 'receiver' and so on. It makes little sense to ask after the social class of the sender, or the gender of the receiver on these accounts and Williams suggests that this is to mask or reduce the idea that what graphic design is doing is producing these social, cultural and economic identities. These criticisms will be explored in more detail in Chapter 4.

The next section will consider semiological models of communication, in which meaning is produced in communication, it is the result of negotiation between designers, clients, marketing people, interpreters and viewers and spectators of graphic design. On these accounts, a different interpretation is just that, not a failure of communication.

SEMIOLOGY

There are three main differences between the communication theories discussed above and the semiological theories to be introduced in this section (Fiske 1990: 2). The first difference concerns the nature of communication itself. The second concerns the nature of the message. And the third concerns the place of meaning and individuals in communication. First, for the theories above, communication is the transmission of messages (signals) and involves senders, signals, channels and receivers. For semiology, communication is the 'production and exchange of meanings' (Fiske 1990: 2). This theory stresses the interaction involved in communication, not the sending and passive receiving of messages. For semiological theories, the cultural position of 'senders' and 'receivers' generates meaning, and the exchange of meanings produces the cultural positions of senders and receivers. Second, according to the theories above, a message (meaning) is something transmitted in the process of communication. According to semiology, the message or meaning is something constructed and interpreted in communication. As Fiske (1990: 3) says, the message is a 'construction of signs which, through interacting with the receivers, produce meanings'. This interaction, or negotiation, is what happens when the 'receiver' interprets the signs and codes of a message in terms of their cultural beliefs and values. Third, meaning and individuals were 'already there' for communication theory, but for semiology, communication is a part of the social interaction in which both meaning and individuals are produced, or constituted. There is no meaning before that 'receiver' interprets the meaning of the message, producing themselves as a member of a cultural group in that interpretation, and the meaning is not separable from the interaction of communication (cf. Derrida 1981: 23–4).

An example or two might help. As a white, middle-class European male, my reactions to, or interpretations of, *Sex and the City* are roughly the same as other members of my class, gender and age group. The beliefs and values that I hold as a member of those groups generate my interpretation of the show: meaning results from the interaction between those values and the show. In turn, it is that interpretation or negotiation that produces me as a member of that cultural group. A black Muslim woman's or a teenaged girl's reactions to the show would be entirely different and their interpretations would constitute them as members of very different cultural groups. The interaction, or negotiation, between their beliefs and values and the show will produce the meaning that the show has for these other people. There is, then, no meaning that pre-exists the interpretation of the show and no sense of communication failure resulting from the different interpretations. Similarly, a teenaged western metal fan's reactions to the typefaces, colours and layouts of *Kerrang* or *Metal Maniacs* magazine are likely to be roughly the same as other members of that subcultural group. That interpretation of the graphic design is one of the ways in which membership of the cultural group is constituted. The liquid gold metallic typeface, lurid contrasting colours and lumpen layout of *Metal Maniacs* will mean something entirely different to an ageing folky and that different interpretation will constitute them as a member of an entirely different subcultural group.

Signs and codes

For semiological theories, signs and codes are the twin cultural bases of messages and meanings. Communication is the construction and exchange of meanings for semiology and meanings are explained in terms of signs and codes. The message, or meaning, then, is a construction of signs that is exchanged and interpreted according to codes, or cultural rules.

In semiological theory, the sign is what the linguist Saussure calls a 'unity' (1974: 66–7). It is a unity of signifier and signified. The signifier is the 'material vehicle' and the signified is the associated concept. By 'material vehicle' is meant the sign's image as we perceive it: the written, drawn, printed or displayed piece of graphic design. The shapes, lines, colours, textures and layouts of graphic design are all signifiers. By signified is meant the concept associated with the signifier, what the signifier refers to. The signified of the signifier 'dog' (the perceived shapes and lines making up the word) is either 'four-legged canine', or 'follow'. Depending on the code being used, or the context the signifier appears in, one or other signified would be correct here. In a set of traffic lights, the signifier that is the red light is associated with the concept or signified 'stop'. The signified of the signifier (the shapes and lines making up the image shown in http://www.apple.com/ipod could be 'woman listening to music on her iPod' or just 'dancing', depending on the code, the context in which it was found.

It sounds odd at first, but the relationship between the signifier and the signified is what Saussure (1974: 67–70) calls 'arbitrary'. What he means by this is that there is no natural, legal, personal or God-given reason for any signifier being associated with any signified. The relation is 'arbitrary' in the sense that the colour blue could just as well be associated with 'stop', the word 'cat' could just as easily be associated with the concept of a 'four-legged canine' and the image in the iPod ad could just as easily be associated with the concepts of 'youth', 'fun', 'freedom', 'carefree', 'flirty' or 'nice bracelet' as with those mentioned above. It is not my personal decision that the signifier 'red' is associated with 'stop', nor can I decide tomorrow that from now on it will be associated with 'Go' (see the section on Expression and Individuality in Chapter 8 for more on this). There is nothing natural about the relation between the word 'dog' and the signified 'four-legged canine': the word 'cat' would do the job just as well and other words in other languages (*chat, felis, katze, gato* etc.) do the job perfectly well. Nor could any government legislate for the relation between the shapes and lines in an ad and what they are to be associated with.

Because the relationship between signifier and signified is arbitrary, it is conventional. And because it is conventional, it is cultural. Another way of saying this would be to say that, because the relationship is arbitrary, it is only the differences between signs that generate meaning. Signs are meaningful only because they differ from other signs, within a code or a structure that organises those differences. Meaning is, therefore, a product of difference. The word 'dog' means different things in the sentences, 'this dog is lost' and 'melancholy thoughts dog my every move'. The image in the iPod ad would mean something different if it were to be found in a book of cool dance moves or a bracelet catalogue. The sentences and the context are codes or structures within which the elements have meaning. These codes are cultural in that they are the rules shared and followed by a community of sign-users. The code for the traffic lights has to be learned (from *The Highway Code* in the United Kingdom) and it is shared by all road users. The code that operates in the case of traffic lights is very simple: 'red' means stop, 'red and amber' means get ready to go, 'green' means go and 'amber' means get ready to stop. The coloured lights are made meaningful by their place in that structure. And the code is cultural in that a community of sign-users (drivers) learn it and adhere to it.

(It is worth noting, parenthetically, that as the relation between the signifier and the signified is arbitrary and because, therefore, signs make sense only within a coded, culturally specific, set of differences, Isotype cannot be the universal language it was designed to be. The Isotype for liquid refreshment, for example, is a cocktail glass, as opposed to a wine glass, a champagne glass, a beer glass and so on. This choice from the paradigm of different glasses is 'very American', as Lupton and Miller (1999: 42) say, and its meaning, that you can get a drink here, has to be learned. A picture of a bottle might be 'more universal', but would still have to be learned. They also point out that the only other depiction of a woman (apart from the one wearing a stylised version of a garment 'sometimes worn by western women' (Lupton and Miller 1999: 42), is in the sign for 'ticket sales'. Here, culturally specific gender roles are reproduced by having the women assisting the man (compare it with the USAir advertisement in Chapter 4). There is no entirely non-arbitrary and purely iconic signifier and therefore Isotype cannot be 'universal'.)

The code may be explained as a structure. A structure is a set of ways in which different elements can relate to each other. In semiology, there are two ways in which elements can be different from, or can relate to, each other. They can come before or after each other and they can substitute for each other. The technical term for the difference between things that come before or after one another is 'syntagmatic difference' and a sequence of elements (an entire layout, for example) can be called a 'syntagm'. The term for elements that can substitute for each other is 'paradigmatic difference' and the name for a group of elements that could substitute for each other (fonts in MS Word, for example) is called a 'paradigm'. In the United Kingdom traffic lights example, red can be substituted for green or amber, but not by blue or pink, and it comes after amber, but not after green. Red, green and amber are thus a paradigmatic group and the sequence 'red, red and amber, green' is a syntagm. In a comic strip, the meaning of any one frame is produced by its syntagmatic relation to the frames preceding and following it. It is also produced by its paradigmatic relation to the frames that could, but do not, replace it.

To summarise: the semiological account of communication may use some of the same words that are found in communications theory's account (message, for example), but the ways in which those words are used and understood differs in each theory. So for semiology, communication is the production and exchange of messages and meanings, not the transmission of messages. A message or meaning is something constructed in communication, not something that pre-exists communication. The 'receiver' in semiology is not really a receiver; in the active interpretation of the message, meanings and receivers are constructed and reproduced according to the cultural identity of the interpreter. Signs and codes are the bases of meanings in semiology. And signs and codes are explained in terms of learned and variable cultural rules. For semiology, then, communication is a cultural phenomenon, not an engineering problem, as it is in communication theory.

CONCLUSION

This chapter has tried to explain what graphic design is and what the function of individual examples of graphic design could be. It has tried to explain what communication is and it has looked at potential explanations from communication theory and semiology. It has been argued that the semiological theories are more appropriate to graphic design. The latter are not handicapped by starting from an engineering or telecommunications background, in which the emphasis is on the efficiency of signal transmission. Instead, they are fully able to account for the social and cultural production and exchange of meaning through signs and codes. There is a sense, then, in which Kalman is correct when he says that 'graphic design is a language not a message' (quoted in Bielenberg 1997: 184). Graphic design does in fact deal with messages, but not in the way that communication theory suggests. This is borne out, to an extent, by the terminology that graphic designers and design journailsts use to describe what they are doing. In the March 2004 edition of the British journal *Design Week*, for example, a mixture of communication theory metaphors and semiological concepts is to be found. Mel Maynard, design director at Brandhouse, says that their new packaging for Sanctuary Spa's beauty products use 'self-pampering cues' and creates an 'impression' of a sanctuary. The use of the word 'cue' suggests that a specific response is being invited by the packaging, not that a message is being delivered. Martin Grimer employs a mixture of the two approaches, suggesting on the one hand that his work 'gives' Hellmann's products a consistent visual style and on the other that it encourages different 'associations'. 'Gives' in this context suggests that meaning is an object that pre-exists the interpretation of it while 'associations' (of freshness and honesty) are connotations (*Design Week*, March 2004: 4–5). The account of semiology begun here suggests that the emphasis should be on graphic design as one of the ways in which meaning is socially and culturally constructed and negotiated, that is, like a language. The use of semiological theory will be continued in Chapter 3, which will investigate the notion of meaning in more detail, using the ideas proposed by Barthes and others.

FURTHER READING

- For more on **Derrida's account of communication**, see his 'Signature, Event, Context', in Derrida (1982a) *Margins of Philosophy*, Hemel Hempstead: Harvester Wheatsheaf.
- The best **introductory text**, to which this chapter is clearly indebted, is John Fiske's (1990) *Introduction to Communication Studies*, London: Routledge. It contains a detailed, approachable and critical account of both communication theory and semiological theory. See especially his explanation of the relation between highly motivated or constrained signs (which resemble the things they are the signs for) and less motivated signs (which do not) and iconic and symbolic signs (pp. 52–6).
- David Crow's (2003) *Visible Signs*, Crans-Près-Céligny, Switzerland: AVA Publishing SA, is a superb, visually stunning introduction to **semiology for graphic designers**.
- For a summary of the debate between **communication theory and semiological theory**, see Marilyn Crafton-Smith (1994) 'Culture is the Limit: Pushing the Boundaries of Graphic Design Criticism and Practice', *Visible Language*, 28(4): 297–315. Crafton-Smith critically discusses Jorge Frascara's (1988) 'Graphic Design: Fine Art or Social Science?', *Design Issues*, 5(1): 18–29.
- Ellen Lupton's essay 'Reading Isotype' and the chapter on 'Modern Hieroglyphs' in Lupton and Miller (1999) contain more detailed argument and discussion on the role of culture in the understanding of **Isotype**.
- An **internet semiotics encyclopedia** can be found at http://www.arthist.lu.se/kultsem/encyclo/intro.html. Produced by the University of Lund, it contains material on visual semiotics as covered here. The University of Wales Aberystwyth website at http://www.aber.ac.uk/media/ contains material on advertising and visual analysis.

3

MEANING: WORDS
AND IMAGES

INTRODUCTION

This chapter will develop the themes of the previous chapter. Chapter 2 established communication as the production and exchange of messages, which were explained as meanings. Meanings were seen to be the products of signs and codes and the nature of signs and codes were introduced. Chapter 3 will look at the notion of meaning in more detail. It will first define three different types of signs: icon, index and symbol. Then it will explain two types, or levels, of meaning (denotation and connotation) and show how they are the result of differences and relations between signs, codes and cultures. It will then move on to consider the relations between words and images and illustrate the different functions that words can have with regard to images. Some areas of graphic design, such as illustration, can be predominantly dependent upon image alone. Other areas, what is most commonly thought of as 'graphic design', perhaps, involve the use of both images and words. And other areas, typography, for example, concentrate on (the form of letters and) words alone.

For example, on the morning after the Hutton report was published in the United Kingdom, the *Independent* newspaper entirely eschewed illustration on its front page (Figure 3.1). (The Hutton report was intended to be a description of the events preceding the death of the civil servant David Kelly, who had been identified as having leaked sensitive information concerning the Labour government's policy on weapons of mass destruction and the war on Iraq to a BBC journalist.) The *Independent*'s front page raised the question whether the report was a 'whitewash', whether it covered up the government's duplicity and responsibility, by using a white front page with only twelve lines of type. Advertising for the Clinique company in the 1990s characteristically used only a photograph of the product in their advertisements, while some recent advertising for the Standard Life building society (Figure 3.2) and the *Big Issue* used only a variety of different typefaces to make their point. In the graphic design industry, the company emediadigital.com concentrates solely on the use of

THE INDEPENDENT

No 5,392   www.independent.co.uk   THURSDAY 29 JANUARY 2004   (Republic of Ireland €0.95) 60p

WHITEWASH?
THE HUTTON
REPORT
A SPECIAL ISSUE

Eight months ago, BBC reporter Andrew Gilligan broadcast his now infamous report casting doubt on the Government's dossier on Iraq's weapons capability, a vital plank in its case for war. In the ensuing furore between No 10 and the BBC, Government scientist David Kelly, who was revealed to be Gilligan's source, was found dead in the woods. Tony Blair appointed Lord Hutton, a former Lord Chief Justice of Northern Ireland, to hold an inquiry into the circumstances surrounding Dr Kelly's death. He listened to 74 witnesses over 25 days, and yesterday published his 328-page report. In it, he said Gilligan's assertions were unfounded and criticised the BBC, whose chairman has now resigned. He said that Dr Kelly had broken the rules governing civil servants in talking to journalists. He exonerated Tony Blair, cleared Alastair Campbell and attached no blame to the government for the naming of Dr Kelly. So was this all an establishment whitewash? And what of the central issue which Lord Hutton felt he could not address? If the September 2002 dossier which helped persuade the nation of the urgent need for war (and triggered this tragic chain of events) was indeed reliable, where, exactly, are Iraq's weapons of mass destruction?

Figure 3.1 Newspaper front page, *Independent* (January 2004).
Courtesy of the *Independent*

typography in advertising. The second part of John Hillis Miller's (1992) *Illustration* analyses many examples of the different 'balance' that may exist between word and image; while drawing on this work, this chapter will concentrate on a few key concepts.

So, having first explained the different types of sign, Chapter 3 will consider the relation between meaning, words and images in the production

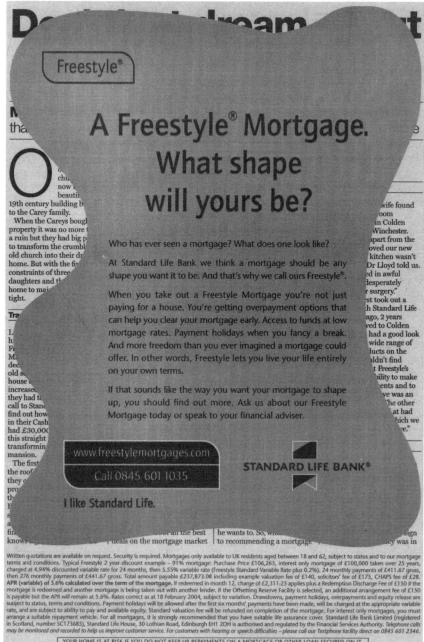

Figure 3.2 Advertisement, Standard Life Bank (2004).
Courtesy of Standard Life

of meaning from a cultural perspective and from a formal perspective. Formally, the relation of words and images has been considered under the heading of 'layout' or composition. Gunther Kress and Theo van Leeuwen's (1996) work on 'composition' will be used here to explore the links between culture, meaning and the different ways in which pages can be laid out. In terms of the relation to culture, the relation has been considered in terms of various concepts; denotation, connotation, anchorage and relay, for example. Roland Barthes's account of these terms will be explained and used to show the connection between culture and meaning. Having introduced and explored these issues, the approach followed by Foucault, in his correspondence with Magritte and in his *This is Not a Pipe*, will be explained. The interrelation between the formal and the cultural, the way the cultural construction of meaning and identity relates to graphic devices will thus be made clear. Finally, the chapter will introduce some more concepts from semiology. Metaphor, metonymy and synechdoche are the names for some of the different visual operations that are performed by graphic designers on ideas and things in the world. Visual examples of these operations in advertising, photography and illustration will be explained here.

TYPES OF SIGNS

The basic structure of all signs (the relation between signifier and signified) was explained in Chapter 2. This section will explain the three different forms that that relation can take: it will explain three types of sign. The typology of signs to be used here comes from the work of an American philosopher, C. S. Peirce (1839–1914), who was living and working at the same time as Saussure (1857–1913) but apparently unaware of his work. Peirce's definition of the sign is remarkably similar to Saussure's. Peirce (1955: 99) says that 'a sign . . . is something that stands to somebody for something in some respect'. On Peirce's account, then, most things can function as a sign. It is the relation between the sign and its object, the thing it stands for, that concerns us here because Peirce says that there are three different ways in which the sign (the signifier in Saussure's terms) can relate to its object (the signified in Saussure's terms). For the sake of convenience, Saussure's terminology will be adopted in order to explain these types of sign. If there are three ways in which the signifier can relate to the signified, then there are three different types of sign. These types are known as 'icon', 'index' and 'symbol' (Peirce 1955: 102).

In iconic signs, the relation between signifier and signified is one of resemblance. The signifier resembles or looks like the signified in some way. Good examples of iconic signs are photographs, in which the signifiers (the shapes, lines, colours and textures) resemble the thing that the photograph is of. The photograph in a passport or student identity card is almost guaranteed to resemble or look like the person it is the photograph of; that is why photographs, rather than charcoal sketches, are used. Cultural codes still play a part here, however. The story of how Picasso sympathised with the man who showed him a 'realistic' photograph of his wife by regretting that she was only two inches tall indicates that, only within certain learned and understood limits, does the photograph 'resemble' its object. Some paintings (representational portraits and landscapes, for example) may be said to be iconic. There is a sense in which maps and diagrams are iconic: the signifiers must resemble the signified in some way for them to be useful maps and diagrams.

Indexical signs are those in which the signifier is causally or existentially related to the signified. An advertisement in which the model's hair streams out behind her as she drives her open-top car contains an indexical sign: the streaming hair (the signifier) is caused by the speed of the car (the signified). An advertisement for holidays in Barcelona which contains a picture of the Sagrada Familia is indexical in that the cathedral (the signifier) is, it exists, in Barcelona (the signified). And the drops of perspiration on the sweaty workmen ogled by attractive women in Coke ads are indexical signs. The perspiration (the signifier) has been caused by hunky masculine hard work (the signified).

Peirce's symbolic signs are the same as Saussure's sign. Here the relation between signifier and signified is conventional, or 'arbitrary' as Saussure says. A community of sign-users has agreed that a signifier will stand for a particular signified. In an Interflora advertisement, it is the roses and not the gypsophila alongside them that stand for love. There is nothing to prevent the gypsophila from standing for love, but the culture this advertisement is part of has agreed and conventionalised the relation between the signifier (the roses) and the signified (love). The roses are thus a symbolic sign on this account.

It should be noted that a single example of graphic design will often contain iconic, indexical and symbolic signs. As Fiske (1990: 48), for instance, has pointed out, the road sign for a crossroads in the UK Highway Code is iconic, indexical and symbolic all at the same time. The red triangle is symbolic: according to the Highway Code signs that are triangular with a red border (and not circular, or blue) are warnings. The shape in the middle is a mixture of icon and symbol. It is iconic in that it resembles a crossroads and it is symbolic in that we have to know the convention that means it is not a church, for example. Located by the side of the road, the sign is indexical: the sign alerts drivers to the existence of a crossroads ahead. The Isotype is also a mixture of iconic, indexical and symbolic. The sign for 'woman' is iconic in that it looks like a woman wearing something that some women wear in some cultures (Lupton and Miller 1999: 42). It is indexical in that, when seen at an airport or station, it indicates the presence or existence of a lavatory for women. And it is symbolic because the conventions surrounding its use must be learned in order to understand it; it does not mean 'Only skirts to be worn' or 'Brothel', for example (Lupton and Miller 1999: 42). To the extent that it is symbolic, it cannot be 'universal'.

MEANING: DENOTATION AND CONNOTATION

Denotation and connotation are two types, or two levels, of meaning. This section will explain that, although both are based on signs and codes and to that extent culturally relative, denotation is sometimes said to be less culture specific than connotation. Knowing what denotation and connotation are and how they work is necessary for the analysis of graphic design. The distinction between these two levels of meaning is analytical in that, although it is not found in our experience, it can help to explain and make sense of that experience (see Baker 1985 for more on this). As Barthes (1977a: 36–7) says, although they are usually experienced and understood at the same time, analysing them can help to explain the ideological function of connotation. Connotation is an immensely powerful type of meaning: all graphic design depends on it in order to be effective and graphic design is effective because of the way connotation works. Connotation enables the individual to be constructed as a member of a social group because it is where the values and beliefs of a culture interact with the texts, images and layouts of graphic design. As such, it may be thought of as the interface between the individual and a culture: it is where the values and beliefs of a culture generate meaning. Barthes provides a diagram, using the idea of the sign, made up of signifier and signified, to explain in graphic form the relation between denotation and connotation (see Figure 3.3).

The denotational meaning of an image is the answer to the question 'What is this a picture of?' The denotation of a typeface is the answer to questions such as 'What typeface is this?', 'What point size is being used here?' and 'Is this a serif?' Denotation is the 'literal' meaning of a piece of graphic design and an account of denotational meaning can be correct or incorrect. In the iPod advertisement mentioned in Chapter 2 the denotation of the image might be 'woman, dancing, listening to headphones, wearing

Figure 3.3 Diagram, Barthes on denotation/connotation (1977)

bracelet, shortish hair' and so on. If it was suggested that the denotation of the typeface was Times New Roman italic then the denotation would be wrong. Barthes (1977a: 36) says that all that is needed to understand this level of meaning is 'the knowledge bound up with our perception'. What he means is that, in order to understand or construct the denotation of a photograph of a woman dancing, or of a shopping bag, all one needs to know is what an image is and what a woman dancing, or a shopping bag, is. As he says, this knowledge is 'not nothing': one needs to be a member of the sort of culture that has photography, goes dancing and uses shopping bags in order to understand or construct such an image. The construction or understanding of denotational meaning requires a low-level cultural knowledge, but it is still a culture-specific knowledge (see Baker 1985).

The connotational meaning of an image is the answer to the question 'What does this image make you feel?' The connotation of a typeface is the answer to the question 'What does this typeface make you think of?' Connotational meaning is the associations a piece of graphic design has for an individual member of a culture; the way the image makes you think or feel and it cannot be correct or incorrect. If you say the woman in the iPod advertisement makes you think of nights out dancing in town, then that is the connotation of the image for you. If you don't live in the sort of culture that has 'nights out dancing in town' then the image will not have that connotation for you. Another connotational meaning might be that dancing is a sin. If you are not part of a culture that thinks that dancing is sinful, then this connotational meaning will be unavailable to you and you will not be constructed as a member of that culture. This level of meaning requires a much higher level of cultural knowledge in order to be constructed or understood than denotational meaning. In Barthes's famous account of the Panzani pasta advertisement, he identifies four connotative signs: the 'return from market', 'Italianicity', the 'total culinary service' and 'still life'. In order to be able to construct or understand these connotations, one needs to be a member of a culture in which going to a supermarket or shop to get the shopping for oneself is practised. One also needs to be a member of a society that is wealthy enough to offer holidays to other countries. In the case of the last connotation, 'still life', one needs a relatively specialised education in western art history. A member of the sort of culture where hunting animals in the bush, or having other people to do that sort of thing for you, is the way in which food is procured will not understand what is involved in going to the supermarket and will not be able to construct or understand the connotations of the advertisement.

Barthes's example concerns the image that is found in the advertisement. He is concerned with the the copy, or text, that appears, but his interest is linguistic, not visual. However, the concept of connotation may be used to analyse and explain typefaces, as well as images. An example of how connotation may be applied to the visual explanation of typefaces is to be

Figure 3.4 Typefaces from Morgan and Welton (1986)

found in Morgan and Welton's (1986) *See What I Mean*. They ask the reader to consider these signs (Figure 3.4). As Morgan and Welton (1986: 31) say, they look 'odd'; there is something wrong about them. This oddness or wrongness may be explained in terms of meaning, as the result of connotation and cultural values. What is happening here is that two sets of connotations, two sets of cultural expectations, are conflicting. In British culture, cream teas are associated with 'rural holidays, picturesque scenery and old cottages' (Morgan and Welton 1986: 31). These are the values, associations or connotations that 'cream teas' has for those brought up in British culture. However, the typeface which has been selected for the words 'cream teas' has connotations of 'technology, efficiency and the future' (Morgan and Welton 1986: 31). The connotations of the idea of 'cream teas' are not the same as those of the typeface that has been selected and the face is experienced as inappropriate and odd. The same oddness is experienced and the same explanation can be given for the 'computer aided design' example. Here, the words would be associated with technology, efficiency and the future but the typeface would be associated with half-timbered buildings and picturesque old villages. The connotations, the cultural values, of the words are not appropriate to the typeface, and again, the effect is one of oddness. Where the connotational meaning that a type-face has for a cultural group is not matched to the connotational meaning that the words have, the effect is disconcerting.

Connotation is central to the account of communication that is being proposed here. As already noted, it is where the beliefs and values held by members of a culture interact with the text and imagery of graphic design. Given this, it is therefore where graphic design meets what Marxists call ideology. One of the simpler definitions of ideology in Marxism is that it is the set of beliefs, ideas and values held by a social class. For Marxists, social class is a product of economics; one's position in capitalist economy determines one's social class (see Chapter 4 for more on this). The values, ideas and beliefs (the ideology) held by a member of a social class are also the product of one's economically defined class position. Although Barthes is not concerned with social class, he is concerned with the nature and ideological function of connotation. Barthes (1977a: 49) says in 'Rhetoric of the Image', 'the common domain of the signifieds of connotation is that of ideology'; connotational meaning and ideology share a common space. Connotational signs are made up of a signifier and a signified. The signified is the meaning. The signifiers of these signifieds are therefore the 'signi-fiying aspect of ideology' (Barthes calls the signifiers of these connotational or ideological meanings a 'rhetoric', hence the title of his essay). In the iPod ad, for example, the image of the dancing woman may be understood in certain cultures as the signifier of the signified connotation that dancing is great fun. This is an ideological message in that it represents the beliefs and values of a specific culture.

Clearly, graphic design is a rich source of these ideological signifiers; every graphic text, image and layout is a visual signifier of ideological beliefs and values. Images, texts and layouts produced by graphic designers may now be understood as the signifiers of ideology and the meanings of those images and text (connotations) may be understood as ideological meanings. The function of the images and texts produced by graphic design is to naturalise (to make appear natural and legitimate), the culturally specific meanings of connotation. The image in the iPod ad functions to naturalise the idea that dancing is great fun; simply by showing the activity in a positive way. A culturally and historically specific idea about dancing (which is not naturally or eternally true), is made to appear natural. As will be seen in the following chapters, however, ideology may also be challenged or contested by graphic design.

MEANING: LAYOUT

As noted above, it is not only text and image that generate connotations. Layout also has connotations. Again, these connotational meanings are culture-specific: different cultures will react differently to layouts and produce different interpretations of them. Gunther Kress and Theo van Leeuwen (1996) explain some of the main features of layout in western graphic design in their *Reading Images: The Grammar of Visual Design*. They analyse layout in terms of three systems: information value, salience and framing.

Information value in graphic design layouts is explained in terms of three structures, a 'left–right' structure, a 'top–bottom' structure and a 'centre–margin' structure. The left-hand side of a layout, a page for example, is generally where what the viewer 'already knows' is found. The right-hand side of a page is where the new information is presented (Kress and van Leeuwen 1996: 186–7). In the Diesel advertisement (Figure 3.5), the women flicking through the catalogues are a familiar sight in western culture and they are placed on the left of the ad. The woman critically inspecting the sperm sample is something new and is placed on the right of the ad. In a layout with a pronounced top–bottom structure, Kress and van

Figure 3.5 Advertisement, Diesel (1995). Courtesy of Diesel

Leeuwen (1996: 193) suggest that the 'ideal' is found at the top and the 'real' is found at the bottom. Their example is a 'Fenjal' advertisement where the photograph at the top of the page is an illustration of the 'promise' the product makes and the photograph at the bottom is an illustration of the 'real' products. Giovanni Pintori's 1953 and Tadaaki Kanasashi's 1975 advertisement posters for Olivetti typewriters employ the same technique. An illustration of the 'real' typewriter is placed underneath an 'ideal' image (see Timmers 1998: 209–10). And this structure is also used by Ocean Spray fruit juice packaging. The design for the Cranberry Classic juice pack depicts a bunch of 'real' berries beneath a splash of juice. A 'centre–margin' structure is self-explanatory: whatever is placed in the centre of a layout is perceived as the 'nucleus' of the information, to which other elements are 'subservient' (Kress and van Leeuwen 1996: 206). The ways in which cultural difference generates differences in connotation are shown when it is noted that the centre–margin structure is not common in western design but that is is more common in certain eastern cultures (pp. 203–4). Kress and van Leeuwen (1996: 204) suggest that it is the 'greater emphasis on hierarchy, harmony and continuity in Confucian thinking that makes centring a fundamental organizational principle in the visual semiotic of their culture'. Here, the values of a culture are used to explain a difference in preferred layout; connotation is directly related to membership of one culture or another.

The top–bottom structure is exploited to grisly effect in the package design for Drum 'Gold' hand-rolling tobacco. In the top two-thirds of the pack, the 'ideal' section, one finds the words 'Class A tobacco', 'Gold', 'Excellent' and 'Premium Quality'. The typestyles are a visually interesting mixture of different sized serif, sans serif and calligraphic. The colours used here are the primaries (clean and bright hues of red, white and blue) and gold. In the bottom third, in stark black lower-case sans serif on a white ground, is the government's health warning: 'Smoking can cause a slow and painful death'. All the words in the 'ideal' section are positive, connoting the best. And all the words in the 'real' section are negative, connoting the worst. As if it were needed, the top–bottom structure is emphasised by two vertical lines, in gold and black, running from top to bottom on the left and right sides of the pack.

Guitar magazine provides an example of the 'left–right' structure (Figure 3.6). As part of the 'Songwriting workshop' column, in which professional guitar tutors provide tuition, the left–right structure might be expected. On the left of this double page spread is a photograph of John Martyn, with whom readers of *Guitar* will be familiar. This is consistent with Kress and van Leeuwen's account, in which the 'given' is often found to the left of a layout. On the right of the spread is the new material: diagrams of the C and F chords in CFCCGD tuning and some exercises using these chords. However, within the right-hand page of the double-page spread, the left–right structure is repeated: it is as if the left–right structure of the double page is duplicated on the right-hand side of the spread. Here, the chords on the left stand to the exercises on the right as 'given' and 'new'. This is because the knowledge of the new chords must become 'old', or given, in order for the exercises on the right to be successfully tackled.

These are not necessarily discrete structures, nor are they immune from being 'played around with' by graphic designers. They can be combined with each other and they can be reversed, to create new and possibly unsettling structures and therefore meanings. The 1989 poster 'Do women have to be naked to get into the Met. Museum?' produced by the Guerrilla Girls, for example, reverses the conventional left–right structure to sub-versive effect (Figure 3.7). On the left of the poster is a picture of a reclining nude woman with a gorilla's head and on the right is a plain background with black text. Where one would expect the expected, on the left, one finds the new and threatening, a 'gorilla-girl'. The cultural values of a society which routinely underrates and excludes women artists, but which over-rates and includes pictures of naked women in every art gallery, are challenged by the layout of the poster as well as by its content. Having been asked to provide a poster for the Public Art Fund (PAF) in New York, the Guerrilla Girls were surprised when the PAF rejected their design on the grounds that it was not 'clear enough' (http://www.guerrillagirls.com/

posters/getnaked.shtml, March 2004). One explanation for the perceived lack of 'clarity' might be that the critical poster did not follow the culture's gendered rules for poster layout. It might also be that the male-dominated PAF were so challenged and unsettled by the layout that they could not understand it.

Another example of the ways in which these structures can be manipulated for shock effect is found in the *Independent* front page (see Figure 3.1 on p. 31), where the central section of the page is emphasised. The placing of text and the use of white space creates the central section. This is where the important question whether the Hutton report is a 'whitewash' or not is placed. The centrality of the question to British political life is signalled, not by placing it conventionally at the top of a page, but by adapting or inverting the structure and placing it in the centre of the page. As Kress and van Leeuwen (1996: 193–4) say, salience is usually signalled by an item's appearing at the top of the layout. Here, salience has been signalled by putting the question in a different place. In upsetting this conventional structure, the designers at the *Independent* have drawn attention to the political significance of the question and ensured that it cannot be ignored. Similarly, in constructing a layout with little or no left–right movement, or structure, the designers have also subverted the conventional given–new structure. This also has the effect of drawing attention to the question. Where in Kress and van Leeuwen's account a cultural group would expect their eyes to move from left to right, the layout here minimises that movement and disrupts the viewer's normal habits. With such a symmetrical layout, there is very little left–right movement. Such a device alerts the viewer to the idea that the *Independent* believes that this issue 'isn't going anywhere' and 'isn't going away' and stresses again the centrality of the question to British political life.

Salience refers to the prominence or conspicuousness of elements in a design and to the amount of attention they are designed to attract. Kress and van Leeuwen explain salience as the ways in which the viewer's attention is attracted to different elements in a layout to varying degrees. Some elements of a design are to stand out and others are not. The ways in which graphic designers can regulate salience, the degree of attention an element commands, include foregrounding, relative size, tonal contrasts and focus, for example (Kress and van Leeuwen 1996: 183). Foregrounding and relative size are used, for example, in the Wrigley's chewing gum advertisement (in Hine 1995: plate 9). Both the little girl and the policeman are behind the pack of gum and both are dwarfed by its size. Tonal contrasts are used by Ocean Spray fruit juices to regulate the viewer's attention. In the packaging design, the splash of juice noted above is in an eye-catching blue while the berries are in a subdued, natural red. This may be read as inviting the viewer to pay more attention to the ideal or the promise of the juice than the mundanity of the real berries.

SONGWRITING WORKSHOP

John MARTYN

Master of the acoustic guitar, John Martyn has proved himself on the UK's finest singer/songwriters over the past 30 years. Douglas Noble runs you through the tunes and the tunings...

Though John Martyn emerged from the late '60s folk scene, he has, by his own admission, 'never been very interested in the "folk scene" or the "jazz scene". Music's much bigger than that; these places can be so negative, and by its very nature music is a harmonious, all-embracing thing.'

Influenced by folk singer Hamish Imach, eclectic folk guitarist Davy Graham and blues musician Skip James, Martyn's first two albums; *London Conversation* ('68), and *The Tumbler* ('68) also revealed a distinct jazz influence. The acoustic-based

Bless The Weather ('71) typifies Martyn's spontaneous approach, being largely written in the studio and then improvised by the band.

For *Glistening Glyndebourne* from *Bless The Weather* Martyn uses a delay, while his amplified acoustic guitar was fitted with a pickup to create one of his trademark sounds. Inspired by the Glyndebourne opera festival, Martyn recalls in the sleeve notes to his *Sweet Little Mysteries* anthology ('94), 'There was this small country station and hundreds of people in evening gowns and dinner jackets poured onto the train. It was so formal and I think

music should be informal. I wanted something very loose that could change every time I played it,' Martyn's masterpiece *Solid Air* ('73) highlighted his important musical relationship with double-bassist Danny Thompson.

Martyn is a man who likes his two-chord vamps. The title track of *Bless The Weather* is based on a vamp in the minor key of Im IVm, as is the title track of *Solid Air* – that is, Am Dm in the key of A minor, or Cm Fm in the key of C minor. *Couldn't Love You More* from *One World* ('77) is based on a I IV vamp in the major key with chordal embellishments – A D in the key of A,

Figure 3.6 Magazine layout, *Guitar* magazine (January 2002), 12(8): 62–3.
© 2002 Guitar/Focus Network. Reproduced with permission by IPC Media Ltd. All rights reserved

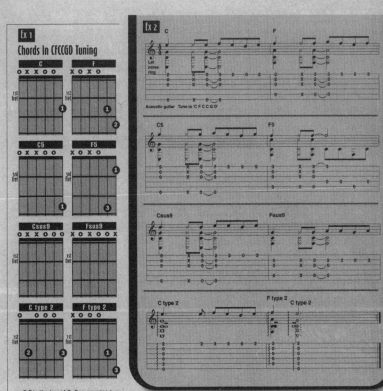

Ex 1

Chords In CFCCGD Tuning

or C F in the key of C. See exercise two for an exploration of this technique.

Much of Martyn's songwriting is heavily influenced by his use of open tunings, claiming that the greater note gap between the bottom and the top strings made it easier to achieve a warmer, yet bigger sound when playing solo. Though he often plays acoustic blues in open tunings, Martyn does employ the folk standard DADGAD for a number of songs. His favourite tuning, though, is one that he picked up from Dick Gaughan: CFCCGD. Based on a violin tuning, Martyn has explained that he likes the simple sweetness of this tuning, particularly the nuances that he can get from the C-tuned third and fourth strings. Martyn uses this unusual tuning in a number of his compositions, including *Couldn't Love You More*, *Small Hours*, *Dealer*, *One World*, *Some People Are Crazy*, *Lookin' On*, *Sweet Little Mystery* and *Hurt In Your Heart*.

DADGAD tuning is used for *Make No Mistake*, *Over The Hill*, *Spencer The Rover* and *Bless The Weather*. He also uses DADGAD variations: *Head And Heart* is in BADGAD; *May You Never* is in DADGBE. The title track of *Solid Air* is in DAFGCE. All these tracks can be found on *Sweet Little Mysteries*.

The following musical examples explore the textures created by CFCCGD and DADGAD tunings. Since the music notation reflects these unusual tunings, with notes on different frets from normal – drastically different frets in the case of CFCCGD – it is perhaps easier to get the notes from the tablature and take the timing from the music, rather than reading the music on its own.

Ex 1 Chords In CFCCGD Tuning

Going down to this tuning is difficult with light strings, as they'll either buzz horribly or go out of tune higher up the fretboard. As a way round this problem, instead of tuning all the way down, you could tune to C#F#C#C#G#D#, or DGDDAE, as both of these tunings have

the same relative intervals between the strings as CFCCGD. The first six chords are to be fingerpicked to avoid the unwanted open strings. The C type 2 and F type 2 chords are six-string and five-string voicings respectively, fully exploiting the resonant qualities of this tuning – especially the unusual unison C's on strings four and three.

Ex 2 I IV Progression With Percussive Accompaniment In CFCCGD Tuning

Martyn often uses a percussive 'thunk' in his chord work, as shown by the 'x' symbols shown in both the music notation and the tablature of the exercise. This can be achieved by firmly placing the right fingers back onto the strings, or by firmly placing the side of the right hand back onto the strings – the 'thunk' sound is produced ▶

63

43

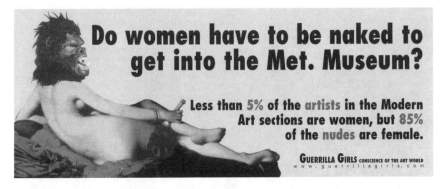

Figure 3.7 Poster, Guerrilla Girls (1989). Courtesy of Kathe Kollwitz for the Guerrilla Girls

Framing refers to the ways in which a layout connects or disconnects the elements within it. Graphic devices such as lines, or frames, are used to indicate that elements within a layout either do, or do not, 'belong together'. Kress and van Leeuwen (1996: 183, 217) suggest that horizontal lines have a 'weak' framing effect but that vertical lines have a 'strong' framing effect. In a recent Clinique advertisement for 'Happy' perfume, there is a very strong vertical frame which divides the women shown on the left from the product shown on the right. The same framing device also divides the word 'clinique' on the left from the word 'happy' on the right. The strong framing here establishes the 'given' or familiar material from the 'new' or unfamiliar material and establishes the connotation of the advertisement. Crudely, this is that the (new, unknown) product will make you 'happy' (given, familiar). A frame is also the name given to a development in website design (http://webreference.com/dev/frames/, March 2004) and html frames perform many of the functions described by Kress and van Leeuwen. Dan Brown, the creator of the webreference.com pages, says that frames may exist with or without borders and that they serve to 'segment the browser', keeping things apart. They are also useful for keeping something onscreen (navigation tools, or an index, for example), while something else changes. Whether they are seen or not, then, website frames are a graphic device that serves to indicate whether or not elements of a layout belong together.

The meaning of layout, the connotations generated, will vary from culture to culture. It is probably a consequence of the fact that western writing goes from left to right and from top to bottom that ensures that Kress and van Leeuwen's (1996) analyses are relevant to western graphic design. Left is where western writing begins from: it is appropriate that the left-hand side of a graphic layout contains material that one is already familiar with. When writing, what is already written appears to the left of the writer. The right-hand side of the page, where the writing goes toward, seems appropriate to contain new, undiscovered, material. In a culture where writing goes from right to left, it is reasonable to suppose that the meanings of layouts will be different, as they are with centre–margin layouts.

MEANING: ANCHORAGE AND RELAY

The explanation of meaning in the previous section uses ideas that could apply to images alone as well as to images that contain text: denotation, connotation and layout could be used to account for the production of meaning in image-only graphics, as well as in graphic design that employs image and text. This section will consider some central concepts which have been used to explain the ways in which combinations of words and images are meaningful. It will consider two of the main ways in which the relation between image and text has been conceptualised, anchorage and relay. There is a sense in which no images are at all meaningful without words. This is the sense in which words are necessary even to see or experience an image: without using language, one could not even identity what a picture contained, let alone describe that content or experience to someone else. To this extent, all experience is experience of meaning, as Derrida says (1981: 30). Without language, the image would not be experienced in any meaningful or communicable way at all and could, therefore, hardly be described as a experience at all.

Anchorage and relay are the metaphorical terms used by Roland Barthes (1977b, 1977a) in the essays, 'The Photographic Message' and 'Rhetoric of the Image' to describe the functions of text in relation to imagery. In the latter essay, Barthes describes anchorage and relay as the two functions of the 'linguistic message'. Where there is text and image in a piece of graphic design, then, the function of the text is first to anchor the meaning of the image and second to advance the action or scene appearing in the image. Because all images have many potential interpretations – they are 'polysemous' in Barthes's terms (1977a: 39) – and thus many possible meanings, the text functions to limit those interpretations, to fix the meaning. There are two forms of anchorage, both of which 'fix' or limit meaning. The first operates on the denotative level and limits denotative meaning. On this level, the text fixes the meaning of an image by answering the question 'what is it?'. This usually takes the form of the text simply naming or identifying what is in the image and Barthes (1977a) calls it the 'denominative' function. The second form of anchorage (anchorage 'proper') operates on the connotative level and serves to settle or to stop the 'drifting' of connotative meaning. On this level, anchorage prevents the proliferation of connotations, limiting or guiding the interpreter towards one preferred connotative meaning rather than another. Barthes (1977a: 40–1) claims that anchorage is the 'most frequent' function of the linguistic message in graphics design and that it is most commonly found in press photographs and advertisements. Relay is less common in graphic design, but Barthes (1977a: 41) says that this function of text is found in comics and cartoons where the text functions to 'advance the action'. The text within or above the image in a comic or cartoon is to move the story on, to help proceedings.

Barthes's example is an advertisement for jam or jelly, in which a 'few fruits' are scattered around the base of a ladder. The caption reads 'as if from your own garden'. The text anchors the connotational meaning by 'banishing' or excluding some alternative possible meanings; that the harvest has been very poor, that these are windfalls or that the product skimps on the fruit. Rather, the interpreter is 'oriented' towards a preferred or more 'flattering' reading; the natural and private bounty of your own garden (Barthes 1977a: 40). In the advertisement for the iPod, the text anchors the denotational meaning of the image by naming the product, iPod. On the connotational level, it anchors the image's meaning by excluding certain meanings (bracelet catalogue, dancing as a sin and so on) and guiding the interpreter towards the preferred reading (technological sophistication, perhaps).

Although Barthes provides no examples of relay, he seems to have the speech bubbles in comics and cartoons in mind, rather than the captions to frames. In the page from *2000AD*, however (Figure 3.8), the relay functions of both speech and caption can be seen to operate. The first caption announces that 'They make a brief stop at Vienna's apartment. The boy should know his family'. The function of the text here is clearly to get the reader into the next sequence of events and to tell the reader where they are, and why. The reader now knows that they are at Vienna's apartment and that she, and they, are to be acquainted with the 'family'. The page reproduced here is the sequence of events and the caption introduces the reader to the meeting between Rico, Dolman and Vienna in which Dolman meets his 'family' in the form of Vienna (who, genetically, could be Rico's daughter or his sister). The third caption reads 'She makes a pot of tea . . . '. Here, the action is advanced because tea-making is time-consuming and probably not the sort of thing that readers of *2000AD* want to see. Relay is being used in the service of the cultural group's perceived interests here. The caption advances the action by enabling the illustrator to fast-forward, omitting the kettle-boiling, the pot-warming and so on. The text in the speech bubbles also performs relay. In the final frame, for example, Vienna says 'Sit down . . . '. This prepares the reader for the next page, in the first frame of which the two Judges and Vienna are sitting round the tea-table, politely drinking their steaming mugs of tea.

Hillis Miller begins from the same place as Barthes, the problem of the relation between words and images. He raises the question 'Is a picture worth a thousand words?' and his provisional answer is 'Perhaps' (Hillis Miller 1992: 61). In expanding this 'perhaps', he takes the example of Mark Twain, who, on seeing Everett Julio's 1869 painting of *The Last Meeting of*

Figure 3.8 Extracted from *2000AD* (3 March 2004). © Rebellion A/S. The script
for 'Judge Dredd: Brothers of the Blood' is by John Wagner, the art by
Carlos Ezquerra and the lettering by Tom Frame. All Rights Reserved.
Used with permission. http://www.2000adonline.com

Lee and Jackson, answered the question with a resounding 'No'. Twain's position was that, without words, the image could mean any of at least eight things (including Jackson asking Lee for a match). The image is 'helpless' without a title or label and the interpreter is left to vacillate between alternative interpretations. Hillis Miller (1992: 65) then looks at some more complex examples, including the illustrated books of Edward Gorey, who 'exploits . . . the indeterminacy of pictures' in a different way from Twain. What Hillis Miller (1992: 65) is interested in is sequences of text and image 'that present pictures with captions placing them within a narrative of which the other parts are missing'. In *The Haunted Tea-Cosy*, for example, there is a story 'going on behind the scenes in the firmly labelled pictures' (it is a version of Dickens's *A Christmas Carol*), but the story is 'constantly interrupted by false clues'. In Figure 3.9, for example, Gravel, the Bahhum Bug and Nub are facing right with their arms raised. The caption reads:

The cynosure was a cake taller than everything else in the room, a conflation of Chartres Cathedral and the Stupa at Borobudur iced in dazzling white sugar; inside was a quarter-ton of fruitcake.

Figure 3.9 Illustration from Edward Gorey (1997) *The Haunted Tea-Cosy*, London: Bloomsbury, and New York: Harcourt. Courtesy of the publishers

What Gorey is doing is subverting the syntagmatic and paradigmatic structures that were explained in Chapter 2. Without any explanation, Nub, the orphan, has suddenly reappeared in the story, having been absent for the previous four frames. In the preceding frame, 'No sooner than they were back', Gravel is writing invitations and the Bahhum Bug watching. In the next frame, 'giggling, dancing and shrieking prevail', as the Bahhum Bug dances with Gravel and an unidentified woman; at the same time, an arm intrudes from the left and a leg from the right. Hillis Miller's point is that the words describe the images but that meaning is nevertheless subverted. The text provides anchorage, as denomination, but the syntagm is so incomplete that confident interpretation is impossible. Gorey undermines the way the meaning of the story is produced by paying little or no attention to the 'before and after' sequence that conventionally structures a narrative and thus generates meaning.

FOUCAULT AND GRAPHIC DESIGN

Michel Foucault is not often mentioned in connection with graphic design, but his work on Magritte has implications for the understanding of the relations between words and images (Foucault 1983; see also Lupton and Miller 1999: 66–70; Jobling and Crowley 1996: 280). In this work, Foucault begins with Magritte's 1926 or 1929 drawing entitled either *The Treason of Images* or *This is Not a Pipe* (Foucault 1983: plate 3) gives one date and title and Mitchell (1994: illustration 12) gives another). In the drawing, a meticulously observed pipe appears above the text 'Ceçi n'est pas une pipe' – 'This is not a pipe'. One aspect of Foucault's reading of this image is that it undermines the relation between image and text as that relation is normally experienced. On being shown such a drawing of a pipe without the text and being asked 'What is that?', most people will reply 'It is a pipe'. On being shown Magritte's drawing, most people will say, 'Well, of course it's only a drawing of a pipe, but you know what I mean'. The temptation is to dismiss the image, and the questioning, as either 'elementary or perverse' (Foucault 1983: 30). And yet what Foucault and Magritte are up to here is questioning the relationship between all images and all language, all relations between text and image. They are showing how the relations that most people think apply most of the time between text and image (that texts 'denominate' or 'anchor' images, or that images 'illustrate' and 'shed light on' the text) fall apart under the slightest pressure. How the text 'anchors' one's interpretation of Magritte's drawing is no longer clear. And how the image 'illustrates', illuminates or sheds light on the text has become obscure.

The level of meaning that is being undermined here is denotation. The question 'What is that?' is a question about the denotation of the image. The answer, 'It is a pipe', is supplying the denotative meaning of the image. By writing 'This is not a pipe' beneath the drawing, Magritte is drawing attention to the role of representation in our everyday understanding of the relation between words and images. Pointing out that this is not a pipe is to draw attention first to the fact that it is a representation of a pipe and second to the fact that we routinely refer to representations as though they were the actual thing represented. Representation is what happens when one thing stands for another thing and the sign is defined in terms of representation: one thing (the signifier) stands for another thing (the signified). So Magritte is highlighting the role of representation in our everyday understanding of the relation between words and images. The sense of 'anchoring' as 'fixing' has been made problematic in that it is now perfectly clear that 'anchoring' only anchors the meaning of one form of representation (visual) to another form of representation (verbal). There is nothing 'outside' of or 'beyond' representation to anchor meaning to. This also has implications for illustration's role in 'shedding light on' or illuminating the text. Illustration may shed light on the text, but only to the extent that it is one form of representation (visual) that is 'illustrating' another form of representation (verbal). Again, there is no outside of, or beyond to representation which might be used to illuminate representation.

The last implication of Foucault's and Magritte's work is that even denotation, even the most innocent illustration, is the product of cultural selection and agreement. Strictly, denotation is not a literal meaning and illustration cannot innocently or neutrally depict (shed light on) its subject. If one representation can only be explained in terms of another representation and if representation is a signifier standing for a signified, then whatever is selected as the literal meaning or as shedding light and must be the product of culture. This is because the relation between signifier and signified is arbitrary and therefore the result of cultural selection, negotiation and agreement. Any representation that is used to shed light on another representation will therefore be the product of cultural choice and agreement. As a product of cultural choice and agreement, it cannot be innocent and 'neutral'.

METAPHOR/METONYMY/SYNECHDOCHE

These terms are the names of figures of speech, or 'tropes'. Like the terms 'icon', 'index' and 'symbol', they name different ways in which something can stand for something else. Following the account of the sign that has been given so far, metaphor, metonymy and synechdoche are therefore explicable in terms of signifier and signified. They are also indicative of the construction and reproduction of a cultural group's beliefs and values. Unlike 'icon', 'index' and 'symbol', they describe an operation that is performed on the element(s) of a sentence. In the phrase 'She is a pillar of the community', the operation that has been performed is substitution by a similar thing. 'She', a person, has been substituted by something, a 'pillar', that is like her, but is not a person. Something from one context (architecture) has been used to replace something from another, different context (people). The quality that is similar is 'upstanding', or 'solid and dependable'. This is called metaphor. In the sentence, 'The suits are running the university', the operation that has been performed is substitution by a different thing. The 'suits', an item of clothing commonly worn by managers, has been substituted for the managers themselves. What has been substituted is an associated detail of something (the suits) that now replaces that thing (the managers). This is called metonymy. And in the sentence 'Have you seen the Professor's new wheels?' the operation performed is substitution of part for whole. What has been substituted here is a part of the car (the wheels) for the whole (the car). This is called synechdoche. Synechdoche also works when the whole is substituted for the part, as in 'Then the law arrived', when a single police officer turned up. Although they were originally used in the study of literature, they may be applied to graphic design. This section will explain how the visual forms of metaphor, metonymy and synechdoche work. (These tropes have been chosen from the thirty or so possible tropes as they are the most common and the post powerful used in graphic design. Chapter 8 of Gillian Dyer's (1982) *Advertising as Communication* contains a clear, illustrated and exhaustive account of what these tropes are and how graphic designers have used them in advertising. This section will follow her account of the difference between metonymy and synechdoche.)

As with denotation and connotation above, analytically, if not in our actual experience of it, graphic design is metaphorical in two ways or on two levels. The first is the way in which, merely by representing an object or an idea in two dimensions, graphic design takes something from one context and places it in another. An object has been 'carried across' or transported from one context (the world) to another (a drawing) and this is the operation that metaphor in general performs. The second concerns the specific operation that is performed on the idea or object. Some examples might help. In the advertisement for Barclays bank (Figure 3.10), the graphic design takes something from one context (personal finance) and transfers it into another context (visual representation, a picture). The graphic design is already metaphorical on this level. Next, the savings account has been represented specifically and visually as a leak in a boat. Again, something from one context (personal finance) has been represented in a different context (boating). There is something about, some quality of, the leak which is similar to the savings account (that you cannot ignore it). This is the second metaphor. It should not have gone unnoticed that the advertisement also happens to use a mode of transport (a boat) as a metaphor (that is, a mode of transport) for a financial product, thus complicating the metaphorical structure even further. Incidentally, although the copy at the

Figure 3.10 Advertisement, Barclays Bank (2004). Courtesy of Barclays Bank

bottom of the advertisement says 'Ideal for a buoyant bank balance', the connotation of the leak as potentially disastrous is another thing that cannot be ignored and there is a conflict between metaphor and connotation here. The recent Clinique 'Happy' advertisement uses a two-dimensional image to stand for a product in the world: this is the first level on which the design is metaphorical. Secondly, it says that there is some quality common to both product and image. This quality is 'feminine happiness' and it has been transferred across from the visual representation to the product: this is the second level on which the advertisement is metaphorical.

Visual metaphors are very common, especially in advertising. All perfume and many cigarette, food and drink advertisements, for example, employ metaphor. This is because they are obliged to use one thing, an image, to substitute for another, different thing, the product. They are compelled to use one form of representation to communicate something about a product or service that exists in the world. The perfume ad which contains an illustration of a beautiful woman, or man, is metaphorical because it is trying to communicate a quality of a smell by using something different from a smell, a picture. The cigarette ad which uses a picture of an American landscape is metaphorical because it substitutes the unprintable experience of the product with an image.

All graphic design that uses photography contains visual synechdoche. This is a result of the nature of photography. Any and all photographs 'capture' the subject in a fraction of a second, either on a sensitised film or electronic sensor. The image thus selected and 'captured' is necessarily a part, or a detail, of a larger whole: the sports photographer captures maybe 1/500 of a second and this is used to stand for the whole baseball game or test match. Any manually produced graphic design that depicts a still picture of some action or process also contains synechdoche. In these cases, however, it is not guaranteed by the nature of the mode of representation, but is the result of selecting a part or a detail of that action or process and 'freezing' it in the image. Martin Aitchison's 1970s illustrations for the Ladybird children's books *People at Work* and *Public Services*, for example, are synechdochic. They take a moment in time (in which a kindly policeman warns a little girl of the dangers of riding her bicycle near a busy road, for example) and that moment stands for a whole middle-class and English way of life (see Bracewell 2004: 30). The graphic design on the packaging for Ocean Spray cranberry juice uses synechdoche. The 'splash' of juice at the top of the pack is a frozen moment of the whole splash. Daniel Chandler (http://www.aber.ac.uk/media/Documents/S4B/sem07.html) uses Nissan's 'Ouch' advertisement to illustrate the idea of synechdoche. Chandler says that:

> The ad is synecdochic in several ways: it is a close-up and we can mentally expand the frame; it is a 'cover-up' and the magazine's readers can use their imaginations; it is also a frozen moment and we can infer the preceding events.

The advertisement uses synechdoche in that it shows a part of the man's body to stand for the whole of his body. It also shows an instant in time which refers to other events that happened before and will happen after that instant. And it provides a clue to the nature of the relationship between the man and his partner. In all of these aspects of the advertisement and with pun fully intended, a part is standing for a larger whole.

In the advertisement for nail polish (Figure 3.11), both metonymy and synechdoche are present. Metonymically, where an associated detail of something is used to represent that thing, the car represents 'the high life' or 'a glamorous and exciting social life'. The car itself is not the exciting social life but a detail or aspect of it, it is something that is a facet or a feature of such a life, and it stands in here for that life. Similarly, the blurred lights in the background operate as a metonym of 'urban entertainment'. They are not literally that urban entertainment but they stand, as an associated detail, for it. The visually represented bright lights stand metonymically for 'the bright lights' of modern urban entartainment here. In the same ad, the young woman's foot functions as a synechdoche in the same way as the

Girl's Night Out : 9:30 p.m. Drying my nails.

Figure 3.11 Advertisement, Nail Polish (2004). Courtesy of Superdrug Stores plc

man's torso functions above. And the women's faces are metonyms for the rest of their bodies. They are parts from which the rest of the bodies can be inferred.

CONCLUSION

This chapter has introduced some of the ways in which meaning is generated in graphic design. It has also tried to show how the production of meaning in graphic design is related to culture and communication via codes and signs. Two levels or types of meaning were identified and explained. Denotation and connotation were explained as types of meaning that were conditional on different levels of cultural knowledge. Both types of meaning required some cultural knowledge or membership in order to be constructed and understood, but connotation required far more than denotation. Layout was seen to be meaningful as a result of culturally specific codes concerning left–right, top–bottom and centre–margin structures and the ways in which those codes could be manipulated in order to disrupt the meanings conventionally produced by a dominant culture were explored. Barthes's account of anchorage and relay was outlined and applied to comic strips. Again, the relation to culture was explored by noting the way in which relay may be used to 'edit' the action that a cultural group is not expected to be interested in showed the role of cultural codes. The apparent perversity or childishness of Magritte's and Foucault's treatment of the illustrated text was shown to be an analysis of the cultural expectations regarding the relation between two forms of representation. And three major tropes were taken from literary theory and used to explain the most powerful operations performed by graphic designers.

Having explained the production of meaning in graphic communication in relation to cultural codes here, Chapter 4 will explore the social, cultural and economic functions of graphic design. Since no example of graphic design has ever been produced outside of a society, a culture and an economy, the ways in which graphics and these 'contexts' relate to each other will be explained in some detail.

FURTHER READING

- Another perspective on the **relation between words and images** may be found in Katherine McCoy's (1988) 'Graphic Design: Sources of Meaning in Word and Image', *Word and Image*, 4(1): 116–20. She pays particular attention to modernist typography and discusses Polish, Japanese and Russian graphic design. She begins from a similar problem in her (2001) 'American Graphic Design Expression: The Evolution of American Typography', in Heller, S. and Ballance, G. (eds) *Graphic Design History*, New York: Allworth Press. The chapter raises the problem of **visual and verbal understanding** in graphic design, with particular, but not exclusive, reference to typography.

- As argued earlier, there can be no '**anchoring**' of connotative meaning. Anchoring and drifting are metaphors and the problems with metaphor were outlined in Chapter 2. For more on this, see Derrida (1978a), where the 'drifting' of metaphor, and the impossibility of (a proper sense of) 'anchorage' is connected to communication.
- The problem of how verbal representation relates to visual representation is known as '**ekphrasis**' and is discussed in W. J. T. Mitchell's (1994) 'Ekphrasis and the Other', in *Picture Theory*, Chicago, Ill.: University of Chicago Press. Mitchell also provides a long discussion of the issues raised by Foucault's account of the Magritte drawing on pp. 64–70.
- In addition to the Lupton and Miller (1999) reference, Ellen Lupton's (1989) 'Reading Isotype', in Margolin, V. (ed.) *Design Discourse: History/Theory/ Criticism*, Chicago, Ill.: University of Chicago Press, provides another perspective. An extract from Otto Neurath's (1936) *International Picture Language* can be found in Ashwin, C. (ed.) (1983) *History of Graphic Design and Communication: A Sourcebook*, London: Pembridge Press. Philip Meggs (1983) *A History of Graphic Design*, New York: Viking, surveys the use of **isotype**-type symbols at the 1968 Olympic games.
- **Magritte's advertising work** is discussed by Georges Roque (2001) 'The Advertising of Magritte / The Magritte in Advertising', in Heller, S. and Ballance, G. (eds) *Graphic Design History*, New York: Allworth Press.
- The University of Wales Aberystwyth website at http://www.aber.ac.uk/media is good, again, for visual semiology. For **visual metaphor, metonymy and synechdoche**, see especially Daniel Chandler's contribution at http://www. aber.ac.uk/media/Documents/S4B/sem07.html (all 3.3.04).

4

SOCIAL, CULTURAL AND ECONOMIC FUNCTIONS

INTRODUCTION

This chapter will begin to investigate the social, cultural and economic functions of graphic design. It will ask how graphic design relates to society, culture and capitalist economy and it will investigate what roles it plays there. Drucker (1999: 42) suggests that graphic design points to the 'ideological values and cultural attitudes' of a society, but it will be argued here that it does more than point or indicate. This chapter will show that graphic design is one of the ways in which those values and attitudes are constructed, reproduced and challenged. It will therefore show that graphic design produces social, cultural and economic relations; to that extent, graphic design is productive of society, culture and economy. Strictly, these matters are closely interconnected; as the following sections will show, it is impossible to deal with any one of them without having to refer to the others. However, it is impossible to write about all of these things all at the same time and some attempt must be made to separate them, in the interests of clarity, while retaining a sense of their interconnectedness. The chapter will deal first with the relation between graphic design, society and culture, explaining the nature of society, the nature of culture and the functions of graphic design with regard to society and culture. It will then deal with the relation between graphic design and economics. This is partly because of the problem already mentioned and partly because economics seems to 'straddle' social and cultural issues; consumption, for example, will be shown to be as much a social matter as it is a cultural matter and the anti-consumption movements are as much about global economics as they are about cultures and societies.

THE RELATION TO SOCIETY AND CULTURE

Most students of graphic design would agree that there is some relation between graphic design and society. A majority of such students would also agree that there is some relation between graphic design and culture.

Unlike the situation that obtains in art, there is no question of anyone suggesting that graphics is independent of society or culture: were it not for the existence of different classes and cultural groups (another name for which might be 'audiences' or 'markets'), there would be little call for advertising graphics at all, for example. The idea of a 'graphics for graphics' sake' movement, along the lines of the nineteenth-century 'art for art's sake' movement, makes no sense at all. And, if pushed on the matter, most people would probably agree on the nature of the relation between graphic design and society and culture. The existence in pre-degree and degree-level curricula of what is variously called 'Contextual Studies', 'Complementary Studies', 'Historical and Theoretical Studies' and so on provides a clue as to the assumed nature of this relation. Such titles commonly describe two possible relations between graphic design and society and culture. The first is that society and culture exist as a backdrop, a background or a setting for graphic design. In this case, it is simply asserted in 'survey' courses that Art Deco graphics came after Art Nouveau graphics but before Swiss design and that they all took different forms in different countries. Of the former, it might be said that French Art Nouveau was floral and luxurious and that Viennese Art Nouveau was simple and more geometric, for example (Meggs 1983: 257). The second is that graphic design points to or reflects the society and culture it is found in. Graphic design is considered as a mirror or an indicator of something going on elsewhere, in 'society' and 'culture'. In this case, it is argued that social and cultural values and attitudes can be seen reflected in graphic products such as advertisements and that many advertisements from 1970s Britain contain stereotypes of women, because the culture of the time was 'sexist'. These are both ways of suggesting that graphic design operates within the context of society and culture.

In general, the courses with names such as these ignore the Latin derivation of the word 'context' (which would suggest a weaving together of two things), and it can be taken to mean a setting within which graphic design happens, and from which it could easily be removed. As noted, context may be used to mean 'backdrop', as in the theatre, and society and culture are conceived as the scenery before which the main action takes place. The other sense of context is that in which social and cultural beliefs and attitudes can be seen 'reflected' in graphic design, or in which graphic design can be used to point to and identify those beliefs and attitudes. Among the meanings of 'complementary' is 'parallel' and 'that which completes'. The sensitive theorist might take this to imply that graphic design and society or culture never meet (as parallel lines never meet). Or they might assume that graphic design could exist and operate perfectly well without society or culture, like a car with a broken radio, but that it would merely be 'incomplete'. This chapter will argue that the relation between graphic design and society cannot be described in these ways.

Instead, it will suggest that the metaphor buried in the word 'context' is in fact a useful one: it refers to a textile, with weft and warp, which would not exist were it not for the threads holding each other together.

This chapter will go so far as to argue that all these conceptions of the relation between graphic design and society and culture are mistaken to the point of being offensive to designers. The mistake lies in conceiving of society and culture as 'contexts', as either backdrops to graphic design or as being reflected in graphic design. Some of the offence lies in the implication that, as at the theatre, the actors and their actions have no effect upon the background and that the background has no influence on the actors. And some of the offence lies in the implication that all graphic designers do is mirror or signal something that is going on somewhere else. It surely does nothing for a designer's dignity to be told that their work has no effect on the culture or society around them, or that their work is just a mirror of something else, after all. This chapter will argue that, far from being backdrops to graphics or that without which graphics is incomplete, graphic design in fact produces and reproduces society and culture. The following sections will show that graphic design, society and culture are mutually conditioning: each is one of the ways in which the others are made possible. So, this chapter will show how graphic design makes society and culture possible, and how society and culture make graphic design possible.

SOCIETY

The component parts of society to be focused on here are class and institutions. Graphic design is one of the ways in which the identity and existence of social classes and social institutions are established and assured. It is also one of the ways by means of which that identity and existence may be challenged, or resisted. According to a Marxist account of society, every society is a class-based society (Marx and Engels 1985: 79) and social class is defined in terms of economics (Marx and Engels 1968: 170–1). In a much simplified Marxist account, one either owns, manages or works with the means of production (the machinery, property, money and knowledge, for example, necessary for the production of goods and services), and one's social class is defined in terms of that relation. Those who own the means of production in a capitalist society are called capitalists, or the bourgeoisie, in Marxism and those who work with it are called the proletariat. Immediately, there is class difference and one will notice that there is also an inequality or hierarchy here: there is a social structure. The presence of a social structure indicates that there is a political relation between these classes: where two or more classes exist there will be a power relation between them; there will be a political relation between them. The bourgeoisie have more money and power than the proletariat and they enjoy a higher social status than the proletariat. Members of the bourgeoisie have more money because they appropriate the profit that is made from the labour power of the proletariat. They have more power because they own and control the means of production. And they enjoy a higher social status because the possession of money and power is how status is measured in capitalist economies.

One should also notice that there is a conflict of interests here, a conflict of class interests. The different interests of the classes arises from their different relations to the means of production. Briefly, the bourgeoisie has an interest in promoting cheap, efficient and continuous production: they own the means of production and want to make as much money (or profit) as they can from both it and the workers they employ. The proletariat does not own the means of production and has an interest in benefiting from the profits of its own labour. These different and opposing interests give rise to different and opposing ideologies, sets of ideas and beliefs concerning the world and one's place in it. If members of the proletariat believe the idea that they are free and equal (free to choose to enter into employment, and equal to the person employing them, for example), then they are likely to continue turning up to work every day. If they believe the idea that their freedom to choose is their freedom to starve and that they are in fact exploited by their employer, then they are not so likely to turn up to work every day. Marx says that the ruling class also rules as a producer of ideas and dominant classes will produce dominant ideologies (Marx and Engels 1970: 64–5). Where a dominant class's ideology is seen as legitimate and natural and that class is able to exercise its authority, Marxists use the word 'hegemony'. Gramsci uses the word to refer to a sort of moving battlefield where different social classes continuously fight for social supremacy (Hall and Jefferson 1976: 401).

Institutions are groups of people organised for a purpose. The family, religion and education are well-known institutions and they may be explained as groups of people organised for a purpose. In some societies, the family consists of a mother, a father and children. Its purpose is the raising of the young and preparing them for a life in society. Education consists of teachers, students and administrators and some say its purpose is to develop an individual's potential, bringing out their abilities, skills and interests. It will be noted that institutions are affected by ideologies, the sets of ideas held by members of dominant or subordinate social classes. Consequently, different classes will have different ideas as to the functions of these institutions. There will be those with a different ideology who see education as a form of training, of fitting people with marketable vocational skills, rather than of enabling people to reach their potential. There will be those who want to include grandparents, uncles, aunts and others in the family personnel, or who see the family as ensuring the continued existence of a willing labour force. These are ideologies, they are political and they modify what people think about institutions.

SOCIAL FUNCTIONS

Now, the relation of graphic design to classes and institutions must be addressed. On the one hand, graphic design in general may be said to support the interests of the dominant classes, operating politically to enhance the power and status of those classes. As Raymond Williams (1980: 51) says, the means of communication are a means of 'social production', part of the way in which social class is made possible and reproduced. Apart from the dominant classes, with their financial and political power, which other classes would be able to afford to employ graphic designers? But on the other hand, graphics has a history of alternative employment, supporting the interests of subordinate classes. Graphic design, therefore, may be seen as one of the ways in which political power is reproduced and contested in society. James Curran (1982) analyses the relations between society, institutions and the mass media in his 'Communications, Power and Social Order'. He explains how the early medieval Christian Church used the mass media of the time, which included what we would now call graphic design and illustration, to construct and maintain its position of power in society. Sculptures, paintings and stained-glass windows were used to illustrate the life of Christ and the horrors awaiting the ungodly in hell, thus persuading people of the fact of his divinity and reminding them of God's omnipotence, both on Earth and in Heaven (Curran 1982: 207). The 'basic tenets of papal ideology' were communicated through graphic design in the interests of encouraging the population to believe the Christian tenets and not question the power of those who were running the church. As Pope Gregory the First said, the people could 'read by looking at the walls what they could not read in books' (Curran 1982: 207). The function of graphic design here was to help keep an elite social class in power over the lower, illiterate, classes.

On the other hand, Curran's essay also provides evidence of graphic design being used to challenge or contest the social order, to support the interests of the subordinate classes in their conflict with a dominant social class. He refers to the growth of print media from the thirteenth century onwards (Curran 1982: 217). During this time paper became more widely available, making it cheaper and quicker to produce manuscripts; more people were employed in the copying of books, either in commercial or university scriptoria; and an international book trade was established. Following the invention of movable type in 1450, productivity rose while costs fell. Printers, typesetters and designers were all involved in these developments and all contributed to what Curran (1982: 218) calls the undermining of the 'ideological ascendency of the Church'. So, movable type, cheap print processes and increasing numbers of people involved in graphic design, allied to the introduction of new media such as fly-sheets and pamphlets, all posed a serious and critical threat to the authority of the Catholic elite. Indeed, Curran (1982: 220) goes so far to say that 'Protestantism was, in some respects the product of print'.

More recently, the representation of the British royal family shows evidence of both aspects of graphic design's social function. Much of the British press automatically adopts a supportive and uncritical position regarding this family, but some of it is more critical. Some graphic design, then, is used to reproduce the social position of this particular branch of the aristocracy and some graphic design is employed in the interests of a more egalitarian social order, contesting the existing hierarchy. In February 1992, for example, *Hello* magazine saw fit to celebrate the fortieth anniversary of the accession of Queen Elizabeth II to the throne. That month's edition contained a series of photographs of the Queen and the family. The photographs used in this edition depicted the sorts of scenes that are found in all family photo albums: a young woman standing in the garden, a young mother watching her son playing in his toy car in front of the house, group portraits with her mother, son, daughter-in-law and grandchildren sitting on the sofa, and so on. The connotation of these images is that the royal family is just like any other family and the function of the images is to make their social position and status appear to be natural and normal. The facts that the 'garden' is Windsor Great Park, that 'the house' is Sandringham (just one of the houses), that 'mother' was the wife of the previous king and that 'son' is, potentially, the next king are effaced by the ordinariness of the subject matter. Such effacement and the resulting legitimisation of the social position and status of the family are part of the process in which that social status is reproduced.

A more critical attitude to the royal family is shown by the *Guardian* newspaper, which uses graphic design to mount a gentle attack on the same family (Figure 4.1). The G2 section for 27 July 1993 features an illustration by Steve Caplin and Paul Jeremy of the Queen, along with Princes Philip and Charles, sitting on a sofa reading books. The caption reads 'The books one ought to take to Balmoral'. Prince Philip is reading *The Ragged-Trousered Philanthropists*, a socialist novel by Robert Tressell, and he looks suitably irritated and revolted. The Queen, wearing curlers and a greedy, gleeful grin, is reading a book about tax. And Prince Charles is having his eyes opened by Madonna's book *Sex*. Of course, Philip is correct to react the way he does: the introduction of social justice and the abolition of class-based, unearned privileges would mean the end of his class's way of life. The Queen's expression is probably referring to the way in which the world's richest woman demonstrates a marked reluctance to pay tax. And Charles, like the rest of them, would not be in the position he is in were it not for his being the chance product of the right two people having sex. In July 1993, Charles's sex life was the subject of much media speculation; he had allegedly been recorded telling Camilla Parker Bowles that he wanted to be her tampon and had been legally separated from his wife in 1992. The

Figure 4.1 Illustration, Steve Caplin and Paul Jeremy (1993).
Courtesy of the designers

graphic designers here, then, are not reproducing the social status and position of this family, or of the social class they represent. Caplin and Jeremy are pointing out the ideological, financial and ancestral interests of a social class and, by so doing, they are questioning the legitimacy and persisting operation of those interests.

Not surprisingly, the French and Russian revolutions of 1798 and 1917 are rich sources of graphic design whose function is to contest and challenge the social order. The image of the social pyramid, which is wide at the bottom and narrow at the top, is a popular motif in such graphics. One example, entitled 'Pyramide a Renverser', or 'The Pyramid to be Overthrown', was produced by the Socialist Press in France. At the top of the social pyramid is royalty, in the form of the king: the caption alongside him reads 'I reign over you'. Beneath him are two clerics, praying, and the caption reads 'I pray for you'. Three soldiers support the clerics, saying 'I shoot upon you'. Four seated and fat capitalists, smoking and drinking hold up the soldiers: 'I eat for you'. At the very bottom of the pyramid, propping up the entire structure, are 'the people', whose caption reads 'I work for you'. The depiction of working people, at the bottom of the social order, but sustaining and carrying the entire edifice, challenges the fairness of that social order and encourages the revolution to overthrow, or reverse, the structure. The political caricatures and cartoons of William Hogarth, James Gillray and Thomas Rowlandson in the eighteenth century are also good examples of graphic design being used to support or oppose political groups. Gillray supported the Tories and opposed the Whigs and Radicals such as Tom Paine, while Rowlandson and Hogarth satirised anyone and everyone. Hogarth's 1743 series of paintings entitled *Marriage à la mode* (in the National Gallery in London), which he also produced as a series of engravings, is an uncompromising satire on the morals and practices of both the emerging middle classes and the aristocracy. In the first of this series, we see the newly rich merchant and the aristocratic Lord Squander haggling over the marriage contract. Squander, gouty, heavily in debt and with his mortgage overdue, is displaying his family tree, while the merchant is so vulgar as to put cash on the table. As the lawyer, Silvertongue, chats up the bride-to-be, her potential husband admires himself distractedly in the mirror. Hogarth's point is that wealth should be earned, not inherited or married and he effectively skewers both aristocratic and middle-class beliefs about marriage.

A contemporary example of political graphics is provided by Steve Bell's cartoons for the *Guardian* newspaper and in his work for *Leveller* and *New Statesman* magazines (see Bell 1999). While Bell claims to have been influenced by Leo Baxendale and Robert Crumb (Bell 1999: 9), his work may also be placed in the tradition of cartoonists such as David Low, Vicky (Victor Weiss) and Fougasse (Kenneth Bird). Bell takes a left-wing political stance and uses it to castigate any and all political leaders. In Figure 4.2, the British Prime Minister appears, heavily caricatured and in the process of terrorising the British public with the prospect of 'Really evil terrorists! Behind you!!' Bell is making the point that Tony Blair needs to scare the British population into believing that the threat of terror is real in order to drive through a series of Bills limiting civil liberties and increasing the role

Figure 4.2 Cartoon, Steve Bell (2004). Courtesy of the artist

of the surveillance services. He is thus critiquing the actions and policies of the 'New Labour' government.

All of the examples analysed so far have used representational imagery (recognisable pictures of people, for example) to provide an alternative to or a critique of an existing social order. It is worth pointing out that abstraction (where shapes, line and colour alone stand for people or ideas) can be used to contest a social order. El Lissitzky's (1919) *Beat the Whites with the Red Wedge* is probably the best known example of this. Meggs (1983: 312–13) suggests that El Lissitzky even moved into a more abstract version of graphic design, as opposed to fine art, in order to assist the social transformation of Russia begun by the February 1917 revolution. Following the 1917 revolution, in which Tsar Nicholas II was overthrown, there was a series of provisional governments in Russia. Then, in October 1917, the Leninist Bolsheviks, known as the Red Guard, overthrew the provisional government to form the first Soviet government. However, Tsarist forces regrouped to oppose the new Soviet regime and there was civil war. In El Lissitzky's work, the white circle, representing the Tsarist forces led by Kerensky, is shown being penetrated, or pierced, by the red triangle, representing the revolutionary Bolshevik forces. The work, then, is encouraging people to join the communist forces, who want to establish some form of socialism in Russia, and to defeat the Tsarist forces, who want to retain the aristocracy, the royal family and the social order that prevailed before the revolution. The function of El Lissitzky's graphic design is to encourage political opposition to the old and unjust social order.

Finally, the ability of a social system to incorporate critical material and render it harmless should not be underestimated (see Fox-Genovese 1987; Barnard 2002: 138–41). Capitalism is infinitely accommodating and able to make a profit from the most challenging graphic design. The case of Banksy is indicative of what was referred to above as a 'moving battle'. His anarchist graffiti (reproduced at http://www.banksy.co.uk) is now available as a silk screen print at Simon Finch Art in London for £200 a print (see

http://www.simonfinchart.com/picture.php?id=Graffiti&picid=33,   March
2004). The website advertises the sale of Banksy's 'artwork' known as *Rude
Copper*, saying:

> Original signed silkscreen by London's most notorious and
> probably most political graffiti artist. This image is a great example
> of his stencil technique and demonstrates how he uses it to produce
> a contemporary slant on his punk heritage.

The 'punk heritage', the anarchic, violent and subversive attitude to
consumption, fashion, music, politics and graphic design (see Hebdige 1979:
114), has itself been made into a commodity to be bought and sold. Using
many of the most potent terms of art history, Banksy's graffiti has been
turned into a work of art; it is 'original', 'signed' and a 'silkscreen'; it evinces
'his stencil technique'. In this way is the 'most notorious . . . most political'
and most critical graffitist transformed into an 'artist' and made available
for conservative middle-class consumption.

CULTURE

There are many definitions of culture. Not all of them are of much use when
it comes to explaining graphic design. According to some of them, for
example, graphic design does not count as an example of cultural activity. It
is an easy target, and one which your present author has aimed at before
(see Barnard 1998), but Kenneth Clark's (1969) *Civilisation*, which surveys
numerous attempts to 'enlarge' or 'develop' the human mind (Clark 1969:
xvii) omits any reference to graphic design as it has been explained thus far.
A few illuminated manuscripts are included (the Book of Kells and the
Lindisfarne Gospels) and printed translations of the Bible are mentioned.
But neither the Book of Kells nor the Lindisfarne Gospels is mechanically
reproduced and it is the translation, rather than the printed book, that
interests Clark (1969: 160). Even a more recent book entitled *Visual
Culture* (Jenks 1995) contains only one chapter on anything recognisable as
graphic design; all of the other thirteen chapters concern themselves in
some way with 'art' or terms from art history. Books such as these think of
culture in what has been called a 'unilinear' and elitist fashion. Unilinear
means 'one line' and unilinear conceptions of culture hold the view that
there is only one course or direction for a worthwhile, valid culture to
follow. Those cultures and artefacts that are not on that route are deemed
either immature or deviant. Clark (1969) believes that European aristocratic culture, including oil painting, sculpture and architecture, is the only
proper culture and he explicitly omits non-western cultures. Graphic
design, whether printed text or image, including printed ephemera and
lower-class or mass cultures, is nowhere to be found and the impression is

that graphic design is not a part of 'civilisation'. Unilinear conceptions are closely related to elitist conceptions of culture. To concentrate on 'art' in a book on 'visual culture' is elitist in that it privileges the culture of the educated upper classes over those of other, lower, classes.

According to others, culture itself is a form of communication, like graphic design. Colin Cherry (1966: 4), for example, says 'A group of people, a society, a culture, I would define as "people in communication"'. Although this is rather too vague to be of much use here, it does make the point that cultures consist in groups of people who communicate with each other, who talk to each other, show each other pictures, read and understand each other's books, magazines, newspapers and so on. Graphic design is one of the ways in which people can communicate with each other, it is one of the ways in which people can understand each other. It is therefore constitutive of cultures. And James W. Carey (1992: 30) argues that 'to study communication is to examine the actual social process wherein significant symbolic forms are created, apprehended and used'. Effectively, he is arguing that the study of communication is the study of culture, and that culture is the creation and use of meaningful forms, which would clearly include graphic design. These conceptions of culture are multilinear and more democratic than those discussed above. Multilinear means 'many lines' and multilinear conceptions of culture take the view that there are many different cultures, each of which is as interesting and valuable as the others. These conceptions are democratic in that they do not emphasise the culture of a dominant, or 'superior' social class. Rather, mass-produced artefacts, printed images and texts and everyday products are included as examples of culture. Unsurprisingly, this book allies itself more closely to the second two definitions than the first two and it explicitly deals with Raymond Williams's (1961) formulation of precisely this problem concerning communication and creativity in Chapter 8.

However, it is with Williams's (1981) definition of culture as 'the signifying system through which . . . a social order is communicated, reproduced, experienced and explored' (1981: 13) that this section will be concerned. It should be obvious by now that graphic design may itself be considered as a 'signifying system'. Chapters 2 and 3 presented various models of communication and introduced a number of semiological concepts all of which were used to explain the ways in which graphic designers constructed and communicated meaning. So, graphic design may be thought of as a signifying system, within a much larger system, which includes and accounts for all of the other ways in which a society constructs and communicates meaning (fashion, literature, music, language, art, philosophy and so on: Williams 1981: 13). The social order has been at least partly explained in the section above as social classes, ideologies and institutions. And that graphic design is one of the ways in which people, beliefs and institutions are variously experienced, communicated, reproduced and explored should need no emphasis here. One might want to add the idea of challenge, or resistance to Williams' list. It is not the case that all graphic designers simply reproduce the social order, its inequalities or its ideologies: some attempt to oppose what they see as inequity, discrimination and injustice through their work.

To summarise: culture may be thought of as the beliefs and values (the ideologies) of groups of people and the ways (the signifying systems – both products and processes) in which those beliefs and values are communicated, reproduced and contested. The beliefs and values may concern any and all aspects of the world and its contents as they are experienced by the group in question: nature, children, material goods, gender, other people and so on. Graphic design is a cultural activity in that it is one of the signifying systems in which those beliefs and values are communicated, one of the ways in which those beliefs and values may be reproduced or challenged. Its products and processes are examples of culture in so far as they reproduce or resist the social order.

CULTURAL FUNCTIONS

This section will consider some examples of the cultural function of graphic design. It will take some examples of western cultural beliefs and show how examples of graphic design have either constructed and communicated or provided challenges and alternatives to those beliefs.

Childhood

The first example is that of childhood. Childhood is something that all cultures think important and concerning which they hold identifiable, if not always entirely consistent, beliefs. The strength and intensity with which these beliefs are held can be gauged by the regularity with which stories about children appear in the mass media. Features on the nature of children, what sorts of things they are, the correct or appropriate way for adults to relate to them and the scandal of their mistreatment, are regularly occurring features in western press and television media. At the time of writing, for example, the pop singer Michael Jackson features heavily in print and broadcast media as a direct result of his personal opinions as to what sorts of things children are and what is the best way to behave towards them. Pete Townshend, another musician, was investigated for allegedly accessing child porn on the internet for research purposes. And paedophiles are routinely demonised by certain sections of the press until they have become the ever-present and threatening parental nightmare. This section will investigate the cultural function of graphic design, how graphic designers have constructed and communicated the beliefs of the culture they are part of.

The dominant cultural belief concerning children includes the ideas that they are innocent, vulnerable and that they should not be thought about in a sexual way. In 2003, the charity Barnardo's ran a series of advertisements alerting people to the evils of child abuse. They showed computer-enhanced images in which children and babies were shown injecting drugs, drinking in alleyways or apparently having just had sex with an adult (Figure 4.3). Whoever has been involved in the production of this poster has clearly been paying attention to his or her culture's position on the nature of children. The loss of innocence connoted by the computer-generated face of the girl and the brutish backside of the man on the bed torments the viewer, the terrible vulnerability of the child's pose and gaze is almost tangible and the case for supporting Barnardo's protective work is powerfully made. In this poster, then, the graphic design reproduces a dominant view of this culture's view of children. One suspects that the graphic design team here was also paying attention in their 'Complementary Studies' class (see p. 58). Edvard Munch's (1895) painting known as *Puberty* would appear to be the source of the illustration in the Barnardo's poster. In this painting, Munch is not simply reproducing a view of children as being innocent and vulnerable; it is almost as if he is suggesting that innocence and vulnerability are themselves sexually enticing. Such a portrayal is not to be critical of the culture's dominant view of childhood, but it is to present an alternative and it may be indicative of the inconsistency in the beliefs held by a culture that was noted above. The young woman in Munch's work assumes a similarly defensive pose; with arms crossed and knees together, she inevitably suggests innocence and vulnerability. But Munch's young woman has hips and breasts: she is sexually mature. Moreover, she returns our gaze: she may be wide-eyed, but she is presented as not entirely innocent. One begins to feel quite uneasy looking at her, as though Munch were offering her as a sexual object.

Another example of this inconsistency in the dominant beliefs and values of a culture, and of the way in which examples of graphic design can construct and communicate such inconsistency is found in recent Armani advertisements. One advertises Armani for women and the other advertises Armani for children. Both are promoting luxury fashion products which are intended to make the wearer feel or appear more attractive: both use black and white photographs of a female model and both models are returning the gaze of the viewer. Both adverts use a full-face portrait, although the one featuring the adult woman is more closely cropped than the one representing the child. The Armani for women advertisement shows an attractive and mature woman returning the spectator's gaze and the Armani for children advertisement appears to show an attractive but immature child returning the spectator's gaze. Seduction, like beauty, may well be in the eye of the beholder, but it also seems to be in the eyes of both these models. Similar, if not identical, graphic and persuasive techniques

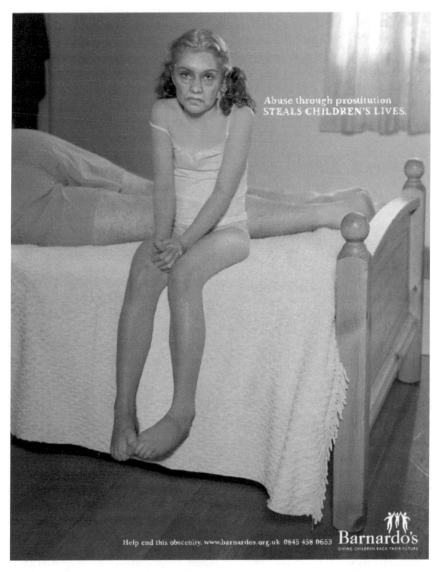

Figure 4.3 Poster, Barnardo's (2002). Courtesy of Barnardo's

are being used to sell adult products as are being used to sell children's products. One of the connotations of these advertisements, therefore, is that children are the same sorts of things as adults. It would not be implausible to suggest that what is being communicated by the Armani Junior advertisement is the idea that children are sexy, they are attractive and that it is acceptable for one to relate to them as one would an adult, including, apparently, thinking sexually about them. The graphic design in

70

this case is constructing, communicating and reproducing beliefs regarding children that are distinctly at odds with the dominant cultural view of childhood.

Nor is this the only example of such beliefs being communicated. There is an entire genre of magazines for teenaged girls published in UK magazines such as *Sugar*, which bills itself as 'Britain's best-selling girl's magazine'. In the December 2001 edition, advertisements for perfumes, body products and clothing are found alongside the 'Sex Q&A' page in which 13-year-old girls receive advice on oral sex and the horoscope page in which the majority of predictions concern the 'fab new guy' to be encountered next week. That the graphic designers, art directors and artists who design, illustrate and layout such magazines are helping to produce an alternative view of childhood from that held by the dominant culture is borne out by the controversy that such magazines regularly generate. Also in 2001, Calvin Klein got into trouble for using pictures of young boys and girls in their advertisements: the highly sexualised images, in which the young model's underwear was visible, upset many people (see http://employees. oneonta.edu/farberas/arth/Images/ARTH200/body/Calvin_klein.html for the images, August 2004). There is a long tradition of graphic designers and illustrators communicating a view of children that does not fit into the dominant view held by the culture, that children's innocence and vulnerability is to be protected by adults. In *Strewwelpeter* (2000), for example, which was first published in 1844, Heinrich Hoffmann's 'pretty pictures and funny stories' show Harriet burning to death, Conrad bleeding after his thumbs are cut off with scissors and Augustus dying of malnutrition. Hilaire Belloc's (1907) *Cautionary Tales for Children*, illustrated by Edward Gorey in the Harcourt edition (2002), features children eaten by lions (Jim) and burned to death (Matilda). In *The Gashleycrumb Tinies*, first published in 1963, Edward Gorey (1998) presents, alphabetically, all the comical and rhyming ways in which little children can die. 'Q', for example, is for Quentin, 'who sank in a mire' and 'R' is for Rhoda, 'consumed by a fire'. Willans and Searle's (1999) *Molesworth*, published in the 1950s, contains Ronald Searle's pen and ink illustrations of 'Kanes I Have Known' (1999: 13), including the 'Nonpliant . . . with silencer attachment to drown victims cries [sic]' and the 'Table of Grips and Tortures for Masters' (Willans and Searle: 48–9), which recommends shaking, also known as 'The cork in the storm for violent temperaments'. Molesworth's innocence is clearly open to question but, while the other characters are both innocent and appallingly vulnerable, the glee with which their demises are drawn suggests that an alternative view of the unsuspecting defencelessness of children is both possible and profitable. It is an ambivalent culture that finds a space in which child abuse is acceptable, hilarious even and, as members of such a culture, the cultural function of graphic designers and illustrators can only be to communicate that ambivalence.

Gender

The second example to be dealt with here is gender. As with childhood, gender is something that all cultures think important and concerning which they also hold identifiable, if not always consistent, beliefs. Theoretically at least, gender is to be distinguished from sex. In humans, sex is to do with reproduction and is made possible by physiological differences. Reproduction requires genitalia and one's sex is determined by which set of genitalia one possesses, male or female. Gender is the meaning or the significance that a culture gives to sexual difference. As a cultural phenomenon, a gender identity is the product of a set of beliefs or ideas concerning what it means to be male or female and, being cultural, different gender identities are accorded different values. Being emotionally stunted and inarticulate may mark you out as masculine and being nurturing and domestic may indicate that you are feminine in many western cultures, but not in certain Middle Eastern cultures, for example. Ways of behaving are said to be masculine or feminine, and masculinity and femininity are not accorded equal value in any culture. So, sexually, one is usually male or female, with one or other set of genitalia. Culturally, one is more or less masculine or feminine, according to how one's culture defines and assigns meaning to masculinity and femininity. 'Proper' or 'appropriate' characteristics and ways of behaving are assigned to the categories 'masculine' or 'feminine'.

The following paragraphs will explore the ways in which the dominant cultural beliefs concerning masculinity and femininity are communicated and reproduced by graphic designers. Then some attempts to challenge or resist those dominant beliefs will be proposed. It is worth noting that another word for the dominant beliefs concerning or values ascribed to masculinity and femininity is 'stereotype'. Originally the name of a photographic print-making process, to stereotype means to present a simplified and generalised image of a group of people accompanied by an implicit or explicit judgement concerning the social, cultural or moral worth of that group (see O'Sullivan et al. 1994: 299–301). Dominant beliefs, or stereotypes, are dominant because they are produced (in graphic design) on the behalf of dominant cultural groups. In a culture where middle-class white males are dominant, one might reasonably expect the non-white, the non-middle-class and women to be stereotypically devalued. The cultural function of graphic design in stereotyping is therefore to construct, communicate and reproduce the dominant group's simplified and generalised images of what are in fact diverse and complex groups of people.

In the USAir advertisement (Figure 4.4), various men and women are portrayed performing various activities. One smiling woman is staffing the check-in desk, another is serving food and drinks. There are four non-smiling men: one is ordering an airplane around with some light-sticks, another is on the telephone, and the third is reading papers and writing. In

You'll find it's easier
doing business with USAir.

Now daily to Baltimore/Washington, Philadelphia and Charlotte.

Everything USAir do for you, makes it easier to do business in the USA.

Our non-stop flights leave Gatwick at civilised hours and arrive at convenient local times.

Our in-flight service is amongst the most hospitable in the skies.

The key hubs we fly to are some of the most modern and least congested gateways into the USA. Customs and baggage reclaim is quick and hassle-free.

Onward connections couldn't be easier. From these three gateways alone, you can fly direct to over 120 US cities and centres of business, without changing airlines.

And, until March 31st, we're offering free round trip airport transfers in 14 U.S. cities for anyone who flies Business Class or Full Fare Economy.

So if you're flying business to the USA, make it easy on yourself. Call your Travel Agent or phone USAir direct on 0800 777 333.

USAir

USAir begins with you

Figure 4.4 Advertisement, USAir (1999)

terms of gender, however, two gender identities are portrayed, masculine and feminine. Femininity declares that certain characteristic qualities are exemplified by women, who are thus recognised as feminine. In western cultures, these qualities include being submissive, passive, caring and decorative. Hence the women in the advertisement are smiling and attending to the men's requirements. Masculinity is the association of

73

certain characteristic qualities with men, who may thereby be recognised as masculine. These qualities include being assertive, dominant, active and rational. Hence the men are non-smiling, ordering things about and engaged in serious business-related activities. This is part of what it means to be masculine or feminine in western culture: these activities have been ascribed masculine or feminine status. The graphic design's cultural function here is to communicate and so reproduce that meaning and that status.

The following paragraphs will explore the other cultural function of graphic design, to challenge or contest the dominant cultural beliefs and values of a society. In the Diesel advertisement seen in Chapter 3 (Figure 3.5), three young women are visiting the sperm bank. One sits flicking through a catalogue of donors, one stares into space, pondering her choice and the third inspects the test tube containing the 'Special Offers' donation, given to her by a an older nurse figure, who holds a tray of test tubes. In the background, the wall is covered with mug-shots of men, including one that looks like Andy Warhol. The first line of the copy reads 'Men. Who needs 'em?' and in the body copy the words 'designed for women' appear in a different colour, in bold and a larger point size than the rest of the copy. The use of text and image here constitutes an alternative to the dominant gender identity of women in that these women are not passive, they are not submissive and they are not pandering to the needs of men. The text suggests that men are unnecessary and that the products are designed for women: women are the centre of attention, not a peripheral attraction. Indeed, although they have not managed to do without men entirely, they have managed to do without having to relate to them emotionally. Their relation will be purely financial. Men have become the commodity, to be assessed, judged and purchased purely on the basis of their looks and this is a significant reversal of the usual gender roles, in which, as John Berger (1972: 47) says 'men act and women appear'. The role of women in advertisements is more commonly that of the surveyed object than of the active subject and the graphic designer here has provided a critique of, and a challenge to, that role.

Homophonically, and in terms of gender, recent Siemens advertising is entirely appropriate here. In one of the ads, a man with the hint of a smile on his face carries bags of vegetables through a blond-wood floored and white-walled room to the stainless steel refrigerator. Above and to the right, the copy says that the refrigerator is both stylish and 'good'. The critique of dominant gender roles here lies in the portrayal of a man in a domestic setting. This is unusual because, as Buckley (1989: 256) points out, a 'relatively constant feature of the sexual division of labour is the delineation of women's role as housewives and carers for the family'. The dominant conception of women's gender role in western culture is that of housewife and carer and as designers usually assume that 'women are the sole users of home appliances' they present women as housewives in advertisements for products (Buckley 1989: 256). In this case, the designer has gone against the dominant portrayal of gender roles and provided a challenge to those roles. So, where it is traditionally, or ideologically, held to be the woman's job, the man is shown performing a domestic task and smiling while he does it. To that extent, the graphic design here functions as a critique of the cultural ascription of gender identity.

THE RELATION TO ECONOMICS

It was suggested earlier that most students of graphic design would be happy to entertain the idea that their practice was related to society and culture, and that it had social and cultural functions. At first glance, the relation to economics, beyond the simple assertions that graphic design is part of 'the design industry' or that design briefs specify a budget, might be less cordially received. Graphic design is said to be part of a country's design industry. It is part of the economy, part of the means of production, and its contribution to the gross national or domestic output of a country is confidently asserted. But how that contribution is to be measured is not clear. To argue by analogy: it has been claimed that a corporate identity or a trademark has an economic value, but as Saul Bass says, there is no way of putting a figure on that value. It is difficult, if not impossible, he says, to separate the economic contribution of the trademark or corporate identity from all the other things in the 'marketing mix: advertising, sales promotion, packaging . . . etc' (Bass, quoted in Meggs 1997a: 71). It is difficult, if not impossible, then, to assess the contribution of a nation's graphic design industry to the national economy because it is impossible to re-run history with graphic design absent from the 'mix'. What this section is concerned with rather is, first, the function of graphic design within capitalist economy as a whole and, second, how graphic design mediates the relation between economics, culture and society.

As Walker points out, design cannot be separated from the economic system in which it is found; a particular mode of production and exchange 'permeates' design so profoundly that it is 'largely invisible to those in the profession and those in design education' (Walker 1989: 35). Economics is at the centre of the explanation of social class, as it was explained previously. For Marx, class identity is a product of an economic relation to the means of production. As well as being part of the economic means of production, graphic design was also shown to be one of the means of social production, one of the ways in which class identity is constructed and challenged. Similarly, economics is central to the account of culture in that consumption is part of the 'social process' in which 'symbolic forms are created, apprehended and used' (Carey 1992: 30). On Williams' account, consumption is a part of the 'signifying system' by means of which a social order is experienced and made meaningful (Williams 1981: 13). At its simplest, the argument is that a cultural group's beliefs and values are established and communicated through consuming products different from those consumed by other cultural groups and that graphic design encourages consumption (largely, but not only in the form of advertising). Consumption, then, is the economic 'bridge' between society and culture, and graphic design's most important economic function is either to produce and reproduce, or to challenge and resist, consumption.

Marx is clear on the central position of consumption to economics. 'Without production no consumption; but also, without consumption, no production; since production would then be purposeless' (Marx 1973: 91). So, the production of commodities creates consumption. But consumption in turn produces or creates production itself. It does this in two ways. First, because a product becomes a 'real product' only by being consumed. There is a sense in which a product is only properly a product as and when it is consumed. As Marx (1973: 91) says, a house where no one lives in not a real house. Second, because 'consumption creates the need for new production' (Marx 1973: 91). Consumption ensures that production itself is reproduced because, once the product is consumed, another one is needed. When your printer cartridge is used up and empty, you have to buy another one. Graphic design encourages (produces and reproduces in Marx's terms) consumption largely, but not only in the form of advertising. Chapter 5 will explore this topic in more detail, using examples that are not advertising, but here it should be noted that advertising is essential to the continued existence of the economy. As Williams (1980: 186) says, capitalism and advertising could not continue without each other. Advertising would not exist without a capitalist, class-based society and modern capitalism 'could not survive' without advertising.

Consumption is therefore related to identity and to politics. It is related to identity in that social and cultural identity are the result of choices made between different commodities. In buying and wearing Gap clothing, for example, one is constructing an identity by associating with the perceived values of the brand and differentiating oneself from those who buy and wear Brooks Brothers or Austin Reed clothing. In the same way, a magazine which uses a loose 'cut-and-paste' technique, with bold colours and a cluttered page is constructing an identity that is different from a magazine which uses a severe grid-based layout and a limited number of colours. A surfing magazine will construct a different identity from a stamp-collecting magazine, by selecting and using (consuming) a different layout, typefaces, shapes and colours. Social and cultural identities and differences are thus constructed and communicated by the consumption of different graphic techniques, processes and styles. And consumption is related to politics in that the social and cultural groups that are the result of the different choices and uses relate to each other in a structure: as noted above, some groups are high status and powerful and others are not. As soon as there is social or cultural difference there is a hierarchy, there is a difference of power and status and there is politics.

Consumption

Advertising is only the most obvious way in which graphics relates to consumption. Adverts persuade people to consume some commodity or other. They also have a social and cultural function: creating and reproducing social and cultural identities. Adverts also consume in so far as designers select and use graphic styles and techniques that they think will 'appeal to' or communicate with the social and cultural groups who are to purchase the commodities advertised.

All of these aspects are present in some recent advertising for the British department store Selfridges. The advertising takes the form of a booklet, which is constructed after the manner of an academic journal. It has a matt front cover (Figure 4.5), with issue number and date, there is text sloping up from left to right, in white sans serif capitals on pink ground, an editorial information page, a contents page and it contains articles, essays and illustrations. The spoof 'Editorial' inside the 'journal' urges the reader to think 'Maybe I should go to Selfridges?', thus fulfilling its advertising function. But the text on the cover instructs the reader to consume and refers to the social function of consumption. 'Shop until you drop*' it says, and the asterisk refers to some small type at the bottom of the page which reads 'Thereby fulfilling your role in society while simultaneously finding happiness'. As a piece of advertising, the booklet is persuading some people to go to Selfridges and buy some clothes. The white on pink text, the matt finish and the sans serif typestyle have been selected and used in order to construct and reproduce a social and cultural identity. Such choices will be identified with by certain types of people: if you are young, interested in slightly unusual, non-High Street, fashion and a little bit 'ironic' and 'knowing', you will understand that this shop is for you. The older and more conservative flannels-and-blazer brigade will understand these graphic signs to mean that the store and its fashions are not for them. The ironic practice of knowingly participating in your economic contribution to capitalism, fulfilling your social function by consuming these commodities, does not stop that contribution from happening.

Anti-consumption

Not consuming is the most (possibly the only) potent weapon possessed by anti-capitalists. Not consuming is a way of refusing the social, cultural, political and economic structures, practices and institutions of capitalism. Not surprisingly, there are few examples of graphic design whose economic

Figure 4.5 Booklet front page, Selfridges (2004). Courtesy of the publisher: John Brown Citrus, the designer: Scott King, the client: Selfridges

function is anti-consumerist. In the 1990s, however, there existed a brand of cigarettes called 'Death' (also wittily available as 'Death Lights'), whose packaging depicted a skull and crossbones and whose advertisements urged one not to smoke them (see Barnard 1995: 31). In the early twenty-first century, there is a movement called 'culture jamming', which produces spoof advertisements, adds graffiti to existing advertisements and supports International Buy Nothing Day (26 November). Adbusters.org and sub-vertise.org are probably the best known examples of culture jamming (see Klein 2000: 279 ff.). 'First Things First 2000' is a group made up of graphic designers, art directors and visual communicators explicitly concerned with graphic design's function in a capitalist economy. They propose 'more democratic forms of communication' to 'challenge' consumerism (McCarron 2001: 123; see also http://www.x54all.nl/~maxb/ftf2000.htm, August 2004). These groups are explicitly political as they are attempting to curtail or undermine the power of multinational corporations and the omnipresence of capitalist economy.

There are two main strategies employed by these groups. The first is the undermining of existing corporate messages. This may take the form of adding graffiti to existing advertisements or producing spoof versions of advertising, as practised by the Australian BUGA UP (Billboard-Using Graffitists Against Unhealthy Promotions), subvertise.org and adbusters.org. An example of their work may be found in Pavitt (2000a), where an advertisement for KB lager showing two male hands holding the two ends of a can of lager is ridiculed as a 'masturbation fantasy' (Pavitt 2000a: 192). Another example would be the 'Follow the Flock' anti-ad, which pillories Tommy Hilfiger fashions, suggesting that buying the products is a form of unthinking herd behaviour (see Barnard 2001: 2). Paul and John's work in Bristol includes the defacement of a Scottish Widows ad so that, where the widow, with half-covered face, had been advising consumers not to take chances with their pensions, she now advises them to 'mask up when rioting' (Fleming 2002: 13). And the second is the critique of capitalism in general. An example of this tactic is adbusters' (anti?) promotion of 'Buy Nothing Day'. Their 'Christmas Gift Exemption Voucher' and posters urging the celebration of Buy Nothing Day (in Pavitt 2000a: 188–9) use recognisable graphic images to undermine capitalism in general, as an economic system. The poster, for example, includes the 'Eye in the Pyramid', also found printed on US dollar bills and the Exemption Voucher borrows its style from any number of 'professional' certificates. Appropriating the images and styles used by the dominant and offensive group to use them in an unfamiliar and subversive way is a familiar ploy, suggesting a meaning that is at odds with the original offensive meaning (see Barnard 2001: 138–41).

CONCLUSION

This chapter has investigated the social, cultural and economic functions of graphic design. It has argued that society, culture and the economy are not the mere 'contexts' within which graphic design sits or appears. It has shown that and how graphic design is a way of producing, communicating and challenging social, cultural and economic values.The ways in which graphic design has been used to create and contest social and cultural identities and differences has been explained. And the ways in which graphics may relate to economics have been described. Chapter 5 will consider graphic communication in relation to its markets and audiences. On one level, this will be to approach the same kinds of questions from a slightly different angle. The markets and audiences are the social and cultural groups which have been explained here, and the functions of graphic design are those that have been explained here. But, having already explained these topics, Chapter 5 will be able to use a wider range of examples and build on the analyses of this chapter.

FURTHER READING

- Andrew Howard (1997) provides a practising graphic designer's take on the relation between **graphics and society** in his chapter 'There is Such a Thing as Society' in Bierut, M. et al. (eds) *Looking Closer 2*, New York: Allworth Press. Katherine McCoy (1997) argues that graphic designers are in fact part of wider political debates in her chapter 'Countering the Tradition of the Apolitical Designer', in the same volume. The section entitled 'Public Works' in *Looking Closer 2*, contains a number of relevant contributions.
- On **gender**, see Joanne Entwistle's (1998) 'Sex/Gender', in Jenks, C. (ed.) *Core Sociological Dichotomies*, London: Sage. Barbara Kruger is an artist, or a graphic designer, who explicitly plays with and cleverly critiques gender roles in her (1983) *We Won't Play Nature to your Culture*, London: ICA Publications. She is making the point here that, in western society, women have been closely associated with 'nature' and men with 'culture' and she uses text and image to counter this association. Pamela A. Ivinski charts the work of women's groups such as the Guerrilla Girls and SisterSerpents in her (1997) 'Women Who Turn the Gaze Around', in Bierut, M. et al. (eds) *Looking Closer 2*, New York: Allworth Press.
- See Barnard (2001: 137–8) and Gen Doy's (1998) *Materialising Art History*, Oxford: Berg, pp. 190–6, for an account of how Malevich's **abstract** 'Black Suprematist Square' (1914) provides a critique of the social order.
- One of the best **Marxist accounts** of the relation between meaning, communication and capitalism is found in Sut Jhally's (1990) *The Codes of Advertising*, London: Routledge. W. Leiss, S. Kline and S. Jhally (1990) *Social Communication in Advertising*, London: Routledge, pay rather more attention to graphic design in explaining the production and reproduction of capitalist society through advertising. On the relation of graphic design to **consumption**, see Jonathan Schroeder's (2002) *Visual Consumption*, London: Routledge.
- For more on the relation of graphic design to '**commerce**', see Maud Lavin's (2001) *Clean New World: Culture, Politics and Graphic Design*, Cambridge,

Mass.: MIT Press. Chapter 5 considers how designers should react to corporate enterprises and Chapter 8 considers the place of **women** in contemporary graphic design culture. In this connection, Angela McRobbie's (1998) *British Fashion Design*, London, Routledge, argues against the idea that designers are simply '**designing for capitalism**' (McRobbie 1998: 1). Susan Sontag's (1970) chapter on Cuban revolutionary posters is in Bierut, M. et al. (eds) (1999) *Looking Closer 3*, New York: Allworth Press.

* For more on **subvertising** go to http://www.subvertise.org; http://adbusters.org and http://www.videonetwork.org will provide a short film about subvertising. www.micahwright.com is a sort of online version of M. I. Wright (2003) *You Back the Attack! We'll Bomb Who We Want!*, New York: Seven Stories Press, with added shopping facilities. Both 'alter' First and Second World War posters to oppose President George W. Bush's **attack on Iraq**. Steve Bell's cartoons critiquing the United States and Britain's attack on Iraq may be found at http://www.guardian.co.uk/cartoons/archive/stevebell/0,7371,337764,00.html (March 2004).

* More British **political cartoons** may be found at http://www.political cartoon.co.uk/index.html (March 2004) and American cartoons at http://www.politicalcartoons.com (March 2004).

5

AUDIENCES AND
MARKETS

INTRODUCTION

This chapter will develop the analyses of Chapter 4 by examining the ways in which the audience, or market, of graphic design work affects and is affected by the content and the form of that work. The notions of class and cultural groups that were introduced in Chapter 4 will be revisited and dealt with in more detail, as markets or audiences. However, these 'markets' will not be explained in terms of their relative spending power or the choices they make in consumption; this chapter is not interested in aiding a capitalist economy by carrying out market research for it (see Modleski 1986: xii). Markets or audiences here will be understood as different cultural groups, with different sets of values and beliefs. The ideas of previous chapters will be used to explain the relation between the content and form of various examples of graphic design and audience and market. Case studies for this chapter include magazine and website design, advertising, illustration, comics, greetings cards and packaging. The selections made in typography, illustration and layout are all subject to variation, according to which segment(s) of a market the magazine or product, for example, is to communicate with. Similarly, packaging needs to take account of the social status and identity of the market in order to communicate with that market. Advertising is probably the most obvious example of how graphic design interacts with audiences and markets, but some of the less well-covered ways, such as magazine and website design and packaging, in which race/ethnicity, age and gender impinge on graphics will be covered in this chapter.

In Chapter 2, meaning in graphic design was said to be a product of difference. Visual and signifying differences were meaningful because they were organised into structures, or cultural codes. The problem in this chapter is analogous. Cultural identity is a also a result of signifying difference. As soon as there is cultural difference, there is a structure and a hierarchy (see Hall 1997: 234–8). However, a group's position in the hierarchy is culturally produced, it is not the work of nature. The structures are cultural, not natural, and this is as true of racial/ethnic, gender and other cultural identities as it is of semiological structures. It was argued in Chapter 4 that social and cultural identities were constructed, reproduced and challenged through graphic design. The ways in which a culture's understanding of childhood and femininity, for example, were communicated by means of graphic design were examined. Those identities are constructs: therefore, it must be made clear that there is and can be no 'essence' of any of the identities thus constructed. All such identities are constructed in specific times and places, in existing historical and social locations, and they cannot, therefore, be eternal or trans-historical identities. In this way, this chapter hopes to avoid reproducing any essentialising fetishes, which might lead to the legitimation of prejudice based on perceived differences. That is, it is the case that the 'new right' has used the notion of difference, whether racial/ethnic, gender or sexual, and used it to peddle old and offensive prejudices under the new name of cultural difference (see Popeau 1998: 175). This chapter has no wish to contribute to the propagation of these prejudices and no wish to see graphic designers propagating them either. This is why it stresses the idea that the identities and differences to be discussed are socially and historically specific; they are not permanent, essential or in any way natural. They may not, therefore, be used to vindicate the unjust treatment of any cultural groups.

This is not to say that cultural groups do not get represented unjustly, offensively or stereotypically in graphic design. They clearly do (see the 'Adjudications' pages on the Advertising Standards Authority website, http://www.asa.org.uk, for example). It is rather to point out that representation and stereotyping are culturally constructed and therefore may be challenged and contested. So, this chapter will consider cultural identities involving ethnicity/race, age and gender, and it will consider them as some of the audiences or markets with which graphic designers communicate. Consequently, the shapes, lines, colours, typestyles and imagery that graphic designers have used to communicate with these groups will be analysed and explained. Because identity is constructed, reproduced and challenged in the process of communication (as was argued in Chapter 3), this chapter may be read as further investigating the ways in which graphic design contributes to the construction, reproduction and challenging of identity.

TARGET PRACTICE

The graphic design for a book about graphic design is a sensitive, reflexive subject and, as I write these words, the cover for this book has yet to be decided. The functions of graphic design were explained in Chapter 2 and the cover must perform some of those functions. Text, image and layout must inform an identifiable group of people of the nature, tone and approach of the book. They must be attractive or appealing to that group.

And they must help to persuade members of that group to buy the book. My proposal is for the title and my name to be spelled out in 'alphabetti spaghetti'. I believe this to be a witty and left-field reference to typography and I think it will be appreciated by people who value creativity and originality. The commissioning editor's proposal is to cut out letters from well-known brand names and paste them into the title and name. She believes this to be postmodern and to reflect a variety of different design texts. And she thinks that it will be understood by people who work on many different projects in a cutting-edge industry. Similarly, where the cover design for the 1996 edition of my *Fashion as Communication* (London: Routledge) features five items of fashionable clothing on a white background, the 2002 edition shows a young man posing in an Adidas shell-suit against a blue tile background. The former uses fetishised objects because such objects will be a familiar part of fashion students' worlds and the latter depicts a member of a specific youth culture because fashion students are likely to know about, or be a part of, similar youth cultures. While neither of our ideas may end up on the cover of this book, and while the two covers of the fashion book are totally different, none conceives the nature of communication as aiming a message at a target. What all of the covers are trying to do is communicate with specific cultural groups, people who are interested in graphic design or fashion and who are believed therefore to share a set of values, by graphically producing a sense of the (homologous) values possessed by the book.

Graphic communication has been explained so far as the construction of the individual as a member of a culture (or not) through the negotiation of meaning (the acceptance, rejection or contestation of values and beliefs). The teenaged metal fan in Chapter 2, for example, is constructed as a member of a specific sub-cultural group by his or her reaction to and interpretation of the colours, typestyles and layouts of *Metal Maniacs* magazine and the ageing folky is not. The graphic design and fashion students implied in the previous paragraph are constructed as members of specific cultural groups by their understanding of the covers of these books. Their different responses to the graphics, the different meanings those graphics have, determine that they are, or are not, constructed as members of the sub-cultural group. What has been called the negotiation of meaning in this book is the interaction or interplay between those cultural beliefs and values held by the individual and those beliefs and values encoded in the words, images and layouts of graphic design. The values or attitudes of the teenaged metal fan will different from those of the aging folky and the meanings (connotations) of the graphics in *Metal Maniacs* will consequently be different for each of them. And the values of someone who is interested in graphic design, or fashion, will will be different from those of someone who is not; the meaning (connotation) of the cover will therefore be different for each person. Now, if graphic communication is the construction of the individual as a member of a cultural group through the negotiation of meaning, then the practice of conceiving audiences and markets as 'targets' must be reconsidered. It need not be rejected whole-sale, but it needs to be re-examined because interaction or negotiation is not best described as the movement of an arrow towards its target or a bus towards its destination. The metaphors of the 'target' or the 'vehicle' that were examined in Chapter 2 are therefore insufficient to satisfactorily describe the social operations of communication.

In the light of these reflections, the sense of 'target audience' as 'those people that we graphic designers wish to communicate with' may be retained. The sense of 'those people to whom we will direct or send a message' may not. Communication has been established in the previous chapters as communicating with, not communicating to; it is a negotiation, not sending and receiving. Consequently, it is a more accurate description of what happens in communication and of what graphic designers actually do, to say that they learn, or reconstruct, the beliefs and values of their markets in order to communicate with them. Graphic designers spend a lot of time investigating the beliefs and values of their markets; they are interested in and want to know about people's reactions to shapes, colours, images, layouts and so on. According to the view of communication that this book has followed so far, what they are doing in studying a group's reactions to a piece of graphic design is learning the cultural attitudes of those groups in order to communicate with them. Having clarified the conception of audience or market, the following sections will investigate how graphic design communicates with some of them; they will explain how how graphic design constructs, reproduces and challenges the identities of groups of people.

ETHNICITY/RACE

Before examining the ways in which graphic design is used to construct, reproduce and challenge racial and ethnic identity, the very notions of racial and ethnic identity must themselves be challenged. There is a basic asymmetry here: for socially and culturally dominant white westerners, it is usually non-white non-westerners who are referred to as 'ethnic groups' or as 'other races'. It is often forgotten that being white and western is to be a member of both a 'race' and an 'ethnic group'. The problem then gets formulated as how to refer to and explain the experience and position of the 'other', of non-white non-western people. Common conceptions of race and ethnicity, however, are little help. As Jean Popeau (1998: 167) says, 'the term "race" is often placed within cautionary inverted commas to indicate the dubious scientific meaning of the concept'. The idea that race can be defined in terms of physical, biological, anthropological or genetic criteria is one that neither natural nor social scientists are happy with and it is widely recognised as a 'biological fiction' (Popeau 1998: 167). Popeau's position is not incompatible with that of the United Nations, which argues that

> Because people can be grouped by any number of physical differences (height, foot size, resistance to certain diseases), race is an artificial way to categorize people. Nonetheless, race remains an important concept because of the social and political issues that arise from it.
>
> (http://www.un.org/cyberschoolbus/index.html, March 2004)

They are saying that racial identities are not found in nature: racial identities are cultural, or 'artificial' as the UN has it. As a cultural construct, however, the idea of race raises 'social and political issues'. It is as a cultural construction which raises social and political issues that this chapter will understand 'race'. Ethnicity is not much less problematic. Some (Van den Berghe (1981), for example) have attempted to define ethnicity as a 'basic biological tendency' of related groups of people (Popeau 1998: 170). Others have seen it in more cultural terms as the shared language and social and religious customs of groups of people. However, like race, the notion of ethnicity 'is a socially produced concept which cannot simply be reduced to a "biological" content' (Popeau 1998: 173). There are evidently many problems in the way of referring to the experience and position of the various non-white non-western groups of people. Although Stuart Hall is concerned with black subjectivity and experience, this chapter will follow his definition of ethnicity and use it to try to explain all non-white and non-western experience. Hall says that ethnicity is 'a politically and culturally constructed category' (quoted in Popeau 1998: 174), the black subject and black experience are not the result of natural differences, but 'are constructed historically, culturally, politically' (Popeau 1998: 174). With these cautions in mind, then, graphic design can be described as one of the ways in which the identity and experience of racial and ethnic groups is constructed, reproduced and contested.

Some of the problems surrounding white designers portraying black people are raised by Norman Rockwell's illustrations of racially sensitive topics. The first problem is that a white designer *is* portraying black people; a member of one racial or ethnic group is constructing an identity for another group. The suggestion is not that members of racial and ethnic groups should portray only other members of their own groups, but that some thought needs to be given to the asymmetry noted above, in which a dominant group identifies and represents another group as 'the other'. The second problem concerns representation, Rockwell's identification and treatment of another racial and ethnic group. His painting, *The Problem We All Live With*, was produced for *Look* magazine in 1964. In the work, a little 6-year-old black girl, Ruby Bridges, is shown walking to her newly desegregated school surrounded and dwarfed by four federal marshals. The marshals are there to protect her from a hostile crowd and the wall behind her is stained by the juice of a thrown tomato, which now lies on the pavement. The wall has the word 'nigger' and the initials K.K.K. written on it. Reg Weaver, who is black and who was president of the National Education Association in 2003, suggests that the meaning of the image is that the 'problem' of ensuring that every child receives a good education is 'one that will take all of us to solve' (http://www.nea.org/columns/rw030611.html March 2004). It is, however, possible that the meaning of the painting is that black education, or black people in general, is the problem that 'we' white people have to live with. The 'we' in the title is ambiguous and the community or cultural group that is constructed by it is uncertain. A similar ambiguity envelopes the painting *New Kids in the Neighbourhood* (to be found at http://www.nymuseums.com/lm011201t.htm#5, March 2004), which was produced for *Look* magazine in 1967. In what appears to be a prosperous and comfortable street, three typically American white kids on the right of the image are staring at two black kids on the left who are evidently in the process of moving into the neighbourhood. Again, there are at least two ways of interpreting this image. The first is that Rockwell is celebrating America's well-known love of foreign immigrants by showing black and white people living harmoniously on the same affluent street. The second could be that the image constitutes some kind of warning to white middle-class Americans; the postures of the white kids connote a wary standoffishness rather than a warm welcome.

Uncertainty is found again in the 1946 painting *Boy in a Dining Car* (Rockwell 1988: 97), produced for the cover of the *Saturday Evening Post*. Here, a young white boy sits at the table of a train's dining car, intently reading the menu and holding his purse while a black waiter smiles benevolently down at him. The obvious objection to the image is that it shows a black American in a subservient role, thus reproducing the identity of black people as the social and cultural inferiors of white people. However, the ambiguity of the meaning of the image again stems from the title: to which of these two people does 'Boy' apply to? If it is to the young white boy, then no offence is caused. If, however, it is to the mature black waiter, then considerable offence is caused. It is not sufficient to say that these constructions are inaccurate or extreme and that common sense dictates that they are just harmless, if nostalgic, illustrations. The limitations of anchoring, which were outlined in Chapter 3, are made explicit here in that, despite the presence of a title, alternative and potentially offensive and upsetting readings are still possible. Any appeal to 'common sense' in the interpretation of any of these images must be ruled out as it is precisely the commonality of the sense that is in question here. There is no way of establishing the community that is being constructed and the potential offence is never entirely ruled out.

Other Rockwell illustrations are less ambiguous. The 1961 painting *The Golden Rule* was turned into a mosaic and presented by Nancy Reagan, the US First Lady, to the United Nations on the occasion of its fortieth anniversary. The UN reasonably asserts that the image 'depicted people of every race, creed and color with dignity and respect' (http://www.un.org/cyberschoolbus/index.html, March 2004). And in the image entitled *The Family Tree* (1959), the many different racial and ethnic types that make up the 'family' of Americans are portrayed equally and with the same dignity and respect. In both of these images, the ambiguity is absent. *Southern Justice (Murder in Mississippi)*, painted for *Look* magazine in 1964, shows the murder of three Civil Rights activists. A dead white man lies on the ground while another white man supports the body of the black activist James Chaney. From the right of the image the shadows of approaching armed men can be seen. The painting is clear on the matter of who and what is to be deplored. These images are less ambiguous because there are fewer conflicting structures, or sets of connotations, in terms of which different cultural groups can construct meaning and thereby themselves. The role of the title in 'anchoring' the meaning of the image restricts the number of potential constructions. It does this, up to a point, by providing a single structure (murder) in terms of which the image is to be understood.

The representation of black people in advertising is another sensitive topic. In 1997, for example, McDonald's provoked much discussion when their television advertisement which used only black actors was aired on British television. Harriet Green, then an editor at *Campaign* magazine, points out that, when black people appear in advertising, it is usually to signal either the 'coolness' of the product or the advertiser's 'warm-hearted hopes of harmony between all races' (Green 1997). Another possibility is that advertisers use black people in their advertisements because they hope to make money out of them. Andrew Medd, who was one of the partners at Mother, the graphic design agency which handled the advertising for the 'Caribbean' fruit drink Lilt, disagreed with this last possibility by saying that 'you don't target black people by having black people in your ads'. He argued that 'the idea' is what is important and said that Mother would use whatever people best represented 'the idea'. Assuming that the 'idea' is the meaning of the advertisement, Medd is clear that tokenism would not be tolerated by consumers: they would see straight through it, he says (Green 1997). Tokenism is the practice of inserting a representative of a community into an advertisement, or a television show, for example, in a cynical attempt to signify the absence of prejudice. The third series of the satirical animated cartoon, 'South Park', lampoons this media practice by featuring a black character who is actually called 'Token'.

Other companies have used black people in their advertisements. Gap, Tommy Hilfiger, Nike and Benetton, for example, have all courted controversy by their depiction of racial and ethnic difference. Adbusters. org comment on this practice by recalling the various campaigns:

> Polyethnic plays were deployed and planted, most memorably by Gap, Hilfiger and Benetton. Their ads are a tangle of multicultural- ism: scrubbed black faces lounging with their wind-swept white brothers in that great country club in the sky.
>
> (http://adbusters.org/magazine/49/articles/brand_cool.html, March 2004)

The following paragraphs will outline the causes of the controversy raised by the Benetton campaigns of the 1990s and explain how it arises in terms of meaning (denotation and connotation) and culture (different beliefs and values held by different groups of people). One of the themes of Benetton's advertising in this period was racial and ethnic difference; others were AIDS, environmental issues, the American practice of judicial killing, and violence. The campaigns were entitled 'Race' and 'Contrasts in Black and White'. Ostensibly, the idea was that the ads portrayed racial harmony and promoted the idea that human beings are all members of the same family: as Heller and Pomeroy (1997: 99) say, Benetton intended to 'communicate strong, if unpopular, messages about society and the world'. Tibor Kalman, who worked on the *Colors* magazine, suggests that Benetton were 'challenging assumptions and raising issues' with their advertising (Kalman 1997: 231). One 1996 advertisement showed three allegedly human hearts, with the words 'white', 'black' and 'yellow' superimposed on them. Another showed a black woman breastfeeding a white baby (in 1989). In 1996 a third showed a black stallion in the process of mounting a white mare, and in 1989 there was an ad in which a black man and a white man were shown handcuffed together (Figure 5.1). There were also many advertisements that showed two or more individuals from a variety of different racial and ethnic groups happily poking their tongues out, laughing together, kissing each other and so on. The text in the ads read 'United Colors of Benetton'. Some of these advertisements may be viewed at http://www.benetton.com/ press/ (March 2004).

Unfortunately for Benetton, not everyone interpreted their advertise- ments as promoting racial harmony and the tolerance of difference. In her *Black Looks,* for example, bell hooks (1992) took a different view. She said that the 'racially diverse images' used by Benetton ads merely exploit Otherness in order to increase product sales (hooks 1992: 28). Parenthetic- ally, hooks also uses a graphic device (lower-case text) partly in order to challenge conventional notions of authorial intention (see http:// www.kentucky.com/mld/kentucky/2004/01/28/news/state/7813417.htm, March 2004). Many blacks in America objected to the image of the black

Figure 5.1 Poster, Benetton 'Handcuffs' (1989). Photograph by Oliviero Toscani.
Courtesy of Benetton S.p.A.

woman breastfeeding the white child because it connoted slavery and reinforced the stereotype of the black nanny. The image of the two men handcuffed together was offensive to some black people because the black man was interpreted as a criminal and the white man as a police officer. Both of these advertisements were withdrawn in the United States as a result of the offence they caused. In France, however, a Benetton store was attacked with a tear-gas grenade by neo-fascist racists precisely because of Benetton's perceived support for racial integration and harmony (see http://www.nordicom.gu.se/reviewcontents/ncomreview101/seppanen.pdf, March 2004). The differences in the interpretations here may be explained in terms of the construction and communication of meaning within culture. To recap, different cultures are identifiable groups because they share a set of connotations: what an image, for example, makes them think and feel is common to the members of the group. An individual either shares those connotations or not and thereby either constitutes themselves as a member of the group or not. An individual in the group constructs the meaning according to the cultural code and thus reproduces themselves as a member of the culture. In understanding the black horse as metaphorically signifying a black male, the white horse as metaphorically signifying a white woman and in seeing this as a positive metaphor of racial harmony, one is constructed as a member of a particular cultural group. Where the connotations are negative, and the image constructed as degenerative miscegenation, one is constructed as a member of a quite different cultural group.

It is the case in these examples that all cultures will agree on the relation between signifier and signified at the level of denotation: all will agree that one ad shows a black stallion mounting a white mare, and all will agree that another ad shows a white man and a black man handcuffed together. It is at the level of connotation that differences in meaning, and therefore culture, arise. Differences appear as soon as the signifier of the black man and the white man cuffed together is said to signify or connote black criminality, or that both black and white people are equally likely to commit crime, for example. Some black groups will object that the image reproduces a simplified and generalised stereotype of black males; some white supremacists will see it as confirming their view of black males and some liberals will understand it as evidence of a shared problem. This is a ambiguity similar to that which arises in connection with the Rockwell examples and it has a similar explanation. Some of the images themselves appear to be scrupulously 'neutral'. There is absolutely nothing in the 'Handcuffs' picture, for example, to suggest which of the two men is the law officer and which the felon. Both wear denim and a blue shirt, both hands are in the same 'pose' and both are well manicured. Only the existence of different cultural groups, with differing sets of connotations, explains the contradictory interpretations of this image. Other images are less sensitively composed. In 'Angel and Devil' (1991), for example, it is impossible to deny that the little black girl's hair forms the shape of horns and one is inevitably led to associate her with 'Devil' in the title (Figure 5.2). Even if a 2000-year-old western Christian culture did not associate light with good and dark with evil, the idea that the black girl was associated iconographically with the devil would still be clear and potentially offensive. That is, it is not only the existence of different cultures that constructs the connotation here, although that is crucial: there is also something in the image that supports the offending connotation.

The role of the titles in anchoring the meanings of these images should also be taken into consideration. There is a general title, provided by the text which appears in all of the advertisements: 'United Colors of Benetton'. And there is the specific title of each advertisement, as provided on the Benetton Press Office website. The 'unity' proposed by Benetton is intended as a good thing, but the existence of cultural groups for whom such unity is abhorrent generates alternative meanings. The union proposed by the text is precisely what the French fascists objected to and the text cannot anchor meaning so firmly that a particular connotation is prohibited. In the specific titles, the problem is slightly different. Where the titles on the website mean anything at all, they tend, as with 'Horses', to be scrupulously neutral. The anchoring here operates on a denotational level on which it is difficult to find offence. However, the title 'Angel and Devil' appears actually

UNITED COLORS
OF BENETTON.

Figure 5.2 Poster, Benetton 'Angel and Devil' (1991). Photograph by Oliviero Toscani. Courtesy of Benetton S.p.A.

to invite a particular connotation. Where it would be perverse to object to the title 'Horses' on the grounds that it encourages interbreeding, it would also be perverse not to see the devil in the little girl. Anchorage in this example demonstrates the limits of the distinction between denotation and connotation and suggests a connotation that many will find objectionable.

AGE

This section will investigate the ways in which graphic design uses imagery, typography and colour to construct and reproduce different age groups. It should not need saying, but 'youth', 'adulthood', 'old age' and the other terms a culture uses to indicate an age group are, like race/ethnicity and gender, not found in nature (see Leach 1970: 21ff.). A continuum has been segmented by a culture in order to make sense of or make meaningful the different experiences of the members of that culture. The first set of examples are from the packaging for Tetley tea-bags. These will be examined to show how imagery, typestyle and colour must be changed in order to appeal to or communicate with a younger, less conservative group of people. Tetley tea is also interesting here because Tetley market tea in North America: the differences between the packaging used in the United Kingdom and that employed in the United States can illustrate how graphic designers, art directors and marketing people must take account of different national cultures in their work. Packaging, marketing and the content of Tetley's websites will be examined here. Age and nationality, then, each involve cultural differences (differences of values and attitudes), that design must take account of if it is to communicate with different age groups and different national groups. The second set of examples concern the ways in which different age groups are represented in advertisements and magazines. Three magazines will be examined in order to show how some of the meanings of childhood, middle and old age are constructed and communicated by graphic design's use of typography, imagery and layout.

In the two illustrations (Figures 5.3 and 5.4), the changes between the present packaging and the previous packaging of Tetley tea can be seen. The previous packaging (Figure 5.3) uses a picture of a teapot with cups and saucers on a table. The present packaging (Figure 5.4) uses a picture of two leaves surrounded by an abstract heart-shaped motif. The idea is that the teapot and teacups are part of the paraphernalia of tea-drinking and that they connote the ritualistic process of boiling the kettle, warming the pot, waiting for the tea to brew and then, finally, sitting at the table to drink it. The leaves, however, connote only the naturalness of the product and the heart motif suggests health benefits. To the over-sixties, the earlier image may connote 'teatime' when the family would sit together, or it may suggest friends coming round for a chat. To the under-thirties, a cultural group for

Figure 5.3 Packaging, Tetleys (1995). Courtesy of Tetley UK

Figure 5.4 Packaging, Tetleys (2004). Courtesy of Tetley UK

whom the ritual aspects of tea-making may be tiresome, or who may not regularly sit down with the family for meals, that image will mean something completely different. The connotations of 'health and naturalness' are more likely to be favourably received by a health-conscious younger age group than the 'tedious rigmarole of tea-making'. This is a clear example of how the values and attitudes of different age groups are taken into account when designing the packaging of a product. The connotations that an image is likely to have for a particular cultural group are taken into account when designing the package. Nick Kilby (marketing and development director of the Tetley Tea group) is well aware of the relation between connotational meaning and cultural groups. Talking about Tetley's new iced-tea product, 'T of Life', he says that 'it has a distinctive quirky labelling, designed to appeal to the under-30 age group'. The packaging of this product is designed to communicate 'something new, something fun' to a specific age group: a large 'T' and cartoon images in the package design are intended to communicate precisely that quirkiness, novelty and fun to that age group (see http://www.teaandcoffee.net/0703/coffee.htm, March 2004).

The Tetley company used animated cartoon characters in their British television and press advertising from 1973 until 2001, when they were replaced by a new campaign. These characters were known as the 'Tetley Tea Folk' and they included four flat-capped and white-coated Yorkshiremen (Gaffer, Sydney, Maurice and Gordon) and three kids (Clarence, Archie and Tina). In 2004 the Tetley.co.uk website suggests that the characters have returned from their 'sabbatical' and they may be found at http://www.tetley.co.uk/shop/content/Home_frames.asp (March 2004). All characters appeared as line drawings and all appear to be wearing the same style of slippers. Given the direction Tetley tea is taking, towards a younger, less staid and more health-conscious product, it is surprising that the Tea Folk have not been given a permanent sabbatical. The connotations of middle-aged Yorkshiremen, with unglamorous and faintly comic names, are not consistent with the connotations of the fresh, healthy and natural leaves on the packaging. Sydney's droopy cap, braces and white coat are unlikely to mean 'quirky' or 'fun' to the under-30 age group Tetley are trying to communicate with. While the kids Clarence and Tina could, possibly, connote a younger lifestyle, with their reversed baseball cap and yellow ponytail, Archie wears glasses and a tie and will probably never connote youthful trendiness. In this example, the values held by the group that Tetley want to communicate with are not likely to generate the meanings that Tetley want their product to have.

There is also an American website: 'Tetley Sip' (http://www.Tetley usa.com). There is no mention of the Tea Folk on the American website, but the consumer can 'tickle their brains' by purchasing books, art and music and playing tea-related versions of 'Hangman' and 'Tic-Tac-Toe' ('Noughts and Crosses'). Where the British site has a 'Tea Shop', the

American site has a 'Tea Shoppe'. Both British and American sites show the identical packet of tea and both sites employ the Tetley blue background colour, the picture of the leaves and the trademark typography. The American site, however, also shows a packet of Tetley 'British Blend', which depicts the clockface of Big Ben and the Union flag. Clearly, tea means something different to Americans from what it means to the British. In the United States, tea is not the habitual or customary drink: it is a speciality drink, which connotes Britishness, and possibly America's own inspiring struggle for independence from colonial servitude. In the United Kingdom, the British would no more recognise the 'British' connotations of tea than the Italians in Barthes' account of the Panzani ad would recognise the 'Italianicity' of pasta (Barthes 1977a: 34). Therefore, the absence of the Tea Folk is easily explained. To the British, Yorkshire means 'straight-forward', 'no nonsense' and 'down to earth'. Hence the positive connotations of the Yorkshiremen (to some age groups), in the UK advertising campaigns. Americans are unlikely to have any understanding of the connotational meanings of 'Yorkshire' or flat caps, hence the absence of the Tea Folk from the American website. Cultural differences regarding the interpretation of images and characters, concerning different connotational meanings, determine what both the packaging and the websites look like.

In a recent advertisement for Quorn, a stereotypical image of elderly people is reproduced. The elderly man's infirmity is signalled by a Zimmer frame, spectacles and stooped posture. His cardigan and slippers connote both advanced age and a lack of interest in fashionable clothes. With no name, he is referred to only by his place in the family structure, 'Gramps'. It is the fourth element of the stereotype, however, that the advertisement plays upon; that of being unproductive. Productivity is a central value of capitalist society: being in work, being useful and reproducing one's position as a working and therefore worthwhile individual are important elements of life in capitalist society. Having left the world of paid employment, elderly people are constructed (at least by those still in that world) as being unproductive. Doing no 'proper' work and not producing goods or services for sale is inimical to capitalist society and Quorn's advertisement helpfully suggests a remedy; their shepherd's pie. The idea seems to be that, having eaten a nourishing plate of meat substitute, Gramps will have enough energy to clean the floor for 'you'. Gramps will become more productive and 'you' will 'get more out of' him. The irresistible humour in Gramps's position stems from the suggestion that, as a result of his infirmity, 'you' will have to to tie sponges to his frame and mops to his feet in order that he might clean the floor.

Using terms such as 'you' and 'they' in the body copy is significant because they establish who is and who is not included in the group addressed by the advertisement: 'you' are spoken to by the ad and you are not old, but 'they' are spoken about by the ad and they are old. This rhetorical device is a part of the way in which the community or constituency that is appealed to by the ad is constructed. It is a version of the asymmetry that was noted in the section on Ethnicity/Race and it is likely to be found every bit as offensive here by certain groups as it was there. The beliefs held by the young about what sort of people the old are are what enables this ad to work. Those beliefs include the ideas that elderly people are likely to be unproductive, infirm and uninterested in fashion, for example. They are what the young recognise in the image and what produces meaning (connotation) for them. It is the sharing or not sharing of those beliefs that produces the individual as a member either of 'the young' or 'the elderly'. Depending on whether you are the 'you' or the 'they' constructed in the copy, you will understand the ad in a different way. In portraying Gramps in this way, the people responsible for this advertisement have produced and reproduced the cultural groups referred to in this section as 'the young' and 'the elderly' by constructing meanings that the dominant group will recognise, accept and understand.

Sometimes, efforts are made to challenge or reject these meanings. In a 1991 experiment for *She* magazine, graphic design mock-ups were produced which showed more mature models in advertisements for cosmetics. These older women, with their dimpled thighs and wrinkled eyes, were substituted for the standard, blemish-free 20-year-olds in ads for products such as cellulite creams and facial moisturisers. Groups of students to whom these images have been shown have reacted by saying things like 'It doesn't work' and 'gross'. While admitting that this is anecdote rather than evidence, their characteristically severe responses indicate the ways in which the construction of meaning is being manipulated by the mock advertisements. One's expectations are confounded. Membership of certain western cultures would lead one to expect certain things of a cosmetics advertisement and, when they are not found, one is surprised and unsettled. Then, because the culture does not or has not prepared one for this (because it has not supplied a set of ready-made connotations), one does not know 'what to make of' the ad. One does not know how to construct it in a meaningful fashion. Consequently, 'it does not work'. The structures of signifiers and signifieds are not those of the culture the advertisements are appearing in and the advertisements do not make the sense that is expected of them. In the absence of a conventional code, which would organise the signifiers and signifieds into meaningful structures, meaning is challenged. It may be that this is another way of explaining the 'grotesque'. Philip Thomson (1972: 27) defines the grotesque as an 'unresolved clash of incompatibles in work and response' and as 'the ambivalently abnormal'. The presence of an older model in a cosmetics ad is incompatible with certain western culture's beliefs and values concerning age and beauty and the mock-up ads do nothing to resolve that incompatibility and ambivalence. Such an account of meaning and the grotesque would begin to explain the beliefs of those students who thought the ads were 'gross'.

My Weekly and *The People's Friend*, both published by D. C. Thomson, cater for an older, more mature audience. The following paragraphs will examine their use of graphic design in order to show how that audience is constructed and reproduced. Both magazines produce guides for writers, produced by the Jacqui Bennett Writer's Bureau, in which the preferred contents of stories and other articles are outlined. These guides make compelling reading as they explicitly identify the cultural group's values and attitudes to a range of topics. It would not be unreasonable to expect the graphic designers and illustrators working on these titles to know the market and to at least be aware of these guides. The style guide for *The People's Friend* indicates that the readers range from 30 to 'well over' 80; they do not like 'realistic' material, 'with sex, violence, drugs, drink etc.', that makes them frightened or sad; they are 'traditionalist' and 'like to see their values reflected in their "Friend"' (from http://www.jbwb.co.uk/pfguidelines.htm, March 2004). The style guide suggests that would-be writers read the magazine for several weeks, in order to 'work out' what the readers want. In the style guide for *My Weekly* there is less detail, but it is made clear that the market is 'young mothers, active middle-aged wives, and elderly retired ladies'. The guide says that sex and violence are 'taboo' and that 'we aim to fill our stories with warm, real people striving to cope with the ups and downs of everyday life with pride, dignity – and a sense of fun' (at http://www.jbwb.co.uk/weekly.html, March 2004). It was noted in the section on Target Practice that graphic designers often spend time investigating the values and beliefs of the people they are hoping to communicate with and researching those people's reactions to layout, colours and so on. In order to facilitate communication, the guides produced for these magazines outline those beliefs and values. The guides explicitly say that the readers like to see their values 'reflected' in the magazines and they even go so far as to recommend that possible contributors spend several weeks researching them. While this book is obliged to argue that the values are not merely 'reflected', but are constructed and reproduced in the content of the stories and articles, it is clear that the guides demonstrate a good understanding of what communication involves.

Given the audience or market for these titles, and given their stated attitudes and beliefs, one would expect conservative and traditional layouts, typestyles and illustrations to be used in the magazines. The design might be expected to reproduce the values and beliefs of the audience through the selection of appropriate shapes, colours, styles and imagery. And this is what is found in the edition for 13 March 2004 (Figure 5.5). *The People's Friend* is well known for using an illustration on its front cover and this edition features J. Campbell Kerr's pen and watercolour picture of the harbour at Ballycastle, Co. Antrim. The illustration is framed by banners at

Figure 5.5 Front cover, *The People's Friend* (13 March 2004).
© DC Thomson & Co. Ltd, 2004

the top and bottom of the page announcing the contents (houseplants, embroidery ducks and pistachio recipes), while three modest starbursts advertise a four-page pull-out, an azalea offer and 'twelve tempting stories'. The green of the top banner reflects the greens, whites, greys and blues in the painting of the harbour. Apart from the text in the starbursts, everything is horizontally aligned; the horizon in the painting (of course), but also the road and the gutters of the houses; going from left to right across the page, they echo the banners and the title. Inside the magazine, there is a lot of painted and drawn illustration; each story is accompanied by at least one colour illustration of the ordinary people who feature in them. Pen and ink illustration is even the subject of one of the features in this edition; Douglas Phillips' drawings of Rye are tied to the 'Mapp and Lucia' books of E. F. Benson. All the typestyles used, except those in some of the advertising and in 'The Friend Doctor' column, are serifs and many are based on calligraphic styles and in italics. There is occasional overlapping of one image or piece of text by another and no cut-and-paste style layouts. The overlap that does occur is modest, and involves the background colours of the illustration remaining visible beneath the text of some of the stories, for example.

The connotations of all these graphic features are conservative and traditional. On occasion, they are romantic, too. Watercolour paintings connote genteel leisure and retirement. The pen and ink drawings connote tranquillity and old-fashioned charm, qualities that Phillips draws attention to in his written commentary on his own drawings. Perhaps by countering what Kress and van Leeuwen (1996) say about left–right and top–bottom structures (see Chapter 3), the strong horizontal lines and the top–middle–bottom structure of the layout connote stability and evenness. There is no 'new' on the right of the layout and there is no 'real' at the foot of the page. As noted, serifs abound, as do calligraphic faces and italics. Often, the serif faces have an 'Art Deco' feel to them. The connotations here are all romantic, reproducing the tone of the love stories they adorn. While the content guide suggests a readership between 30 and 80, the values connoted by the graphic styles used in *The People's Friend* would seem to be closer to the values held by the 80-year-olds than to those held by the 30-somethings.

Although the style and content guide would have one believe that its market is much the same as that for *The People's Friend*, the front cover of *My Weekly* is very different. There are at least five different sizes of sans serif type and a colour photograph of a smiling woman wearing a pink shirt in front of a green background on the cover of the 20 March 2004 edition (Figure 5.6). The type is either white or bright yellow. Inside, while there is some painted and drawn illustration, there is a lot more photography than there is in *The People's Friend*. As a rule, the photographic work illustrates the features and the painted and drawn work illustrates the romantic stories. Layouts inside the magazine are occasionally rather traditional,

Figure 5.6 Front cover, *My Weekly* (20 March 2004).
© DC Thomson & Co. Ltd, 2004

with a colour picture at the top of the page and text underneath, but there are many more exciting layouts as well. An article on Francis Rossi (a guitarist from the band Status Quo) employs a strong diagonal line, formed by the leg of a pair of denim jeans, running from bottom left to top right. Text is found above the diagonal and colour photographs overlap the denim. A feature on charity shops uses five photographs in a semicircle, with a sixth in the centre of the circle. The headline text runs across the top of a double-page spread and the body of the text fills in the irregular space formed by the gaps between the photographs. The sans serif on the cover is also found throughout the inside of the magazine, except in the short stories and the knitting column, where highly decorated serif and calligraphic faces are used.

Whether the sans serif connotes 'a sense of fun' or not is debatable, but it certainly gives a cleaner, less cluttered, look to the cover and to much of the inside of *My Weekly*. The colours of the front cover are also brighter and 'younger' than those found on the cover of *The People's Friend*. A 'younger' look is also constructed on the inside of the magazine. The sans serif does most of the work here, especially in a fashion feature entitled 'Timeless Elegance'. In this feature, a relatively large and very narrow white sans serif (Univers) on a black background introduces High Street fashions that recall the style of the young Audrey Hepburn. Where the serif and calligraphic faces are used, in the short stories and the knitting column, they seem to be used in the 'older' or 'more traditional' features. It is unlikely that the age group that is interested in creating for themselves the gamine Audrey Hepburn look will also be interested in knitting themselves a jumper which has a koala bear motif on it. Serif and cursive script connote the romance and escapism of the short stories, one of which is illustrated by a picture of someone bearing an uncanny resemblance to Clark Gable in the film *Gone with the Wind*. On balance, however, one's guess would be that the values connoted by the graphic styles employed in *My Weekly* are closer to those of the young mothers and active middle-aged wives than they are to the elderly retired women specified in the content guide.

Find Out!, a magazine for children published by Tree Top Media, is quite different from *My Weekly* and *The People's Friend*. *Find Out!* uses almost completely different colours, imagery, typestyles and layouts from those found in the magazines for the more mature market. It thus constructs a completely different cultural group from those magazines. Where the two front covers of *My Weekly* and *The People's Friend* contain one exclamation mark between them, for example, the front cover of *Find Out!* (issue 18, March 2004) contains thirteen (Figure 5.7). Where the former's covers feature one main picture each, the latter's cover includes four, three of which overlap one another and all of which are overlapped by text. And where the choice of typeface is between serif and sans serif in the magazines for the older market, *Find Out!* mixes serif and sans serif, combines

Figure 5.7 Front cover, *Find Out!* (Issue 18, March 2004). Courtesy of
Kathryn Hill and Tree Top Media

different point sizes in the same word and makes up its own styles as it sees
fit. The face used to introduce the magazine's Australian theme looks as
though it has been drawn with a stick and the question 'Is there life on
Mars?' has a blobby, alien feel to it, as though it were drawn by a three-
fingered hand. The only text that is sitting quietly on a horizontal line is in

the speech bubble coming out of Henry VIII's mouth, where he invites the reader to 'WIN! A fantastic laptop!' There are banners to the top and bottom of the page, in red and blue, but they cannot contain the images or the text which cut into both of them. All of the primary colours are used, along with black, white, greys and greens (for the Martian).

There is a general problem here in anticipating the reactions of any other cultural group to an example of graphic design; it is that, unless one is a member of that group and shares their values, it is difficult to know exactly how members of that group will respond to the images and texts used in this cover. Because one does not necessarily hold the same values as members of that other group, it is not easy to guess what connotations a piece of graphic design will have for them. However, to this adult the connotations of the colours, shapes, images, typestyles and layout are exhausting. They are energetic, excited, inquisitive, acquisitive, wild, funny, unsophisticated and noisy, much like children themselves, in fact. The inside of the magazine is equally boisterous and the designers (Adam Hall and Emily Smith) must be credited with understanding the values and attitudes of children extremely well and communicating with them in a highly effective manner. It may, by definition, be an adult's perception of a child's likely understanding of a collection of shapes, lines colours and so on, but it seems in this case that that perception is accurate. It is plausible to suggest that the connotations of the graphic design elements will be recognised, accepted and understood by children, who will thus be constructed as members of the cultural group, western children.

GENDER

This section will investigate some examples in which gender poses a series of problems for graphic design. Its examples will include packaging design, advertising and cards. The concept of gender was explained in Chapter 4, on the social function of graphic design and a brief restatement here should suffice. Gender was explained as the meaning a culture assigns to or associates with being male or female. Like race and ethnicity, gender is not found in nature but is politically and culturally significant because it is a way of specifying appropriate masculine and feminine ways of behaving. Graphic design is one of the ways in which those appropriate modes of behaviour are constructed and reproduced. The first example to be discussed here is packaging. The use of shape, line, colour and typography to construct and communicate gender identity in packaging will be explored by looking at the packaging for a product that does the same job for both sexes, razors. In many western cultures, both sexes need to remove unwanted hair. However, the different genders have different meanings in these western cultures and hair removal has different meanings as well. This section will investigate the relation between the packaging of the product, the values and meanings associated with each gender and culture. The ways in which graphic design produces and reproduces gender identities through the use of shape, line, colour and typography will be established. The second example is Mother's Day and Father's Day cards: the gender identities and gender roles constructed, and very occasionally challenged, by these cards will be explained here.

To begin with the shaving products, both are from the Gillette company. First, the names of the products are gendered. The first women's razor was introduced by Gillette in 1915 and it was called 'Milady Décolettée'. The Gillette 'Daisy', introduced in 1975, was Gillette's first women's disposable razor. And in 2000 the 'Venus', a triple-bladed razor, was produced. 'Milady Décolettée' literally means 'A posh woman in a low-cut dress'; the 'decolettage' is the area surrounding a woman's neck, shoulders and cleavage. 'Daisy' is the name of a flower, and Venus is the Roman goddess of love. The connotations of the names are clear. Women are, or femininity is, associated with the body (especially some of the more erotically charged parts), with simple, common-or-garden flowers, with goddesses and with the emotions. The Gillette 'Mach3 Turbo G-Force' refers to the speed of sound, the force of gravity that is exerted on a body and a way of improving the performance of internal combustion engines. The masculine connotations are equally clear. Men are, or masculinity is, associated with machinery, with dangerous, crushing and exhilarating speed and with improved performance. Such connotations accord precisely with the values and meanings accorded femininity and masculinity in many western cultures. These associations are found in other areas of male and female experience. These meanings therefore offer an easy way for men and women to construct themselves as members of those western cultures. In this way the graphic design simply reproduces the stereotypes of masculinity and femininity.

The shapes, lines, colours and typestyles used in the product itself and in the product packaging are also gendered. The 'Venus' is available in two colours – a pale blue and 'Passion Pink'. The packaging echoes these colours, adding a curvy scallop-shell effect and white lettering (Figure 5.8). The lettering itself is not serifed, but it is also 'curvy', and the 'V' in 'Venus' incorporates a squiggle that could be a '3'. The 'Passion' in 'Passion Pink' is script-like and all lettering is shadowed with a darker hue of the pack colour. The 'Mach3 Turbo G-Force' comes in various shades of grey, speckled black and silver. The packaging uses a dark blue, a white and a metallic silver. All the lettering is sans serif and italic: some slants left to right, some from bottom to top and some from top to bottom (Figure 5.9). The typeface used in 'Mach3 Turbo' comes with 'go fast' stripes and is itself shadowed by the go-fast 'T' of 'Turbo'. Again, the connotations are clear. Pink is a feminine colour and dark blues, greys and black are masculine in most western cultures. Compared to the dark blue of the men's product, the

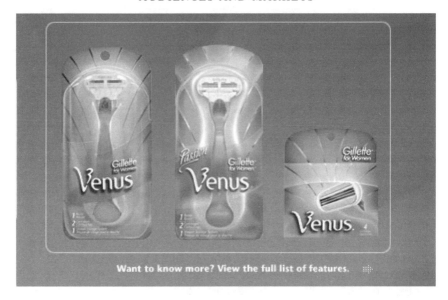

Figure 5.8 Packaging, Gillette Venus (2004)

pale blue of the female product is clearly feminine: in the structure formed by the two colours (light blue and dark blue) one has been associated with men and one with women. Their cultural meanings as masculine and feminine are thus assigned. The sans serif italics on the male product packaging connote modernity, technology and speed whereas the more rounded shapes in the lettering on the women's product seem to connote gentleness and naturalness. The metallic effects used in the lettering also connote machinery and masculinity.

By using these colours and typefaces, the packaging establishes one hair removal product as feminine and another as masculine. While the function and performance of the products is identical (both use a sharpened piece of metal to cut off unwanted hair), the meaning of the activity changes according to whether it is male or female hair that is being removed. Cutting off male body hair is established as a masculine thing to do, by associating it with speed, machinery, powerful forces and metal. By associating cutting off female body hair with nature, love and mythical goddesses, it is assigned a feminine meaning. It is the choice of colours, typefaces and shapes for the packaging that connotes masculinity or femininity and constructs the products (and thus the consumer) as masculine or feminine.

Something not dissimilar may be observed in Mother's Day and Father's Day cards. These 'days' may or may not have been invented as business opportunities by the Hallmark company, but they are opportunities for sons and daughters to express their love for one or other of their parents. The

106

Figure 5.9 Packaging, Gillette Mach3 Turbo (2004)

expression of emotion is also gendered in western society and part of the problem of choosing the 'right' card for one's own mother or father is the problem of selecting the 'correct' gender connotations of the card one sends. The cards on sale in shops and on the internet show how the expression of emotion according to gender is constructed and reproduced. At http:// www.123greetings.com, for example, the Mother's Day cards are resolutely traditional. There are innumerable illustrated cards, all drawn and some animated with Flash, featuring flowers and there are many cards depicting mothers hugging, reading to or talking to their young offspring. Some children are found, flying kites and playing. On the pages of cards for first-time mothers, one page offers five drawn pictures of a baby's head and one photograph of a baby's head. However, there is a genre of cards, and one card in particular, that stand out. The genre that draws special attention to itself is the 'Mother as Angel' card. In these cards, the near-universal, but always metaphorical, understanding that one's mother is a angel is made literal in a series of cards showing mothers as angels, with wings. The card that draws attention to itself is the one that features only a pedal-bin with the word 'diapers' written on it.

Father's Day cards go about the business of constructing fatherhood slightly differently. There is, of course, a huge number of traditional cards, featuring various sports (golf, rugby, fishing and football) and cars. One card may be found in which father and son are fishing. However, there are also many cards with flowers on them. One Flash-animated floral tribute at http://www.123greetings.com uses six pink roses and incoming italic script to tell Dad he's 'the best'. It is impossible to say how popular these are, but 123greetings.com might be thought to be having their cake and eating it by offering one card which shows a bunch of flowers in a car-shaped vase. A little surprisingly, there are many cards in which a relationship and even affection are being shown. Daddy lions are seen hugging little lions, Daddy bears hug little bears and sometimes human Daddies hug little humans.

For the most part, these cards reproduce western gender roles. Mothers are almost never found outdoors and certainly not playing sports. They are often shown relating to, talking to or playing with, their children. The depiction of mothers as angels is hardly remarkable. And the card that reduces motherhood to a pedal-bin full of dirty diapers is merely the *reductio ad absurdum* of the gender identity being constructed, repugnant as it is. Fathers are almost never depicted indoors and they are never found represented as angels. So far, so traditional. But the existence of a number of cards in which fathers are shown in a relationship with their offspring is more surprising. One rather sad card shows father and son apparently not speaking to one another as they sit on a jetty fishing, but many more show affection being expressed and a joy being taken in the relationship. Where mothers are never shown in a non-traditional role, fathers sometimes are. This asymmetry may reproduce the asymmetry in society, where men have always had more freedom to do things outside the home, but the portrayal of men in communicative and happy relationships with their offspring challenges the dominant gender stereotype.

CONCLUSION

This chapter has considered what are often called the 'audiences' or the 'markets' of graphic design, the groups of people commonly said to be 'targeted' by graphic design. The chapter has explained the limited sense in which it is accurate and useful to speak of 'targets' in communication. Rather than explain these 'markets' in terms of spending power, or the number of hours per day they spend watching afternoon soaps on television, it has considered them as different cultural groups, with different sets of values and beliefs. The role of these beliefs and values in constructing the meanings of examples of graphic design, and in constituting people as members of those groups has been investigated and illustrated. Many of the examples investigated have lent further support to the argument that graphic design and illustration are not and cannot be the innocent or neutral conveyors of messages. Rockwell's illustrations and Benetton's advertising, for example, were used to show how different meanings are constructed by members of different cultural groups as a result of the different values and attitudes that identify and define those groups. The children's magazine *Find Out!* illustrated the same phenomenon, but from another angle. The problem here was how to account for a cultural group's understanding of graphic design in terms of connotational meaning and cultural values when that cultural group is by definition incapable of explaining it in those terms. This example also raised the issue of reconstructing the likely responses of one group from the perspective of another group. Erwin Panofsky (1955) discusses this problem under the heading of 'iconological' and 'iconographic' interpretation. His answer is that, in order to understand the meaning that a piece of visual culture has for a group of which one is not a member, one must carefully and sensitively reconstruct the likely values of that other group (Panofsky 1955: 64–6). Barthes (1977a: 34–6) explains what one needs to know or be familiar with in order to understand the connotations of the Panzani advertisement, but does not raise it as a problem for communication. Chapter 6 will begin a more historical theme by considering modernism in graphic design. It will try to explain how graphic modernism raises and solves problems concerning communication.

FURTHER READING

- The potential reading list for **gender** is enormous. With reference to graphic design, however, David Gauntlett's (2002) *Media, Gender and Identity: An Introduction*, London: Routledge, looks at the negotiation of gender identities in men's and women's magazines such as *Cosmopolitan, FHM* and *Maxim*. Anthony Cortese's (1999) *Provocateur: Images of Women and Minorities in Advertising*, Lanham, Md: Rowman & Littlefield, concentrates on how advertisements construct and communicate the meaning of femininity and minority groups. Myra MacDonald's (1995) *Representing Women: Myths of Feminity in the Popular Media*, London: Hodder Arnold, concentrates on the visual construction of femininity in a range of media. Linda McLoughlin's (2000) *The Language of Magazines*, London: Routledge, provides a straightforward approach to the ways in which text and image combine to construct cultural meanings surrounding gender.
- Mike Featherstone and Andrew Wernick (eds) (1995) *Images of Aging: Cultural Representations of Later Life*, London: Routledge, considers the role of advertising and government health programmes in constructing the meaning of **elderly people**. The website at www.geocities.com/lightgrrrrrl/ provides a wideranging survey and bibliography on the portrayal of elderly people in American television and advertising.
- On **race and ethnicity**, see Stuart Hall (ed.) (1997) *Representation: Cultural Representations and Signifying Practices*, London, Sage. And on race, ethnicity and graphic design, see Michele Y. Washington's (2001) 'Souls on Fire', in Heller, S. and Ballance, G. (eds) *Graphic Design History*, New York: Allworth Press.

- For more on **Benetton advertising and ethnicity** see Les Back and Vibeke Quaade's (1993) article, 'Dream Utopias, Nightmare Realities: Imagining Race and Culture within the World of Benetton Advertising', *Third Text*, 22: 65–80, and Pasi Falk's (1997) chapter 'The Benetton–Toscani Effect', in Nava, M., Blake, A., MacRury, I. and Richards, B. (eds) (1997) *Buy This Book: Studies in Advertising and Consumption*, London: Routledge. Henry Giroux (1994) takes the line that the Benetton ads were avoiding issues about political power and substituting aesthetic choice for political choice in 'Consuming Social Change: The United Colors of Benetton', in his *Disturbing Pleasures*, London: Routledge. **Tibor Kalman's work with Benetton** on the *Colors* magazine is discussed on the adbusters.org website: Allan Casey's 1998 interview with Tibor Kalman may be found at http://www.adbusters.org/campaigns/first/toolbox/tiborkalman/3.html (March 2004).
- John Fiske (1990) explains the **ideological functions** of a feature appearing in *Seventeen* magazine in his *Introduction to Communication Studies*, London: Routledge, pp. 178–86. The ways in which femininity is constructed and reproduced by the article are clearly described in these pages. Andrew Wernick's (1994) *Promotional Culture: Advertising, Ideology and Symbolic Expression* (London: Sage), on men in advertising, looks at the construction and reproduction of masculinity in advertising.

6

MODERNISM

INTRODUCTION

This chapter, and the one following it, may appear to have a more historical and descriptive basis than the previous chapters. Chapter 6 will examine European and American modernism and Chapter 7 will investigate postmodernism. However, they will both try to analyse and explain these topics as graphic communication, as the construction and reproduction of beliefs and values. The themes of culture and communication, familiar from previous chapters, will be developed in relation to the notions of modernism and postmodernism. Chapter 6 will first show how modernism may be understood as a set of beliefs and values. The central tenets or features of modernism will be explained as the ideas and practices that a group of people thought were important. It will then show how modernist graphic designers communicated and reproduced those beliefs and values in their work. Different cultural groups, the futurists, the Bauhaus, Swiss design, for example, choose to emphasise different values from those basic principles and the works they produce communicate those different values. In this way, the chapter will be in a position, not merely to describe, but also to explain, the differences between European and American versions of modernism in graphic design. The chapter will observe Meggs' (1983) distinction between European and American modernism. The former developed in the first two decades of the twentieth century, driven by the unfolding of cubism and futurism. Although the United States was exposed to European modernist art and design as early as 1913, an American version of modernism developed only in the 1930s and 1940s, driven by the influx of European émigrés to the United States in the late 1930s.

WHAT IS MODERNISM?

This section will provide a brief definition of modernism, in order to show how modernism appears in graphic design in the later sections. It follows Boyne and Rattansi's (1990) account of modernity and modernism by first distinguishing the one from the other. Modernity is different from modernism in that modernity refers to the experience of living in a modern world and modernism refers to a:

> set of . . . aesthetic movements that emerged in Europe in the 1880s, flourished before and after the First World War and became institutionalised in the academies and art galleries of Post-Second World War Europe and America.
>
> (Boyne and Rattansi 1990: 6)

Modernity, a novel, and distinctly different experience of living in the world was born in Europe around the seventeenth century, as a capitalist economy began to replace a feudal economy. The development of capitalism brought an altogether new range of experiences into being. Increasing urbanisation, the industrial revolution and the French revolution were some of the powerful forces 'unleashed on the world' (Boyne and Rattansi 1990: 3). The period between the seventeenth century and the twentieth century saw entirely new and different experiences being made possible; rapid population growth and the consequent formation of large towns and cities, the progress of science and technology, increasingly industrial production and consumption and new socio-political classes and allegiances all became part of this new experience of the world. In his account of modernity, Berman (1983: 16) explicitly includes the development of 'dynamic' systems of mass communication in his account of the novel experiences engendered by modernity.

As a collection of aesthetic movements, modernism can be hard to define: at first glance, there is little that is common to the work of such dissimilar artists as Picasso, Marinetti, Schoenberg, Schwitters, Joyce, Mallarmé, Heartfield, Matisse, Debussy and Grosz, for example. However, following Lunn (1985: 34–7), Boyne and Rattansi (1990) identify four key features which separate modernism from the various pre-modern realisms and naturalisms. These features embody the values and beliefs of modernism; they are the ideas and practices that modernists think are important and which they think should be communicated and reproduced in their work. This section will identify those values and beliefs and subsequent sections will try to show how how some examples of European and American modernism communicated them. The first feature is 'aesthetic self-reflexiveness' (Boyne and Rattansi 1990: 6). Self-reflexiveness here means to consider, or think about, one's own practice by using that practice (and is also the defining characteristic of modernism in art, according to Greenberg 1993: 85–7). Aesthetic self-reflexiveness, then, is the way in which artists and designers began to thematise, to think about, the practice of art and design by using shape, line, colour and form, for example. It is a painting that takes painting as its subject. Or a piece of design that says something about itself as a piece of design. The second feature is 'montage' (Boyne and Rattansi 1990: 7). This refers to the disrupting of sequence and narrative by juxtaposing items from different sources. It is the construction of a work by editing or putting together previously unrelated elements. Montage is also another way of saying 'cut and paste'. The third character-istic of modernism is the use of 'paradox, ambiguity and uncertainty'. Paradox means 'beyond belief' and alludes to the sense of the absurd or the enigmatic in a work. Ambiguity and uncertainty indicate either the absence of a single, clear meaning or the presence of multiple, contradictory meanings. And the fourth feature concerns the loss of an 'integrated individual subject' (Boyne and Rattansi 1990: 7). These words all mean 'a unity', so the loss of the integrated individual subject means that individuals are no longer consistent or in harmony with themselves, rather they are presented as divided, riven by inner conflict or tormented in some way.

There is a side to modernism, which has already been alluded to above, but which should be stressed. This is the almost contradictory, but always accompanying, belief in progress. This optimism took many forms. It may be seen in the belief in the possibility of a scientific understanding of the world, in the rational nature of human activity, in the advancement of humanity, in the improvement of social life and in the conviction that whatever is done now can be done better in the future. Bauman (1992: 28) says that modernism 'struggled to penetrate the 'deeper' reality, to represent what has been made invisible for the convention-bound eye'. It was an attempt to represent things that had nor or could not be represented before, to improve the understanding of 'reality'. Modernism did this in order to 'attain 'better', correct, true representation' (Bauman 1992: 28). Both Dodd (1999: 1) and Thomas and Walsh (1998: 376–7) see the belief in the progress of history, in the continuous improvement and advancement of humanity as rooted in the Enlightenment of the eighteenth century. To this extent, as Boyne and Rattansi (1990: 8) point out, modernism is a critique of modernity. There is a sense in which modernism represents a dissatisfaction with the modern world and sees a variety of ways in which it may be made better. Modernism does not believe in any simple or unthinking version of science and technology's ability to resolve the problems of the world, but is itself split between a belief in the positive value of the new and a mistrust of the modern world, including itself.

MODERNISM AND GRAPHIC DESIGN

Having outlined the basic values and beliefs of modernism, this section will try to explain them as they apply to graphic design. This section will show how these features appeared in the practice and theory of graphic design. There is a broad consensus as to when modernism in graphic design was. Jobling and Crowley (1996: 139) locate the very beginnings of a 'distinctly modern aesthetic' in the *fin-de-siècle* posters of people such as Bonnard and Chéret, but say that a 'mature' modernism emerges only in the late 1920s and persists until the late 1950s. Hollis (1994) sees the origins of modernism in Italian futurism, around 1914, and lasting until the late 1960s. And Alan and Isabella Livingston (2003: 154) say that modernism embraces a range of graphic styles during the first half of the twentieth century.

There is also consensus as to what modernism was in graphic design. For many graphic designers, the complexity of modernism as it is outlined above gets reduced to two main themes, or values. The first is the rejection of ornament and the favouring of 'clean', 'simple', 'non-decorated' graphics, often in the interests of 'clarity' or the function that the design is to perform. This belief stems partly from Adolf Loos's 1908 essay 'Ornament and Crime' (in Loos 1997), in which he argues that the ornamentation or decoration of objects is to be avoided, because it causes them to quickly go in and out of style. The other source for this belief is Louis Sullivan's 1896 formulation of the 'law' that 'form ever follows function': Sullivan, like Loos, is talking about architecture, but the applicability of the law to graphic design is clear. Although it rather begs the question, the law is that a tall building should look like a tall building; its appearance should result from the job it is to perform. As Walker (1989) says, modernist design theory 'assumed' that the 'machine aesthetic, technology and principles like "form follows function" would determine the shape and appearance of buildings and products': all a graphic designer would have to do in designing graphic products would be 'to find the optimum solution to the design problem' (Walker 1989: 159). A modernist graphic design, then, should be unornamented and free from unnecessary decoration and the way it looked should be a direct result of the job it was to perform. The design historian Jeremy Aynsley, for example, echoes some of these values when he says that 'modernism in graphic design can be identified by stylistic simplicity, a flatness of form, a taste for asymmetrical composition and the reduction of elements to a minimum'(Aynsley 1987: 138).

The second belief is the concentration on modernism's 'improving' energies. In Milton Glaser's view, 'modernism is about progress, the endless frontier and ceaseless development'; its 'origins are in the idea of good coming from boundless technology' and it is 'essentially utopian' (Glaser 1997b: 132). Glaser interprets the scientific and technological innovations of modernity in much the same way as the Italian Futurists interpreted them, as something to be celebrated and welcomed, as something from which good may come. According to Philip Meggs, Mondrian 'saw his art as a metaphor pointing toward a universal harmony and order that might be attained in human society and daily life' (Meggs 1997b: 3). Mondrian's horizontal and vertical lines, together with his limited palette of black, white, grey and the primary colours were a visual metaphor for the 'dynamic equilibrium' that modernism wanted to see in social life (Meggs

1997b: 3). In an essay entitled 'Long Live Modernism!', Vignelli (1994: 51) explains modernism as, among other things, the obligation to improve the world, to fight commercialisation and industrialisation. Kalman et al. (1994: 29) and McCoy (1997: 214) all refer to the modernist imperative to 'improve' the quality of daily life. Jobling and Crowley (1996: 143) even refer to a 'messianic' role for the modernist graphic designer; the modernist designer is seen as someone who is inspired by the hope for or belief in deliverance from the present into a better life on earth. Writing about Moholy-Nagy, they say that the modernist designer's job was to 'prefigure a better world where visual communication would enlighten rather than simply reproduce the prevailing taste, attitudes and conditions' (Jobling and Crowley 1996: 143). Here modernist graphics design is defined as a critical, rather than a reproductive, activity. It will not reproduce the values and attitudes of the culture it finds itself inhabiting. A version of this utopian theme may in fact be found in Sullivan's 1896 essay, noted earlier. When Sullivan concludes his essay by proposing and supporting the idea of an 'art' that shall be 'of the people, for the people and by the people', he is arguing for an art that will be genuinely popular and in the interests of everyone. Bauman's observation, that modernism was an attempt to see 'deeper' into reality is echoed in the view that modernism in graphic design questioned traditional views of what could be known and how it could be known. Modernist graphic design, then, may also be understood as questioning traditional ways of representing knowledge and as posing a series of visual problems to be solved by using new technologies of production, representation and communication.

It is comparatively rare to find either explicit reference to or sustained analysis of any of the other values of modernity in writing on the history of graphic design. Most commentators, historians and designers are content to discuss modernism in graphic design in terms of the utopian impulse and/or the reduction of complex forms to simple and geometric shapes, but few are concerned to explain design work in terms of the disintegration of subjectivity, for example. Before investigating these other values in terms of graphic design, this paragraph will suggest a possible explanation for the reduction of modernism to these principal values. Thomas and Walsh (1998: 377) argue that only selected aspects of what they call 'high modernism' became 'the establishment high art and culture' and that, by the 1950s, these aspects had come to stand for modernism itself. From painting, the dominant cultural groups took abstract expressionism and from architecture they took the stark and functional aesthetic of Le Corbusier: it was these values that came to represent modernism itself and to be accorded the status of a tradition (Thomas and Walsh 1998: 377). If only these modernist values were appropriated by the dominant cultural groups, then it is hardly surprising that graphic designers chose to adopt only the miminalist and functional aspects of the modern aesthetic, allied to a particular utopian train of thought, in graphic design. As McCoy notes, it was her 'faith in rational functionalism' that got her her first job in an international design company. Her account also indicates that by the 1970s, this feature of modernism had been adopted as the corporate style of international corporations. She connects this faith with one in the idea that such an aesthetic constituted progress toward a 'new American design' (McCoy 1994: 50).

The following paragraphs will take each of the four key features of modernism, as identified by Boyne and Rattansi (1990), simply in order to determine whether, and if so how, modernist graphic design used them. The first value is aesthetic self-reflexivity. This idea refers to the way in which designers draw attention to the medium they are using in their work. A piece of design which explicitly announces itself as a product of a particular medium would embody this feature. The most obvious examples of this in modernist graphic design are Man Ray's rayograms and El Lissitzky's photograms. In Man Ray's 1924 *Gun with Alphabet Squares*, for example, the facts that multiple exposures and a moving light source have been used to create a photographic image can clearly be seen. The letters appear twice (evidence of more than one exposure) and the shadows and edges of the objects seem to move (evidence of a change in the position of the light source). Man Ray is drawing attention to the process that was used to create the image and the effects of the ways in which light, shadow and exposures work in the medium can be seen in the work. Some of El Lissitzky's photographic advertisements produced in the 1920s for the German company Pelikan may also be described as aesthetically self-reflexive. In the 1924 poster for Pelikan Ink, for example, one can see a pen, a bottle of ink and the words 'Pelikan' and 'TINTE' (Figure 6.1). The image has been produced by laying a stencil of the word 'TINTE', a pen and a bottle of ink on some sensitised photographic paper and then exposing the paper to a light source from the left. Consequently, the left-hand side of the pen is sharp and the right-hand side, where it casts a shadow, is blurred. The bottle of ink is also clearly defined on its left-hand side and its shadow is cast, fading as it goes, off to the right. The word 'TINTE' is clear, because the stencil, laying flat on the paper, casts no shadow. In this example, the process by which the advertisement has been made can be 'seen' in the image: the image announces itself visually as a product of certain photographic techniques. Because of this, the image is said to be aesthetically self-reflexive.

The second feature of modernist graphic design is montage, the unsettling of temporal sequences or representational images by juxtaposing elements from diverse sources. As a version of cut-and-paste, montage will be familiar to graphic designers. Hollis (1994: 47) distinguishes montage, which he calls 'superimposing', from collage, which he calls 'sticking together', but both techniques are clearly ways in which both temporal sequence and representational images may be disrupted. The Italian

Figure 6.1 Photogram, El Lissitzsky, 'TINTE' advert for Pelican ink (1924).
© DACS 2004

Futurist artist Ardengo Soffici employs montage in the 1915 book cover for his own poems *BIFSZF + 18*. In this book cover he combines various sources (woodblock printed type, letters from existing posters and elements from photo-engravings) to break up the conventional page layout. El Lissitzky provides another good example of modernist graphics in his 1924 *Self Portrait*, which uses collage, photo-montage and multiple photographic prints. In this example, the representational whole of El Lissitzky's face, has been unsettled by printing a hand holding a compass over it. Multiple printing can be seen in the hand, which is in front of the face, while the face itself is superimposed on the graph paper which forms the background, but which can also be seen in El Lissitzky's face, as though his face were transparent. Conventional representational techniques and codes, regarding things being either behind or in front of other things, have been subverted here. Collage was a popular modernist technique, Hannah Hoch, Kurt Schwitters and John Heartfield, for example, all used it extensively in their work.

Third, modernism is characterised by the use of paradox, multiple meanings and ambivalence, or uncertain meaning. Unsurprisingly, perhaps, the El Lissitzky self-portrait also illustrates paradox: the arrangement of space(s) in the image is literally 'beyond belief'; it creates a space that is not like any space encountered in daily life, where, for example, one is usually sure that faces are in front of backgrounds. While the 1923 theatre poster for the *Party of the Bearded Heart*, by Ilya Zdanevitch can be read fairly conventionally, it can also be read unconventionally (Figure 6.2). For example, 'Soirée du coeur barbe' makes sense if one is prepared to read some words from left to right and others from top to bottom. As a result of the way the letters are laid out, however, it is also possible to find other words and to make sense, and occasionally nonsense, out of them. An appropriate example, perhaps, is that the word for 'bristle' may be found by reading the 'soi..' of 'soirée' into the 'e' of 'coeur'. The meaning here is uncertain in so far as it seems to be accidentally found rather than placed or constructed by the poster.

The absence of a unified and consistent subjectivity is the fourth feature of modernism identified earlier. The fracturing of the sense of self one commonly feels in everyday experience, or the presence of more than one self, may be found in many of the montage or collage works discussed already. Hannah Hoch's 1919 collage *Cut with the kitchen knife through the first epoch of the Weimar beer-belly culture* or her 1920 collage *The Pretty Maiden*, for example, employ multiple viewpoints, which give a sense that a single unified subject is absent. In the former, many individuals appear, none of whom is given prominence: it is as if identity and unity have been shattered and now exists only as multiple aspects of a 'personality'. In the latter, various parts of many women's bodies are presented, a hand, a hairstyle, a head and so on. The whole woman is nowhere present; even in

Figure 6.2 Poster, Zdanevitch, 'The Bearded Heart' (1923)

the face that returns the viewer's gaze, one eye has been substituted for someone else's eye. Similarly, in Marcel Duchamp's 1912 painting *Nude Descending a Staircase*, the geometrically fragmented shapes and lines give the impression that the single person coming downstairs has been captured as a series of still time-lapse images, as though they were existing at the same time, but in a sequence of different places. The apparently integrated or consistent subject, then, is both temporally and physically fragmented in this work.

EUROPEAN MODERNISM

The previous section identified and explained the four main features that were identified by Lunn (1985) as being central to the conception of modernism. Those features may be understood as the beliefs or values that were important to modernism. This section will consider a few important examples of European modernist graphic design in order to show how they reveal those important ideas. Meggs (1983: 274) suggests that the whole of twentieth-century graphic design is the product of the 'collision' between cubist painting and futurist poetry. It is with this collision that this section will begin, before moving on to consider some work of the Bauhaus and 'Swiss' design or 'International Typographic Style'.

The end of the nineteenth century saw what might be called the flowering of the industrial revolution. Berman's (1983: 16) description of living at this time as living in a 'maelstrom' must surely be correct. To inhabit and experience an entirely new

> landscape of steam engines, automatic factories, railroads, vast new industrial zones; of teeming cities that have grown overnight, often with dreadful human consequences; of daily newspapers . . . and other mass media, communicating on an ever wider scale
>
> (Berman 1983: 18–19)

must have been confusing and chaotic, if not terrifying. Every institution, cultural tradition, social class, economic practice and political relationship that had existed before had been fundamentally transformed. In such a context, then, it is only to be expected that European institutions and traditions of art, along with beliefs about art and design, were also profoundly shaken. European culture's old aesthetic values, representational practices, and beliefs concerning the very nature and function of art and design also underwent a radical re-examination.

It is in this context that cubism and futurism represent the beginnings of European modernism and, if Meggs (1983) is correct, the origins of all subsequent graphic design. Among other things, cubism and futurism begin a process of questioning the nature of representation: they ask what representation is, they ask how does representation work, and they ask what is it that is being represented. They raise questions about aesthetics, about how colour and form work and about how to communicate using colour and form in a changed and changing world. These are questions about how one sort of thing (shape, line and colour) can stand for or represent another kind of thing (the world and the things in it). These are questions about the nature of the reality that is being represented. And these are questions about the aesthetic codes or rules for representing the world in art and design. Einstein's answer to the question about the nature of reality had been given in his paper on special relativity in 1905 and it led to a deep mistrust of traditional notions of representation and appearances: the Newtonian space in which objects had been experienced and described since the Renaissance was not the space that Einstein described. There was now understood to be a reality behind or beyond the reality that one could see and represent by means of two-dimensional illusionist painting and Bauman's point about modernism being the desire to penetrate to this new and 'deeper' reality can be applied here to the work of Picasso and Braque. Consequently, as Greenberg (1993: 87) says, cubism did not abandon the representation of recognisable, three-dimensional objects, what it did abandon was the representation of the sort of space that three-dimensional objects can inhabit.

Consequently, the cultural conventions for the representation of objects in space began to be questioned and ultimately abandoned by artists and designers. One such convention is perspective. The work of artists such as Picasso and Braque may be read as an investigation of that convention and as a gradual rejection of the codes for the traditional representation of objects in space. The facets and multiple perspectives of analytical cubism that are found in the work of these artists can be interpreted as a way of representing this new understanding of space. The facets or planes are a way of indicating multiple viewpoints, rather than the single viewpoint of traditional perspective theory. Rather than presenting an illusion of three-dimensional space, in which shapes, lines and colours stand unproblematically for things in the world, these facets and planes must be understood as drawing attention to the problem of representation itself: how to represent something that cannot be represented in unproblematic fashion. The multifaceted and fragmented appearance of Picasso and Braque's paintings can also be said to communicate the demise of the unitary subject as it was explained above: the consistent and harmonious individual has been shattered into multiperspectival pieces in the works of this period. Picasso and Braque's use of collage may also be read as interrogating the nature of space. On the one hand, as Greenberg (1982: 105) says, the collages announce the flat, two-dimensional surface of the canvas but on the other they refer to three dimensions. The use of sand, wood-grain wallpaper and sacking in collages introduced three dimensions to works that otherwise emphasised the flatness and two-dimensionality of the canvas suface (Greenberg 1982: 106–7). In these ways, cubism represented an investigation of the cultural codes for representing objects in the sort of space that had been experienced for hundreds of years.

Italian futurist art and design was less interested in the special theory of relativity and its consequences for the understanding of representation. It was, however, very interested in modernity considered as a turbulent and cacophonous 'maelstrom'. In the first of many manifestos that the futurists produced, Filippo Marinetti celebrated the speed, energy, power and danger of modernity:

> We will sing of the great crowds agitated by work . . . the nocturnal vibration of the arsenals and the workshops beneath their violent electric moons: the gluttonous railway stations . . . factories suspended from the clouds by the thread of their smoke; bridges with the leap of gymnasts . . . adventurous steamers sniffing the horizon; great-breasted locomotives . . . like enormous steel horses with long tubes for bridle, and the gliding flight of aeroplanes whose propeller sounds like the flapping of a flag and the applause of enthusiastic crowds.
>
> (http://cscs.umich.edu/~crshalizi/T4PM/futurist-manifesto.html,
> March 2004)

The 1909 manifesto of 'ruinous and incendiary violence', directed against the 'gangrene' of university professors, feminists, libraries and all other forms of antique cowardice, was in no way critical of modernity's values. (And in this respect, therefore, futurism was not a modernist movement.) Although there were manifestos for painting and fashion, this energy and exhilarating violence were to be communicated primarily through the unlikely media of poetry and typography. Marinetti was a poet and his poetry was both impassioned and explosive. The 1914 work *Zang Tumb Tumb* is his 'ear-witness' account of the battle of Adrianopolis in October 1912, where he served as a volunteer (Figure 6.3). Onomatopoeia combines with different typestyles, in different sizes and moving in various directions to give an idea of the noises made by grenades, shells and rifle shots. The name for this new typography, 'parole in liberta', translates as 'words in freedom'. Free typography, as it became known, was an attempt to make typography communicate in an almost tangible fashion, rejecting the stifling horizontal and vertical alignments of Gutenberg's letterpress, which dated from the 1450s. Using the newly available photographic techniques of reproduction, Marinetti and the typographer Giovanni Papini transformed both the ideas behind, and the practices of, layout and typography. Papini's magazine *Lacerba* published Marinetti's manifesto on typography in 1913, in which he called for an end to the 'typographical harmony of the page' and recommended the use of three or four different colours of ink and maybe twenty different fonts. The different typestyles were necessary in order to communicate subtle variations of speed or violence; italics for 'swift sensations' and bold for 'violent onomatopoeias', for example (http://www.futurism.org.uk/books/books.htm, March 2004).

Figure 6.3 Book cover, F. T. Marinetti, *Zang Tumb Tumb* (1914)

It was suggested earlier that futurism was not modernist in so far as it was not at all ambivalent on the desirability of modernity; futurism was entirely in favour of the maelstrom of modern life. Modernism in its guise as a social project, as an attempt to improve life, is absent from the ambitions of Italian futurism. However, in other ways, futurism was a modernist movement. For example, the futurists were modernist in that their work often drew attention to the means of its own construction. The typographic work and layouts of Marinetti and Papini do not even try to efface themselves before the meaning of the text, as more conventional layouts and 'well-behaved' typography does. For conventional typography and layout, to be noticed is to have made a mistake. Futurist typographic and layout shout, 'Look at me! I'm graphic design and I mean something!' The latter draw attention to the codes that had previously governed the construction of meaning and to the ways in which they disrupt them. They do this by rejecting those codes so comprehensively and so enthusiastically: where nineteenth-century use of type and layout would emphasise an element by placing it at the top of a page, or by using a single, bold font, Marinetti's words freely roam the page, in a variety of fonts. Other examples of futurist graphic design that may be counted as modernist in these terms include Apollinaire's concrete poetry of 1918 and Fortunato Depero's book production. Apollinaire's poem 'Il Pleut', for example, provides a sort of visual onomatopoeia as the words fall, like rain, from the top to bottom of the page. Depero's 1927 'nailed book', known as *Depero Futurista* is held together by two aluminium bolts instead of a sewn binding. It draws attention to the means of its own construction and, in so doing, provides a critical perspective on the taken-for-granted, culturally specific conventions of previous book production.

The work of the Bauhaus between 1919 and 1933 provides a series of aesthetic, political and philosophical contrasts with both cubism and futurism, while remaining within the modernist fold. The name Bauhaus is made up from two German words meaning 'to build' and 'house' and indicates the twin desires to learn from the past and to serve the future by adapting and updating the medieval German tradition of the *bauhütte*, with its apprentice–journeyman–master structure. Meggs (1983: 330) says that during its first five years, in Weimar, the Bauhaus was 'intensely visionary' and 'utopian'. Pursuing the legacy of both William Morris and the Arts and Crafts movement, and of the Deutsche Werkbund (both of whom wished to produce cheap, well-made and mass-produced goods), the Bauhaus sought to achieve what they did not, the integration of art and industry in the interests of an egalitarian modern society. For the Bauhaus, all forms of art and design (all forms of communication) were to contribute to the improvement of humanity and society: furniture design, textile design, architectural design and product design as well as graphic design all had a part to play in this utopian vision. The following paragraphs will concentrate on the role that graphic design in the form of typography was to play in the Bauhaus's modernist project.

Herbert Bayer's proposal for a 'universal' type is a good, if an unpopular and ultimately unsuccessful, example of this project. The Universal typeface, containing only lower-case letters, was constructed in 1926 and is made up of circles and straight lines of constant thickness. In his 1935 essay 'Towards a Universal Type', Bayer (1999) explains what he thinks is wrong with contemporary typefaces and what should be done to correct them. He begins with an account of modernity, noting that 'today' we do not build Gothic buildings, travel on horseback or wear crinolines; we construct 'contemporary' buildings, travel in cars and planes and dress more 'rationally' (Bayer 1999: 60). The implication is that we should not be using old-fashioned typefaces. Bayer notes that Roman faces were drawn with a slate pencil and then chiselled into stone and that medieval faces were drawn with a pen. These faces look the way they do because the chisel making the letterforms in the stone has to break into the stone somewhere and because pencils and pens inevitably make thin and thick strokes. His argument is that because most of what is read today is either typed on a typewriter or printed on a press there is no need for typefaces to retain serifs or thick and thin lines. His second line of attack is social and has to do with improving education. He says that a more rational typeface, containing only lower-case letters and no capitals, would be 'less of a burden' for school children, students, professionals and business people (Bayer 1999: 62). It would be easier for children to learn to read and write, and it would be easier to write more quickly if capitals were omitted from the alphabet. Universal, then, is modern in that, being geometrically constructed not bearing the marks of handmade script, it is more suited to contemporary mechanical reproduction. It is also modern in that adopting it would have educational and communicational benefits; it would help children to learn to write and professionals could communicate more efficiently. The typestyle was unpopular with the German public at the time because it contained no capitals (which are more prevalent in written German than in English) and so different from the Gothic or black-letter typestyles they were accustomed to. And it was unsuccessful in so far as Futura, designed by Paul Renner in 1927, has been more widely adopted as a 'modern' face.

The aesthetic differences between the work of the Bauhaus, cubism and futurism constitute a clear contrast between the three. Where cubism presents a variety of perspectives, the Bauhaus is looking for the clearest perspective. Where futurist graphic design is chaotic and noisy, the Bauhaus was the home of ordered, clean and exact design. Meggs (1983: 330) suggests that this was the result of Hermann Muthesius's influence. Having worked alongside the industrial designer Peter Behrens in the Deutsche Werkbund, Muthesius saw that standardisation and absence of decoration was necessary in order to facilitate mass production in Germany's recovering industries. For the Bauhaus, there was an ideal way of constructing visual communication and it would be formed by the demands of mass production. Between them, the absence of decoration and the machine aesthetic determine that Bauhaus graphic design has a clean and efficient look. According to Rudolph de Harak (1997: 137) the main objective of the Bauhaus was to achieve a 'social reconditioning'. Kinross (1989: 138) says that modernist typography was a response to the need to 'save labour, time and money, and to improve communication' and Bayer was keen to stress the savings in both time and money that could be made by adopting a lower-case only alphabet (Bayer 1999: 62). Typography's task was to improve communication and society at the same time: the aesthetic problem of the construction of typefaces and layouts was to contribute to the formation of a better society. This is the main political difference between the Bauhaus, cubism and futurism; the Bauhaus conceives modernism as a social, or even a socialist, project. It thus shares the ambivalence towards the values of the modern world that was noted above as one of the four key features of modernism and wants to eradicate inefficient communication in the interests of improving that world. Futurism and cubism are politically conservative: futurism celebrates modernity, with all its brutality and injustice, and cubism has little, if anything, to offer by way of social critique.

Closely related to the Bauhaus were the 'New Typography' of Jan Tschichold and the subsequent development of the International Typographic Style. In 1923, Tschichold visited the first Bauhaus exhibition in Weimar and appears to have been impressed by the functionality and clarity of the work he saw (see Kinross 1998: xvi). Tschichold's 'conversion' to modernist beliefs took the form of a commitment to purity and clarity along with an understanding of the changed circumstances people found themselves in at the beginning of the twentieth century. His book, *The New Typography*, published in Berlin in 1928, begins by placing typography and graphic design in a 'new world-view' (Tschichold 1998: 11). Here he outlines the idea that the scientific and technological discoveries of the late nineteenth and early twentieth centuries have been created by a 'new kind of man: the engineer' and have engendered in people a 'new attitude to their surroundings'. The modern typographer is to be reconceived, then as an engineer. 'His' work will be characterised by 'economy, precision, use of pure constructional forms that correspond to the functions of the object' (Tschichold 1998: 11). In an echo of Bayer's (1999) formulation (noted earlier), Tschichold (1998: 13) says that just as building Gothic castles now would be incongruous, so practising the 'old typography' today would be absurd; typography must make itself a part of the modern world. In the first section of his book, Tschichold is almost as enthusiastic about the exhilarating energy of modernity as the futurists and he is a keen supporter of the Bauhaus's idea that communicative design needs to be functional and efficient. The key value that Tshichold has taken from modernism, then, is the notion of social progress, which is to be served by practical and precise typographic design.

The New Typography is an enormously detailed, complex and rewarding guide to its topic. However, this section will concentrate on what Tschichold has to say about the principles of the new typography. One of those principles concerns the presence, or absence, of decoration in type and, as Loos and Sullivan subordinated function to form and declared ornament a crime, so Tschichold is against ornament in typestyle design. He says that no ornamented fonts 'meet our requirements for clarity and purity' (Tschichold 1998: 73). The use of serifs in roman type and of curlicues in Fraktur, for example, is neither functional nor modern. Only the grotesque, sans serif or block letter faces are 'in spiritual accordance with our time' (Tschichold 1998: 73). Fraktur dates from the sixteenth century, when the Emperor Maximilian employed it in a series of books, and it attracts much of Tschichold's critical attention. There are two main criticisms. The first is that Fraktur is nationalistic and exclusive. It has associations with the Prussian and Austrian elements of German pre-history: Maximilian was a Habsburg emperor and one story has it that the face was first carved in the town of Schwabacher, for example. Such nationalistic and thus exclusive connotations are unwelcome in Tschichold's understanding of modernity, which stresses and encourages international relationships between different peoples. The second criticism is that, like the roman faces, it is difficult to read and thus distracts from the meaning of the text. Tschichold is utterly scathing; he says that Fraktur is a parody, it is like the uniform of a pompous old admiral that is good only for fancy-dress parties (Tschichold 1998: 75, 74).

So, like Bayer (1999), Tschichold (1998) proposes sans serif for use in modern printing. Unlike Bayer, he is ambivalent as to whether it should be in lower case only. (And neither his nor Bayer's sans serif typestyles ever went into production.) He accepts that a lower-case only alphabet is both logical and 'in harmony' with modern times and says that it is desirable because it would entail economic and aesthetic advantages. But, because redesigning all letters completely would be 'impracticable and unacceptable' (Tschichold 1998: 80–1), he suggests keeping two alphabets, for the time being. Of the sans serif faces available to him, however, Tschichold (1998: 73) finds none that is wholly satisfactory. Most of them, like Erbar and Kabel, are too 'artistic' and 'artificial' for modern demands but he says that Futura (designed in 1927 by his colleague at the time, Paul Renner) is 'a significant step in the right direction' (Tschichold 1998: 74). What Tschichold calls an 'ordinary jobbing sans serif' is 'quiet' and the easiest to read and he seems to have had similar problems finding a face for his own book to those producing the 1998 English edition. Tschichold says that he was confined by the limited number of typefaces held by the printer at the time and the Note on the English edition's design suggests that, as the face closest to Tschichold's original (Aurora Grotesk) was not available in digital form, the designers settled for Imago Light Extended (Tschichold 1998: 75, 236). To summarise, Tschichold proposes the use of sans serif typestyles, such as Futura, as they are undecorated, economical, easy to read and therefore in harmony with modern times. Sans serif faces are also modernist in the term's progressive and liberal sense; as Tschichold says, in replacing faces such as Fraktur, they also oppose nationalism and exclusivity. However, neither Tschichold nor Bayer is modernist in the sense that modernism places a high value on the use of ambiguity and ambivalence: these qualities are precisely what both the Bauhaus's graphic design and Tschichold's new typography were intended to avoid.

This internationalist theme of modernism, developed by Tschichold in *The New Typography*, is also found in the International Typographic Style that originated in Switzerland after the Second World War. Tschichold himself had emigrated to Basel in 1933, having been placed in 'protective custody' by the Nazis as part of their crackdown on what they saw as socialism, or 'cultural bolshevism' (Kinross 1998: xxxvi–xxxvii). Here, he appears to have reversed his opinions on the use of sans serif faces and on the use of asymmetry in layouts and so fallen out with Max Bill, but Tschichold's modernist prescription for the almost mathematical clarity and economy of communicative graphics was also present in Swiss graphics. Hollis (1999: 130) ascribes much of this clarity and economy to the geometric discipline of Karl Gerstner, who developed the notion of the grid, a mathematically ordered pattern of horizontal and vertical lines which provided a unifying and underlying structure for all layouts. The use of sans serif, especially Helvetica (unmodernly, the Roman name for Switzerland), flush left-hand and ragged right-hand margins and the abandoning of drawn illustration in favour of photography all contributed to the style that was heralded as an international style. Jobling and Crowley (1996: 162) note that *Neue Grafik*, the house journal of the Swiss School, was published in three languages; they also record Emil Ruder's enumeration of the main features of the Swiss 'system', which included the use of simple typeforms because they were universal, clear and impersonal. All of these elements (the grid, simple typeforms such as Helvetica, a multilingual house journal), contribute to the emphasising of 'international' in International Typographic Style. Each of them is serving international and 'universal' communication in a way that is quite in keeping with the progressive and socially improving values of modernism.

The International Typographic Style is also modernist in that it is to a certain extent aesthetically self-reflexive; it draws attention to the means of its own construction. Some posters from this period explicitly refer to the grid (e.g. Max Bill 1956 Exhibition Poster for the Kunsthaus in Zurich, Max Huber 1951 Yearbook Cover), and others refer in a way that cannot be missed to the use of colour and shape on a flat surface (Müller-Brockman's 1953 poster for *American Books Today*). Others do both, stressing the grid and the use of large blocks of flat colour (Gerstner's 1957 *Schiff nach Europa*, and 1957 *boît à musique*). In the Bill and Huber posters, the grid is the geometric basis for the visual construction of the poster and, in so far as the elements of the poster draw attention to the grid, the posters are self-reflexive. By using large areas of flat colour, posters such as Müller-

Brockman's effectively announce the flat surface they are printed upon. Arguably, they do this even more convincingly than Greenberg's modernist paintings, because there will be no (three-dimensional) brush-strokes in the prints to detract from the two-dimensionality of the flat surface. In their various ways, then, these works are aesthetically self-reflexive in that they comment on the techniques that they are themselves constructed out of. To that extent they may be seen as modernist in a sense that few other examples discussed so far have illustrated.

However, the idea of 'international' in International Typographic Style cannot pass without comment. Some, like de Harak and Kepes, for example, see modern graphic design in general, and the International Typographic Style in particular, as being somehow universal, or unproblematically international; de Harak (1997: 137) says that the International Typographic Style was a 'timeless style', that it could be easily understood by people from all times. Writing in 1969, Gyorgy Kepes (1969: 13) talks of modern visual communication being 'universal and international'. Indeed, the name itself suggests that the style of the work is such that it will communicate with people from any and all countries. The shapes, colours, simple typeforms (Helvetica) and geometric (grid-based) layouts are such that any communication 'problems' will be overcome. Presumably, the idea is that the 'mathematically' constructed and 'geometric' grids (understood as being non-cultural, or transcultural in some way) will communicate clearly in a non-cultural or transcultural way. Clearly, this book is committed to the idea that there can be no such thing as non-cultural communication: it has argued that all communication is predicated on the existence of signs and codes which, as profoundly cultural, must be learned in order for communication to be possible. There are no signs that are non-cultural, that are not part of the way a culture constructs and interprets its own identity in communication. Thus, the International Typographic Style must be the product of learned, culturally specific signs and codes and it cannot be simply international and timeless as some commentators suggest. Indeed, de Harak contradicts himself in the same paragraph when he, more accurately, says that the International Typographic Style is 'a strong reflection of its times'. It cannot be both 'timeless' and a 'strong reflection of its time'; it can, however, be a product of a specific culture in history and its signs and codes (typestyles and grid, for example) can be learned and understood by people who are not post-war, middle-class European males.

AMERICAN MODERNISM

The United States' initial response to European modernism, as it was manifested in the critical response to the 1913 International Exhibition of Modern Art (known as the Armory Show), was not encouraging. Gallery I, containing French paintings and sculpture, was labelled the Chamber of

Horrors by the press and a prize was offered by *American Art News* for anyone who could find the nude in Duchamp's abstract *Nude Descending a Staircase* (see http://xroads.virginia.edu/~MUSEUM/Armory/galleryI/tour.i.html, March 2004). However, it could be argued that it was precisely the improving, 'modernising' beliefs of modernism that led to the development of American modernism after the Second World War. This is because most of the members of the Bauhaus left Germany after 1933 when the Nazis closed the school and many of them went to the United States. What the Nazis objected to was the perceived 'socialism' of the Bauhaus, the desire for a more egalitarian society that was to be achieved through modern and rational design, even if it was more the Bauhaus's designs for cheap, mass-produced and high-quality housing and furniture than the rationalised typestyles that led to the charges of 'socialism' and thus inspired the Nazis' hatred. Other European modernists also fled. Catherine McDermott (1992: 147) suggests that it was the improving impulse of modernist theory, the link between design and social function, that was seen as being socialist by the Nazis and Meggs (1983: 367) begs the question by suggesting that the dispersal of Bauhaus staff, students and alumni 'made modern design a truly international movement'. Walter Gropius and Marcel Breuer, for example, went to Harvard and Moholoy-Nagy and Gyorgy Kepes went to Chicago, where they formed the financially under-supported New Bauhaus and later the Institute of Design. Herbert Bayer went to New York in 1938 to set up in private practice. This section will attempt to give some idea of how European modernism was understood in post-war American graphic design by looking at two important examples.

The first example here is the Container Corporation of America (CCA), which was based in Chicago. This example has been chosen partly because its founder, Walter P. Paepcke, had an abiding interest in the Bauhaus, possibly, Meggs (1983: 368) says, as a result of the Bauhaus's experiments with paper structures and materials. Indeed, Moholy-Nagy, who had used origami-like constructions for architectural models at the Bauhaus, was encouraged to set up the New Bauhaus and then the Institute of Design in Chicago by Paepcke. It has also been chosen partly because modernists such as Herbert Bayer, A. M. Cassandre, Fernand Leger, Herbert Matter and Man Ray all worked for the corporation.

Egbert Jacobson was appointed as CCA's design director by Paepcke in 1936 and he produced the corporation's new identity, consisting in a logo, trademark and stationery. The new logo included an illustration of a cardboard box, an outline of the United States and three sans serif capitals, CCA (Meggs 1983: 368). The letters appeared in Paul Renner's Futura font, which has already been mentioned as one of the defining fonts of European modernism. The logo was also 'innovative for its time' according to Meggs. It is therefore the uncluttered, efficient values of modernism, found in Renner's font, that are used to construct and communicate the corporate identity of CCA. Two years later, A. M. Cassandre was employed to produce a series of advertisements for CCA and, although he used serifs and representational imagery in 'Concentration', Jacobson's cardboard box and some element of geometric values are retained to create a balanced and almost symmetrical composition. Meggs suggests that this advertisement was modern in that it overturned the longwinded conventions of American advertising (Meggs 1983). Cassandre's take on European modernist values replaced the traditional illustration, headline and rectangle of body text and produced a 'dynamic, asymmetrically balanced composition' of words and images (Meggs 2001b: 285). As Michele Bogart (1995: 263) says, one of the central values of modernist design was a 'concern for creating harmonious visual relationships . . . that could have a transformative effect in broader spheres of life'. This 'Bauhaus-influenced design philosophy remained visible in CCA advertising on into the 1940s' (Bogart 1995: 263), when an increasingly warlike and propagandising approach began to appear.

The cardboard box trademark reappeared in later, more patriotic wartime CCA advertisements, becoming more abstract through the years. In Leo Lionni's 1943 advertisement 'Press the button . . . release bombs', for example, Jacobson's original trademark box appears as a line drawing and as having just been opened. Lionni also uses a classic modernist technique, photo-montage. A gloved hand, about to press the bomb-release button on a joystick, is seen in the foreground over a cloudscape in which six planes can be seen. And in Jean Carlu's advertisement of 1943, 'Gift Packages for Hitler', the same box appears closed, as a highly abstracted version of the Necker cube (see Hollis 1994: 109; Bogart 1995: 264). Carlu's work also uses the modernist technique of montage, in which the boxes 'contain' planes and a hand 'holds' a plane in a box. Montage bombs 'rain down' onto Hitler's upturned face. Other modernist features taken up by CCA's designers include the grid. John Massey's 1967 cover for the annual report, for example, superimposes nearly two hundred half-inch squares over twelve photographs of CCA employees.

Bayer was taken on as a design consultant by CCA in 1946 and, having overseen the CCA's *World Geo-Graphic Atlas* in 1948, began work on what Meggs (2001b: 286) calls 'the most famous institutional advertising campaign in history'. The 'Great Ideas of Western Man' campaign was a series of 200 images illustrating a collection of improving and enlightening quotations from western philosophers, politicians and writers. Paepcke's deeply humanistic idea was:

> to stimulate thinking and discussion about the ideas at the roots of what the philosophers call 'the good life'; ideas that are infinitely more important to the preservation of our society and our liberties than the pursuit of material gain.
> (http://www.mohansamant.com/Happenings.html, March 2004)

The male and western bias is clear and unapologetic. In the Smithsonian American Art Museum's collection of the 'Great Ideas' artworks, Lao Tzu, the sixth-century Chinese philosopher, is the only non-westerner and Jane Addams, the American social worker and feminist who won the Nobel Peace Prize in 1931, and Edith Wharton, the American novelist, are the only women included in the series. (To be fair, there does appear to have been a 'Great Ideas of Eastern Man' series.) However, in this series, artists and designers (including Saul Bass, Josef Albers, Johannes Itten, René Magritte and Leo Lionni) produced images illuminating such texts as Goethe's 'Whatever liberates our spirit without giving us self-control is disastrous'. Bayer himself produced images illustrating Wittgenstein's semiological comment on culture, 'The limits of my language mean the limits of my world' and Roosevelt's warning, 'The things that will destroy America are prosperity at any price, peace at any price, safety first instead of duty first, and love of soft living and the get-rich-quick theory of life'.

In addition to using modernist techniques such as paper collage and photo-montage alongside watercolours and gouache on paperboard, Bayer's 1959 illustration of Roosevelt's warning also provides an account of the curious position of the modernist designer in the United States and of the split within modernism itself. The self-fragmentation of modernism, the way it adopts a critical attitude toward modern life itself was noted above and Bayer's work uses classical modernist techniques (such as collage) to distance itself from modern life. The position of the designer here is often described as being 'between art and commerce'. Bayer's image shows a montage in which appears a laughing woman's face, another woman's leg, fruit, money, a diamond ring, a bottle of champagne in bucket, a lottery ticket and rolling dice. The words 'payola' and 'corruption' appear as cuttings from newspaper articles. Bayer's point is that these items represent parts of the 'soft life' that will destroy the United States. They stand as synechdoches for gambling, lasciviousness, drinking, materialism, political and financial corruption and greed. Bayer is being highly critical of the society he had been a member of since 1938. He is also being paid as an employee by the company that hired him in 1946. The modernist desire to improve society is in conflict here with the economic necessity to make a living from or within that very society; Bayer's socialist critique is ultimately funded by one of the largest capitalist companies in the United States. In this respect CCA's 'Great Ideas' series of advertisements bears comparison with Benetton's 'United Colors' series of advertisements, discussed in Chapter 5.

The second example in this section is Brownjohn, Chermayeff & Geismar (later known as Chermayeff and Geismar Associates), a New York design company that is explicitly located by Meggs (1983: 434) in the 'tradition' of European modernism. In Megg's account, Robert Brownjohn and Ivan Chermayeff, two of the founders of this agency, had a good understanding of European modernism's values and beliefs, having studied under Moholy-Nagy and being the son of Serge Chermayeff (the Russian modernist architect and president of the New Bauhaus in Chicago) respectively. Reinforcing the argument above, that modernism in graphic design was often reduced to one or two of the values identified as constitutive of modernism in general, Ivan Chermayeff (1994: 45) says that he was taught that modernism in design meant 'clean and simple' design. His 1957 album cover for Beethoven's 'Eroica' symphony shows that he also learned the modernist technique of collage and the modernist belief in aesthetic self-reflexivity. The cover uses seven different typestyles, one to identify the conductor, composer and title of the piece and one for every letter in 'Eroica'. Each letter looks as though it has been torn from a different source and glued onto the flat surface. By bringing the viewer's attention to the constructed nature of the cover, the cover announces itself as having been made in a particular way and, as such, shows clear evidence of the values of futurism and cubism. In 1960, as Chermayeff and Geismar Associates, their work for the Chase Manhattan Bank's corporate identity programme uses abstract, geometric shapes and extended sans serif letterforms. While there is little aesthetic self-reflexivity here, there is abstraction and a mathematical precision to the work: the four wedge shapes form an inner square and an outer octagon. The sans serif used here has been extended to make an easy-to-read face even easier to read when approached from 'side on', as it would be by anyone walking down a city street.

A slightly different version of the tension between modernist beliefs and the values of capitalist economics as was seen in Bayer's work for CCA can be seen here. The modernist value of improving society, which the Bauhaus interprets as a desire for clear and functional typestyles and layouts, for example, is incorporated by designers working for capitalist corporations in order to construct an identity for those corporations. Another angle on this tension is the way in which designers are able to experiment formally with geometric shapes and grid-based layouts, for example, but only in the employ of, or under the control of, national and international corporations. Another example may be found in Meggs' assertion that Paul Rand's 1965 trademark for the American Broadcasting Company (ABC) shows the 'legacy' of the Bauhas and Herbert Bayer. Bayer's 'universal' alphabet 'informs' the letterforms, which are lower-case, sans serif and reduced to the simplest of geometric shapes, circles and straight lines (Meggs 1983: 433). Although Rand's 1956 trademark for International Business Machines (IBM) contains slab serifs, it is reminiscent of Matter's trademark for the New York, New Haven and Hartford Railroad and stresses the internal geometric shapes formed by the letters. In all of these examples, one or two of the values that were described above as being characteristic of modernism in design have been taken up, or taken over, by capitalist corporations and used to construct a particular sort of identity for themselves. Milton Glaser's (1997b: 133) position on this is that the 'utopian ideals of modernism' were 'captured' by corporations that wanted to represent themselves as clean, efficient and progressive. Now, as McCoy (2001: 6–7) says, it is difficult to persuade corporate clients to let go of 'Swiss' grids and Helvetica because this aspect of the Bauhaus and the International Typographic Style's versions of modernism has been so thoroughly embraced by the 'corporate world'.

CONCLUSION

This chapter has identified the fundamental principles of modernism. It has explained them as a set of values and beliefs and it has shown how different cultural groups have selected from those values and responded to them in their design work. The works they produce communicate those different selections and responses. The identity of futurist graphic design is different from that of Swiss design, for example, because each group selects a slightly different value and responds to it in a slightly different way from the other groups. Identity is, again, a product of difference. There seems to be no value or belief that is common to all the examples of modernism discussed here. While cubism and futurism are profoundly modernist in that they are aesthetically self-reflexive, they are not concerned with the critique of modern life or the betterment of humanity. The Bauhaus was profoundly modernist, as de Harak (1997: 137) says, in that the social, or even socialist, aim of producing aesthetically respectable mass communications in the interests of a just society was clear, but it was not always modernist in that it was not consistently concerned with self-reflexivity. There is little sense of Bayer's typefaces, for example, self-reflexively drawing attention to the constructed nature of typefaces. There is no essence of modernism that is shared by all these examples of modernist art and design. Rather, there are what Wittgenstein calls family resemblances between them: one includes the social project, but not the fragmented self, of modernism; another has the self-reflexivity, but not the multiple meanings, and so on. This lack of an essential quality or value that is common to all examples raises the problem of to what extent it is possible to talk of a modernist tradition. If there is no one thing shared by all members, then there is no single line of development. However, to the extent that speaking of families is acceptable, because of family resemblance and lineage, so it is acceptable to talk of modernist tradition, for the same metaphorical reasons.

In terms of communication, modernism enacts a movement away from the illusionistic realisms and naturalisms of the eighteenth and nineteenth centuries towards a more semiological notion of representation. What this means is that where pre-modern art and design relied on images resembling the things they were images of, modernism introduces a different set of signs and codes with which to represent the world. In the eighteenth and nineteenth centuries, culturally specific codes concerning perspective, for example, dictated the rules for transcribing three-dimensional reality into two-dimensional images so that a cultural group understood the latter to resemble the former. The facets and fragments of analytic cubism do not resemble or look like people, or guitars, in the same ways that nineteenth-century pictures contain images that 'look like' people or guitars. Rather, one needs to know and understand an entirely different cultural code which determines that and how this collection of triangles represents Picasso's dealer Kahnweiler, or Duchamp's *Nude Descending a Staircase*.

This chapter has described and explained the differences between the various versions of modernism as the result of selecting and communicating different different modernist values and beliefs. For example, in their different ways, both Italian futurist typography and the Bauhaus typographers were interested in new and more effective ways of communicating. Although economics was not their concern, the futurists wanted to break out of the prison-like rules of syntax, grammar and punctuation in order to set words and the imagination free: the Bauhaus typographers wanted to rationalise the alphabet, to perfect letter forms and to clarify communication. Similarly, modernism was often interested in the use of aesthetic self-reflection, using a design to comment on and draw attention to the design's own means of production. These modernist values are the ones that modernist graphic design seems to have used most commonly in constructing corporate identities, advertising and other design products. Although some of the work of Man Ray, El Lissitzky, Hannah Hoch and Herbert Bayer suggests otherwise, the modernist beliefs in ambiguity and in the disintegration of the individual, proved to be not so popular in American modernist graphic design, at least in its corporate forms (some of Bayer's work excepted). This is clearly because ambiguity and fragmented identity are perceived by designers of corporate images as inimical to their practise: CCA and IBM, for example, were hardly likely to endorse a contradictory and fragmented corporate identity. In these cases, the modernist belief in constructing a critical and ambivalent stance with regard to its own values and applying that critique to its own position has been abandoned in favour of clarity and simplicity. Chapter 7 will explain postmodernism in graphic design: postmodernism may be thought of as a response to, and a critique of, the values and beliefs of modernism.

FURTHER READING

- Chapter 5 of Paul Jobling and David Crowley's (1996) *Graphic Design: Reproduction and Representation Since 1800*, Manchester, Manchester University Press, provides a more detailed historical account of **modernist** graphic design and an analysis of the International Typographic Style's understanding of the social role of graphic design.
- A more critical and sceptical view of the **Bauhaus** will be found in Dietmar

Winkler's (1994) 'Morality and Myth: The Bauhaus Reassessed', in Bierut, M. et al. (eds) *Looking Closer*, New York: Allworth Press. And a more critical account of **European modernist graphic design** in general will be found in Part One of Maud Lavin's (2001) *Clean New World: Culture, Politics and Graphic Design*, Cambridge, Mass.: MIT Press. Michele H. Bogart's (1995) *Artists, Advertising and the Borders of Art*, Chicago, Ill.: University of Chicago Press, contains numerous references to the ways in which American pharmaceutical and tobacco companies, for example, were prepared to support modernist designers by employing them to produce adverts.

- Philip Meggs' (2001b) 'The Rise and Fall of Design at a Great Corporation', in Heller, S. and Ballance, G. (eds) *Graphic Design History*, New York: Allworth Press, provides a detailed history of the **CCA's design department** from the 1920s to the 1980s.

- The **futurist** graphic work of Fortunato Depero is discussed in Steven Heller's (2001) 'Fortunato Depero: Cheering up the Universe', in Heller, S. and Ballance, G. (eds) *Graphic Design History*, New York: Allworth Press. And the graphic style of the Soviet magazine *USSR Construction*, as it was designed by **El Lissitzky**, among others, is charted by Victor Margolin (2001) in his 'Construction Work', in Heller and Ballance. Extracts from the writings of El Lissitzky, Marinetti, Moholoy-Nagy, Bayer, Paepcke and many other modernists are to be found in Bierut, M. et al. (eds) *Looking Closer 3*, New York: Allworth Press. See also Philip Meggs' (2001a) 'For the Voice', an account of the relations between El Lissitzky and Mayakowsky, also in Heller and Ballance.

- On the application of the idea that **'form follows function'** to websites, see Nick Finck's essay at http://www.digital-web.com/features/feature_1999–10.shtml, March 2004). He suggests that Sullivan would be turning in his grave. Sullivan's essay, entitled 'The Tall Office Building Artistically Considered', was originally published in *Lippincott's Magazine* in March 1896 and may be found at the New Jersey Institute of Technology website, http://www.njit.edu/old/Library/archlib/pub-domain/sullivan-1896–tall-bldg.html (March 2004).

7

POSTMODERNISM AND GLOBALISATION

INTRODUCTION

This chapter will consider postmodernism and globalisation. In the published history and theory of graphic design, these topics are generally taken to be developments since the early 1970s or so (see Poynor 2003, for example). However, Boyne and Rattansi (1990: 9) report the use of the word 'postmodern' in 1930 and suggest that the term 'gained currency' in the 1950s and 1960s. And Giddens (1990: 63) implies that globalisation is considerably more than thirty years old when he says that modernity itself is 'inherently globalising'. It is clear that some work needs to be done on defining and explaining both of these words and on separating them from their entanglements in modernity. Following the approach of Chapter 6 then, this chapter will provide a definition of postmodernism in order to show how graphic design embodies postmodern values and beliefs in later sections. It will then define and explain globalisation, in order to examine how globalisation appears in graphic production.

The relations between modernism and postmodernism are very complex and potentially confusing. Some idea of this complexity and confusion may be gained by considering the fact that elements of this book are postmodernist. This book produces and reproduces postmodernist values by arguing that there is no god-given or natural meaning. Chapters 2 and 3, for example, explained the production of meaning as the interaction between culturally significant signs and codes: different cultures assign different meanings to signs according to the different values or codes that they hold. Meaning is therefore explained in this book as a product of difference. As we shall see, the idea that meaning is a product of difference is a central principle of postmodernism. However, a cultural product's drawing attention to its own means of production was explained in Chapter 6 as a fundamentally modernist move. Braque and Bayer's collages and montages, for example, were modernist because they announced the means of their own construction. In drawing attention to the fact that it is made up of certain ideas, this (allegedly postmodernist) book has just enacted a profoundly modernist ploy. Such vertiginous complexity is one of the problems faced by any account of postmodernism, and by any account of postmodern graphic design.

Another example of this complexity is provided by Jobling and Crowley (1996: 272), who point out that it is not the case that the modernist 'avowal of clarity and simplicity' has simply been overturned or replaced by post-modernism's 'fascination with complexity and contradiction, decoration and ornament'. To the example that some 'modernist' works exhibit qualities that are described by theorists and historians as 'postmodernist', Jobling and Crowley (1996) add the example of Kurt Schwitters, whose work in the 1920s, they say, seems to anticipate the more recent work of Max Kisman and Studio Dumbar.

WHAT IS POSTMODERNISM?

This section will define and explain postmodernism, in order to show how some graphic design embodies its beliefs and values in the later sections. As Chapter 6 distinguished modernity from modernism, so this chapter will distinguish postmodernity from postmodernism. Postmodernity refers to the social, political and cultural institutions, identities and relations that people enter into at a particular time (cf. Boyne and Rattansi 1990: 9). Postmodernism is a collection of aesthetic movements, or projects. Post-modernity refers to the experience of living in a certain type of society, with certain forms of politics, at a particular time; Thomas and Walsh (1998) summarise some of its main features in the following way:

> Postmodernity is a globalising post-industrial world of media, communication and information systems. It is organised on the basis of a market-orientated world of consumption rather than work and production . . . it is a world of culture in which tradition, consensual values . . . universal beliefs and standards have been challenged, undermined and rejected for heterogeneity, differen-tiation and difference.
>
> (Thomas and Walsh 1998: 364)

This is a useful summary in that it stresses certain key characteristics, or features, of postmodernity. Those central features are globalisation, a post-industrial world of consumption and communication, the challenging of cultural values and difference. Globalisation is one of the qualities that has already been mentioned by Giddens (1990) as being a part of modernity and (in half a sentence) is the sense that, no matter where you go in in the world, you are still in the same place. The post-industrial world of post-modernity differs from the world of modernity in that, where modernity stressed production (the industrial revolution, futurist factories, the noise

138

and speed of mass production, and so on), the postmodern world is one of consumption, media and information. Note that Thomas and Walsh's (1998) account of postmodernity mentions communication systems, as did Berman's (1983) account of modernity. Postmodernity involves the challenging and undermining of traditional cultural values as, indeed, did modernity. Difference, however, is so important to Thomas and Walsh's account that they include it three times, as 'heterogeneity, differentiation and difference'. In the account that follows, difference is absolutely central to postmodernity and postmodernism.

Postmodernism is a collection of aesthetic ventures or projects. As such, and like modernism, it can be hard to define. Dick Hebdige's (1988) list of some of the things that have been labelled 'postmodern' shows how many things have been thus labelled and how difficult it is to ascertain what, if anything, they have in common. A much shortened version of his list includes:

> the decor of a room, the design of a building . . . a television commercial, or an arts documentary . . . the layout of a page in a fashion magazine or critical journal . . . the 'predicament' of reflexivity . . . a fascination for images, codes and styles . . . the 'decentring' of the subject . . . the 'implosion' of meaning, the collapse of cultural hierarchies [and] 'placelessness'
>
> (Hebdige 1988: 181–2)

Some of these items, the layout of a page, for example, are the sort of thing that could be treated in either a pre-modern, modern or postmodern fashion. Others are things that are themselves held to be somehow essentially postmodern, such as the fascination for styles and the collapsing of cultural hierarchies. As evidence of the latter, Jobling and Crowley (1996: 275) mention the 'quotation' of past styles in advertising and they say magazine design is evidence of the former. Andy Warhol's images of mass-produced soup-can labels and washing powder packaging, which have appeared on the walls of high culture art galleries, for example, also question the cultural ranking system in which they had previously been placed. And, it should not go unnoticed, some of the things on Hebdige's list have already appeared, in Chapter 6, as characteristics of modernism; this is a phenomenon that is not uncommon in accounts of postmodernism (Jameson 1991: 4). Forms of reflexivity and the decentring or fragmenting of the subject, for example, both appeared in the explanation of modernism in Chapter 6. All of these things, however, have been labelled 'postmodern', according to Hebdige (1988).

The beginning of an explanation of what all these examples have in common is provided by Boyne and Rattansi (1990: 12), who suggest that all these examples are affected by a 'crisis of representation'. As explained in

Chapter 2, representation is the process in which one thing (a signifier) stands for another thing (a signified). These idea of representation operates on many levels, from shapes and words standing for letters and words to images depicting ethnic and gender groups. What Boyne and Rattansi mean by a 'crisis in representation', then, is that the relation between signifier and signified, as it used to be understood, has dissolved. Where (in modernism) there used to be a series of what might be called 'guarantees', assuring people of the stable relation between signifier and signified, there is (in postmodernism) only the reference to another signifier and another code. For example, where a woman wearing a skirt that did not touch the floor would once have meant that she was 'common', because that was what wearing a short skirt meant in that society, for postmodernism it means only that she is constructing an identity for herself and has done so by choosing not to wear a long skirt, or jeans, or culottes. That identity could be 'liberated', or 'young', or 'modern', or 'independent', for example, according to the code that was used to construct it. What has changed, the crisis, is that the meaning of the skirt is understood in postmodernism to be the product of coded differences, not the product of a relation to a morality that exists outside of the play of codes and differences that is representation. Old identities and concepts (such as gender identities and concepts such as beauty or morality) are perceived as have lost their founding values, from which standards could be set and judgements made.

Where an 'external' and authoritative morality used to guarantee the meaning of the skirt, the relation between signifier and signified, there is now only the reference to more signs and more codes. To take a less inflammatory example: for a modernist Bauhaus typographer, Fraktur was a politically unacceptable, exclusive and nationalistic font, but for a postmodern typographer it is just another font. It is different from all the other fonts and its meaning is a product of those coded differences, not the result of a relation to something understood to be beyond those differences. Postmodern designers might use it to signify or connote 'antique shop' or 'old marmalade recipe' or a German language website about printing (http://www.bfds.de/, March 2004). The crisis of representation here is that for the modernist there was something (a politics) outside of the play of differences that generated or guaranteed the meaning of the type: for the postmodernist, there is nothing outside of the play of coded contextual differences to fix the meaning of the font. Post-structuralist philosophers who developed these ideas identified a number of values that had been held to be outside the play of differences; God, morality, style and taste, for example. Derrida's name for all of them is 'transcendental signified' (Derrida 1976: 49; 1981: 20, 29), by which he denotes a value whose meaning is held not to be produced by its differential relation to all other meanings (signifieds).

Fredric Jameson describes the situation using the example of the video artist Nam June Paik. In some of his works, many television screens are stacked and scattered around the room, among foliage or on the ceiling. Video loops replay sequences of images over and over again on these screens, returning at unsynchronised points on the various screens. Jameson (1991: 31) describes the modernist viewer, accustomed to an 'older aesthetic', who stares bewildered at the screens before trying to concentrate on a single screen 'as though the relatively worthless image sequence to be followed there had some organic value in its own right'. He then describes the postmodern viewer, who (like David Bowie's character in *The Man Who Fell to Earth*) is 'called upon' to see all the screens at once 'in their radical and random difference' and to understand that it is precisely that interplay of radical difference that generates the meaning of the work (Jameson 1991: 31). None of the screens makes any sense on its own or in 'its own right' and there is no 'organic' meaning to any of the screens on their own. Only the relation to other, different screens produces 'meaning'. Other illustrations of the crisis include Derrida's (1986) use of two columns of type, in different styles, on the same page in his book *Glas*. In one column Derrida discusses the idealist philosophy of Hegel. In the other he discusses the life of the thief and homosexual prostitute Jean Genet. Quotations from Hegel or Genet often form a third column of text. Derrida's point is that it is impossible to read and understand the meaning of any column on its own; the other columns constantly intrude to colour one's reading. There is nothing outside of this interaction of different texts (Hegel's 'philosophy' or Genet's 'life') to determine the meaning of either text; one constantly wonders what Genet's gay prison experiences have to do with Hegel's dialectic, for example, and the meaning of one is both produced and undermined by its relation to the other.

For Jameson and Derrida, then, the crisis in representation that characterises postmodernity concerns the relations between signifiers and signifieds. In modernist thinking, there is something that authorises or guarantees relations between signifiers and signifieds and so fixes meaning. 'Politics' in the Bauhaus example, the natural or 'organic' in Jameson's account of Nam June Paik's videos, 'the life of Genet' and 'Hegel's philosophy' in Derrida's *Glas*; all attempt to play this role. In postmodernist thinking, however, there is nothing beyond the relations between signifiers and signifieds that can play this role: Genet's life constantly intrudes upon Hegel's dialectic and Nam June Paik's multiple screens constantly distract from the one the modernist viewer tries to concentrate on. What postmodernism argues is that there there is nothing outside of representation which could generate and fix the meaning of representation 'once and for all'. There is nothing that is not another signifier, with its signified, that could guarantee the meaning of a sign.

The crisis has various consequences. The most significant is that the sign is now what Derrida (1979: 99, 103–5) calls 'undecidable'. What this means is that a sign's meaning is understood as being both produced and destroyed by its relations to all other signs in the various discourses in which it appears (Derrida 1978b: 271). The same culturally coded syntagmatic and para-digmatic relations which produce the meaning of a sign are the same relations that meaning leaks away into as soon as one tries to fix that meaning. For example, Mills (1994) enumerates some of the different meanings of Helvetica: for a postmodern typographer the letterforms are understood as 'functional' when 'used in the context of Hoffman's studies in Basel in the 1950s', they are 'classy' when Vignelli uses them in the 1970s Knoll logo and they are 'trendy' when Neville Brody uses them in the 1980s (Mills 1994: 129). The font means nothing in itself but it means something different in each of these contexts (or 'discourses'). The contexts are the culturally specific codings of syntagmatic and paradigmatic relations that were shown in Chapter 2 to organise differences and so generate meaning. In each of these contexts, Helvetica is one font that is chosen from a paradigmatic group of all existing fonts and used in syntagms (layouts, for example). The meaning changes because the cultures it is found in change. In the culture of 1950s Basel, it is coded as 'functional', because that is what that culture thinks important and what the font connotes to that culture. In the 'designer culture' of 1980s Britain, the font is said to be 'trendy', because being 'trendy' was a central value of that culture. In these ways, the meaning of Helvetica is produced by its culturally coded relations to other different fonts. However, meaning is also destroyed by, or dissipated in, those differential relations in the sense that there is nothing outside of those relations to stop that endless referral to other fonts and other connotations. The meaning 'in itself' of the font is nowhere to be found, as it exists only as the product of a series of references to other different fonts.

POSTMODERNISM AND GRAPHIC DESIGN

For the post-structuralist philosophers, such as Derrida, who investigated what Boyne and Rattansi (1990) call the crisis of representation, the 'undecidability of the sign' was merely a description of how meaning and communication work. Undecidability was a way of taking seriously Saussure's argument concerning the arbitrary nature of the sign and of describing some of the implications of that idea. The undecidability of the sign follows from the arbitrary nature of the sign and it was used to describe how communication and meaning operated, how they had 'in fact' always operated. Fully aware of the (post)modernist implications of the tale, it is tempting to say that, like the blind men confronted by the elephant in Saxe's poem, graphic designers and theorists have responded in a number of ways to the representational crisis of postmodernism and the undecid-ability of the sign. It is also tempting to speculate that these ideas about meaning had an impact in graphic design that was similar in its nature and effects to the impact that some suggest Einstein's ideas about space had in the fine arts. Where Einstein was suggesting that space and time had in fact always been relative, the post-structuralists were saying that meaning had always 'in fact' been undecidable. As modernist artists reacted in different ways to a new conception of space, so postmodern graphic designers reacted in different ways to a new conception of meaning. Also in this connection, it is worth noting that, just as there are marked differences between the European and American versions of modernity, so Poynor (2003: 31ff.) suggests that there is a difference between the American and the British responses to postmodernism. This section will codify those responses and explain them in terms of the definition above.

Analytically, the responses of graphic designers (and graphic design historians) to the undecidability of the sign can be divided into three categories. These responses may be understood as selecting certain values and ideas from postmodernist theory and reproducing them visually. Each position or response selects and communicates different values and ideas and so constructs itself as a position. First, there are those who emphasise what they see as the destruction or dissipation of meaning. These people may take either a positive or a negative view of that destruction. Second, there are those who emphasise what they see as the production or proliferation of meaning. These people may also take a positive or negative view of that productivity. Third, there are those who understand undecidability as a description of the production and destruction of meaning and explore it as such. It is important to note that, as analytical distinctions, these positions will often be found mixed together in actual examples of graphic design; very few people manage to occupy a single position and some work may exemplify more than one response.

The first position is hinted at in the titles of two of Rick Poynor's book titles: *No More Rules* and *Design without Boundaries*. Although it is perfectly clear in the text that the titles are ironic, they nevertheless suggest a response to postmodernism. This response understands postmodernism to be about the breakdown or impossibility of both meaning and the codes that had hitherto generated meaning and sets about producing graphic design that is somehow in tune with that breakdown or impossibility. When Byrne and Witte (1994: 119), for example, say of the work of Joel Katz, Michael Mabry, David Carson and Joe Miller that it 'continues to collapse traditional typographic harmony' and that in their work 'visual coding . . . has begun to disintegrate', they are emphasising this breakdown of conventional meaning and structures. There is no mention in the paragraph describing these designer's work of the other side of undecidability, of the idea that meaning is also produced by difference; the emphasis is on the ideas of collapse and disintegration. Although quotes from David Carson can be found denying it (Poynor 1994: 88), he is sometimes proposed as a designer who abandons the traditional codes of graphic design in order to play anarchically and sometimes nihilistically with type and image. Poynor (2003: 13), suggests that, for some people, it was Carson's self-confessed ignorance of any rules for producing graphic design that enabled him to produce original and striking designs. This represents a slightly different version of this first position in that, although Carson may say he does not use a grid, or a format, and that he never learned the rules of classic modernist typography, he and his supporters are agreed that his design 'works', that it 'ends up in a more interesting place' (Carson, quoted in Poynor 2003: 13).

Kinross summarises some of the main features of postmodernism in the following propositions:

> Meaning is unstable and has to be made by the reader. Each reader will read differently . . . Designers should make texts visually ambiguous and difficult to fathom, as a way to respect the rights of the readers.
>
> (Kinross 1997: 19)

This is his way of berating designers and theorists who take this first position on postmodernism in graphic design. While Kinross names no names, grunge design seems to fit his bill. Elliott Earls' family of typefaces, Dysphasia, Dysplasia and Dyslexia, for example, appear to be calculatedly difficult to read. Dysphasia is a form of brain damage, in which words are difficult to recognise and understand, dysplasia describes the abnormal growth of tissue and dyslexia is a reading disorder: from the perspective of modernist design and design theory, each of them is a dysgraphia and a disgrace. In the example chosen here (Figure 7.1), the layout of Earls' advertisement for the family of faces combines with the typeface to resist interpretation. Even when the text runs almost horizontally, it is not easy to read; when it runs vertically up the page, overlapping and changing background as it goes, it is even more difficult to decipher. The thoughts that the typestyle in general and the advertisement in particular are clever and witty visual constructions of the experience of dysphasia or dyslexia and that, if Dysphasia is a family, then it is a 'dysfunctional' family, are hard to escape. The fonts can be understood as a response to the perceived postmodern destruction of meaning and value. As such, the old values of beauty and function, which used to govern the production of letterforms and typestyles, have been rejected in favour of shapes and styles that are perceived, according to those old values, as ugly and illegible. As a way of constructing and communicating with a community of people who share an alternative set of values, however, the fonts are probably much more successful.

The second response to undecidability emphasises the production of meaning. It reduces the notion of the undecidability of the sign in such a

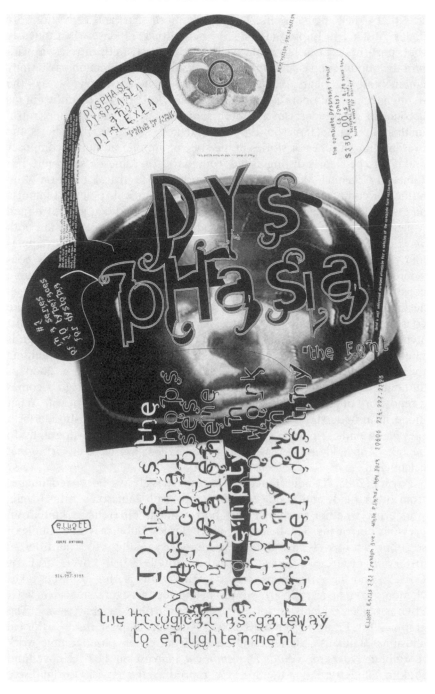

Figure 7.1 Typeface, Elliott Earls, 'Dysphasia' (1995). Courtesy of Elliot Earls

way that it becomes a license to produce more signs and generate more codes. Miller and Lupton (1994: 25) refer to this response when they say that 'post-modernism has replaced [the modernist] faith in renewal with parody, quotation, pastiche and an uneasy alliance with technology'. Many commentators are agreed on this point. Parody and pastiche are two of the defining rhetorical operations that Jameson (1991: 16–19) identifies in his account of postmodernism and both Jameson and Poynor include 'retro' in their accounts (Jameson 1984: 66; Poynor 2003: 79). Pastiche is the presentation of tunes or stories in the style of another author or composer and it is to be clearly distinguished from parody in Jameson's account. For Jameson (1984: 64–5), parody is the humorous or satirical imitation of an author or composer's style: pastiche lacks that satirical (political) impulse and is for him more characteristic of postmodernism. Poynor's 'retro' and Miller and Lupton's 'quotation' fit into this scheme because they are both ways of appropriating material from one context (the past, for example) and using it in another (the present). Where modernism carefully considered the homology, or fit, between aesthetics, style and function, constructing typestyles and layouts that performed their function in an aesthetically satisfactory way, this version of postmodernism abandons the consideration of homology. As Jameson (1984: 65) describes it, 'modernist styles . . . become postmodernist codes'. The undecidability of the sign is interpreted as the absence of any authentic value guaranteeing or guiding the production of text and image and any value is seen as being as 'good' or authentic as any other. Consequently, the history of art and design becomes a repository of styles and imagery to be plundered and used at will. What modernism understood as a series of characteristic styles, postmodernism sees as an endless parade of different styles, imagery and typography to be taken up and used in what Jameson (1984: 64) calls an 'irrational eclecticism'.

Poynor (2003: 72) notes that graphic design has always 'borrowed' images from other fields and is not entirely happy with Jameson's critical tone, wondering whether postmodernist borrowing is different in kind from previous borrowing. The British designer Barney Bubbles is an example of someone who revels in the joyful postmodern raiding of art and design history in order to construct his work. Bubbles' 1979 cover for Elvis Costello and the Attractions' record 'Armed Forces', for example, takes elements from op art, pop art, Mondrian and abstract expressionism in what Poynor (2003: 73) calls a 'riotous *mélange* of art historical allusions'. The graphics for Franz Ferdinand's 2004 CD make at least three historical allusions. Bauhaus-style lettering on the front cover, photographic work resembling Duchamp's *Nude Descending a Staircase* on the back cover and Fraktur-like lettering on the 'live' CD reproduce the gay-ish, Berlin disco/cabaret values of the music. Malcolm Garrett's cover for Simple Minds' 1982 'New Gold Dream' also borrows from the history of design by placing a Christian cross, sacred heart and a book motif, with medieval-looking calligraphic typestyle over a marbled, handmade paper background. Poynor also notes Jon Savage's and Tibor Kalman's criticisms of this aspect of postmodernism, which both align it with a political conservatism and considers the latter's discussion of some of Paula Scher's work. Scher's 1986 poster takes the imagery and layout of one of Herbert Matter's 1934 travel posters and uses them to construct an advertisement for Swatch watches. Her poster is problematic for Poynor because, having no satirical intent, it is not parody and, not being a 'wholly new image in the general style of Matter', it is not pastiche (Poynor 2003: 80). However, as Poynor says, Scher's treatment of the poster is 'literal and descriptive'; there is no implied analysis, explanation or criticism of Matter's original and to that extent her work is politically dormant and hence conservative, as Savage and Kalman argue. To this extent, it is hard not to agree with Poynor's conclusion (if not the exact course of his argument) when he says that Scher's poster embodies Malcolm Garrett's assumption that the past is a 'bottomless pit' to be 'ransacked' at graphic design's convenience. Poynor's chapter is entitled 'Appropriations' and deals with this aspect of graphic design's response to undecidability with intelligence and in great detail.

Moving away from typography and layout, it is possible to see examples of this second position in the postmodern representation of cultural identities and values. The Benetton advertisements that were discussed in Chapter 5 may be revisited in this regard. These ads are postmodern in that they challenge previous founding values of aesthetics and beauty, for example. In western fashion magazines up until the 1980s, the standard or ideal of female beauty was 'white' would have included the values 'white skinned', 'tall', 'straight haired', 'blonde' and so on. This is what female beauty meant to a particular culture, at a particular time and place (and still does mean to certain editors of *Vogue*). These values formed a standard against which all models would be judged and measured and which was not seen as being something that was itself to be judged in terms of anything else. When Toscani started presenting women with black, brown and yellow skin, and with dark or curly hair, however, the ads presented a variety of alternative aesthetic values, showing that beauty exists in many different shapes, forms and colours. The ads are taking advantage of the fact that postmodernism shows the hitherto governing value ('white') to be just another value, deriving its meaning from its relation to all the other values, not a 'transcendental' value existing outside of the play of differences.

The third position is the most sophisticated of graphic design's responses to undecidability. This position attempts to account for both the production and the destruction of meaning that is described by the idea of undecidability and is present in some versions of what is called 'deconstruction'. Katherine McCoy distinguishes her version of deconstruction from other postmodernist work produced by 'people who haven't read about it very deeply [who] conclude that it is just about form and, more than that, that it is about the disassembling of visual language' (McCoy, interviewed in Poynor 1998: 50). She is referring to the first position (above), which sees the undecidability of the sign as the simple evaporation of meaning and in which designers emphasise and reproduce what they see as the difficulties or impossibilities of meaning by using type and layout. But deconstruction, as McCoy says, is not a single, simple, operation in which the terms are merely changed or reversed (Derrida 1979: 81, 95). And McCoy's version of deconstruction does not say 'where there was meaning and communication, let us now stress the absence or difficulty of meaning and communication' as the first response does (cf. Derrida 1981: 41–2). Nor does it unproblematically celebrate and promote the proliferation of text and imagery in pastiche or appropriation as the second position does. Instead, what it tries to do is to graphically enact Derrida's doubled strategy in which meaning is both constructed and deconstructed at the same time.

Some of these deconstructive ideas may be seen in the hard-bound book accompanying a 1990 exhibition at the Cranbrook Academy of Art Museum, designed by Katherine McCoy, P. Scott Makela and Mary Lou Kroh (Figure 7.2). To the casual glance, the catalogue appears to be composed of two columns of text, each with its own set of subheadings and with a narrow margin between them: one might expect a conventional printed layout, albeit one that uses right-hand justification for the subheadings in one of the columns of text. If the casual reader has seen Derrida's *Glas*, they might be expecting a demonstration of how the meaning of one column is produced and destroyed by its relation to the other. On closer inspection, however, each line is seen to run across both columns and the right-hand column of text is set slightly lower than the left-hand column. What appear to be subheadings turn out to be dichotmous pairs of concepts, one of which is set higher than the other. At least two things are happening here. The first is that taken-for-granted assumptions about the presentation of textual material are being subverted in a way that prevents those assumptions from being easily restored (Derrida 1979: 59). What appear to be two columns of text are actually one text. Even when one knows this, the page still looks like a conventional layout, like two columns of text. Visually, one's expectations are constructed and confounded at the same time. The meaning one is expecting is produced and destroyed in and by the same visual material. The second is that the pairs of concepts (including 'art/science', 'mythology/technology' and 'desire/necessity') interrupt, rather than guide, one's reading of the text. They do not operate as subheadings, as either relay or anchorage, but interfere with the passage of the text. They also generate new meanings, as one ponders the appearance of culturally loaded dichotomies within another piece of text.

As Derrida (1977: 236) says in 'Limited Inc', however, the opposing concepts appearing in these dichotomies are not accorded equal value.

Figure 7.2 Front cover, book, Cranbrook Academy (1990).
Courtesy of Katherine McCoy

They are culturally loaded because one of them is always privileged above the other and Derrida's deconstructive strategy is to disrupt the dichotomy in such a way that it cannot recuperate. In certain western cultural discourses, science is valued above art, technology above mythology, and reason above emotion, for example. The Cranbrook catalogue refers to these inequalities by placing one of the terms above the other on the page. However, the placing of the terms or concepts on the page does not always reproduce the cultural valuations of those terms. While 'mathematic' is placed above 'poetic' (thus reproducing the idea that mathematics is valued more highly than poetry in many western cultural discourses), 'art' is placed above 'science' (thus reversing the conventional cultural evaluation). In such deconstructive fashion, the founding conceptual oppositions of western culture, and western education, are confused, generating meanings, but not always the meanings that are expected.

Derrida's own use of graphic devices to indicate the production and destruction of meaning in *Glas* has already been explained; the two or three columns of that work indicating how meaning of a text is both generated by and disappears into the relation to other texts. He also replaces the second *e* in 'difference' with an *a* which, by virtue of being unheard, visual and printed, at once indicates, undermines and permanently disrupts the western privilege accorded in western philosophy and culture to the voice, or spoken language. The practice of writing *sous rature*, or 'under erasure' is another graphic device used to demonstrate the production and destruction of meaning (Derrida 1976: 60). For example, in his *Of Grammatology*, because every sign refers to other signs, because a sign only means anything as a result of its relations to other signs, from which it is both different and absent, Derrida crosses out the words 'is' and 'thing' in the sentence 'the sign is that ill-named thing' (1976: 19). He is making the point that the words 'is' and 'thing' inevitably bring to mind a set of ideas (about what existence is and what things are) which he believes to be inadequate. As there is no meaningful outside to representation, Derrida is obliged to use the words 'is' and 'thing', but he also uses a graphic device to indicate the nature of the problem he has with them. Later (Derrida 1976: 44), 'is' is again crossed out, but remains legible beneath the crossing out, for the same reason. Derrida's deconstructive tactic here follows Heidegger (1958: 83) in which some uses of Being (Sein) appear crossed out but are still legible as an indication that a conception of Being has been forgotten, but still has an effect in human thinking. The meaning is produced and destroyed at the same time: meaning is produced and the word can be read, but the crossing out destroys that original and problematic meaning as soon as it is read. And in *Spurs/Eperons*, the reader is gently chided for having 'skipped over' the drawn images at the beginning of the book, as though illustration had no place in a 'serious volume' (Derrida 1979: 85). He is not reversing the privilege accorded the literal in philosophical texts in favour of the figurative image (or of metaphor), but he is showing how the one is central to the conception of the other in much the same way as he shows how a supposedly literal conception of communication depends for its force on a founding metaphor.

WHAT IS GLOBALISATION?

It was proposed in the introduction to this chapter that globalisation is nothing new. In *The Communist Manifesto*, first published in 1848, Marx and Engels (1985: 83–4) write of modern capitalists chasing 'over the whole surface of the globe' in search of new markets, and seeking new consumers for their products 'in every quarter of the globe'. Where there were 'old wants' that could be satisfied by local production, there are now 'new wants' which can only be satisfied by products from 'distant lands'. Marx and Engels even go so far as to suggest that a 'world literature', part of a global culture, is beginning to emerge. Their analysis is interesting, not just because it suggests that globalisation is as old as capitalism, but also because it prefigures some of the main features of globalisation as they have been identified by more contemporary theorists. Marx and Engels' account refers to what would now be called globalisation as being driven by capitalism. As such, it entails the production of goods and services. It involves consumers, the creation of new wants and desires in those consumers and (in the reference to products from distant lands) it involves the move from local to global consumption. Although Giddens (1990) agrees with Marx and Engels when he says that globalisation is as old as modernity, Tim O'Sullivan et al. (1994: 130) suggest that some recent writers have seen it as a 'telling aspect of the postmodern condition'. It was only in 1968, after all, that Marshal McLuhan coined the phrase 'the global village' to describe the effects of electronic media on the world of communications (McLuhan and Fiore 2001). This section will explain globalisation in order that the postmodern role of graphic design may be explained in the following section.

O'Sullivan et al. (1994: 130) define globalisation as 'the growth and acceleration of economic and cultural networks which operate on a worldwide scale and basis'. By economic networks they mean financial systems made up of banks, stock exchanges, international and multinational corporations and the markets in which they operate. All of these institutions are now held to function on a worldwide scale and to be organised with that worldwide scale in mind. By cultural networks they mean communication technologies such as transport, which enable people and goods to circulate but also the electronic and digital means of communication which enable the distribution of goods and money. Developments in media technologies, such as film, television and the internet, which enable people on different sides of the world to communicate, are also included here. These media are also held to function on a worldwide scale and to be organised accordingly. This definition may be conceived as a series of cultural 'flows'; flows of money, technology, people, images, texts, goods and ideas. Appadurai (1990) identifies five such flows. The first is the flow

151

of people and groups of people in what he calls 'ethnoscapes'. He has in mind 'tourists, immigrants, refugees, exiles, guestworkers and other moving groups and persons' (1990: 297). The flow of mechanical and information technology in 'technoscapes' describes the movement of machinery, technology and plant between different countries and multinational corporations. 'Finanscapes' describes the flow of money through international currency markets, stock exchanges and multinational corporations and banks (1990: 298). The distribution and dissemination of private and state-owned newspapers, magazines, television and film companies, as well as the text, imagery and information which they communicate, is described as constituting 'mediascapes'. Texts and images are also produced and consumed in what Appadurai (1990: 299) calls 'ideoscapes'; these texts and images are 'directly political' and have to do with the dominant groups' representation of such ideas as freedom, and democracy, for example, along with the challenges to those representations. These last two 'scapes' are the most obviously or immediately relevant to graphic design.

The suggestion was made in the second section of this chapter that globalisation was the sense that, no matter where you go in the world, you are still in the same place. This thumbnail sketch is pithily echoed by Roland Robertson (1990) when he says that globalisation is 'the crystallisation of the entire world as a single place' (quoted in Arnason 1990: 220). Given the account of postmodernism so far, it might seem odd for a process that some see as particularly postmodern to result in making places the same. The account so far has laid great emphasis on the role of difference in postmodernity, yet most theorists present globalisation in terms of identity, as the way in which the world becomes a 'single place' or the 'same place'. An alternative, or a necessary supplement, to this 'monolithic' conception of globalisation is provided by Les Back (1998) whose account of globalisation provides a role for difference to play; it locates a space within which difference can operate. Back (1998: 64) says that globalism is not inevitably about making places the same because 'global interconnection cannot completely integrate human societies that remain spatially dispersed'. Even within the 'global circuits of capital and culture' noted earlier, Back (1998: 64) suggests that 'something distinctly local remains . . . or may even be being fostered'. The local, then, may be seen as a source of difference (of different cultural identities), which examples of globalisation cannot entirely eradicate. Global corporations are forced, on this account, to take local and regional cultures into consideration and to give some thought to how to communicate with them. The local and the regional may, therefore, be understood as potential sources of resistance to the homogenising effects of globalisation. Regional identities and local cultures are not guaranteed to be immune from those effects, but they provide some forms of difference which which to counter them.

GLOBALISATION AND GRAPHIC DESIGN

Globalisation raises various problems for graphic design as a form of communication. In this book, graphic communication has been explained in cultural terms, as the visual construction and reproduction of beliefs, values and ideas. It is the construction and reproduction of those beliefs and so on in communication that produces and reproduces cultural identities. The first problem is whether there are 'global' values, beliefs and ideas or whether the values that are presented as such are merely those held by dominant cultural groups. The second problem concerns the possibility of 'global' values; can there be global values or are any putatively global values always going to be those of the dominant cultural groups? The third problem concerns the role of graphic designers in global communication; this is the question whether graphic designers are reproducing or challenging the positions of certain dominant cultural groups. Lupton and Miller (1997: 207) describe the problems of 'international communication' in slightly different terms. They write about the 'promise of an integrated global village' existing alongside the 'dangers of homogeneity and hegemony'. And they say that graphic designers are faced by 'conflicting imperatives' to contribute towards the establishment of the global village but not to contribute to the process in which cultural groups dominate or assimilate other cultural groups (Lupton and Miller 1997: 207).

Of Appadurai's (1990) five ungainly neologisms, 'mediascapes' and 'ideoscapes' are the most obviously or immediately relevant to graphic design. Graphic design is the production of the texts, imagery and information that are communicated by the media and those texts, images and information graphics are undoubtedly both ideological and political. Graphic designers also play a role in producing the advertising that encourages consumption and Appadurai (1990: 307) suggests that the postmodern consumer has been 'transformed' by global advertising. The multinational corporations that produce the goods and services that are advertised all over the world rely on graphic designers for their corporate identities, as well as for their advertising. The highly politicised ideas concerning the nature of both consumption and the consumer are, as Appadurai suggests, produced and reproduced through graphic advertising media. However, before concluding that graphic design as an industry exists only to support and reproduce this monolithic conception of globalism, the role of difference, in the form of multiple regional and local resistances to globalisation should be recalled. The following paragraphs will examine a number of examples in which the issues noted above are raised.

The first example is also one of the most familiar. Indeed, the case against McDonald's is so familiar that the contraction, 'Mc' or 'Mac', has become the prefix used to denote the worst effects of postmodernisation in many

153

areas of human experience: the word 'Mac-job' now refers to any unsatisfying and short-term form of employment in postmodern economies, for example. The argument is that, no matter where you go in the world, there will always be a McDonald's franchise. It will serve the same product and it will look identical to every other franchise. The 'golden arches', the red-haired clown with the yellow knickerbockers, stripy underwear and red boots, the packaging of the food and the decor will all be there, no matter where 'there' is. As Edward Rensi, president of McDonald's USA said, 'people have a vision of McDonald's being identical in 12,000 restaurants' (quoted in Pavitt 2000b: 47). However, Jane Pavitt (2000b: 47) points out that brands such as McDonald's 'nurture their relationship with a locality . . . in order to become "naturalised"', and Russell Belk (2000: 69) describes some of the ways in which McDonald's 'insinuates' itself into local cultural festivals. Both authors note the local variations in menu, mutton featuring in Indian Macs and teryaki appearing in Japanese Macs, for example. Belk also describes how in 1992, the Year of the Monkey, the Singapore McDonald's advertising featured four monkeys, symbolising luck, fortune, longevity and happiness. This adaptation to local cultures, whether it is called 'nurturing' or exploiting, occurs even within the same country: company president Rensi says that McDonald's franchises in Texas offer something different from Boston franchises (quoted in Pavitt 2000b: 47).

It is not the case, then, that McDonald's franchises are unproblematically communicating global values, beliefs and ideas by means of graphic design. While the graphic design (the colours and forms of the arches, or in the packaging, for example) might contain the same formal elements, the argument here is that they are interpreted slightly differently in different cultures. The red that is used by McDonald's in its storefronts and packaging, for example, will not connote good luck in the United States or Europe as it does in China and Singapore. The corporate symbol of the golden arches will not therefore mean exactly the same thing in western cultures as it does in eastern cultures. It functions, as Lupton and Miller (1997: 207) say, as a conventionalised mark, signifying a company, but in which the connotational meaning and identity of that company changes subtly from place to place as it is interpreted by different cultural groups. If the role of culture in communication is taken seriously, then the values of a local culture, in terms of which that culture constructs connotational meanings, have to be present in advertising or packaging. If they are not, then that advertising and packaging will not be interpreted or understood. This is not to say that non-western cultures are not being encouraged to understand western cultures through graphic design, but that this is just what happens in communication. It is little different in this respect from constructing a magazine's front page that will communicate with 'the elderly' or 'teenaged male metal fans' discussed in previous chapters.

The question of the graphic designer's role in global communication is also raised by this example. It does not appear to be the case that McDonald's is straightforwardly imposing a set of global values onto local cultures. In communicating with people from other cultures, the company is taking the cultural beliefs of those other cultures into consideration by referring to some of them in their advertising. McDonald's advertising communicates with members of non-western cultures by including some of the values of that culture in the imagery and colours used in that advertising. The graphic designers have learned that red, for example, signifies a certain signified ('good luck'), and used it to communicate with a different culture. They have discovered that in the Year of the Monkey, monkeys are important to a culture and used them to advertise a product. This is not simply imposing a belief, or a meaning, onto another culture: it is paying attention to how communication works. Consequently, although graphic designers are reproducing the position of dominant western cultures and multinational corporations through advertising, the specificity and difference of the local culture has to be understood in order for the advertising to communicate with that culture at all. Although positions of relative power are being reproduced through communication, they always were: Chapters 4 and 5 showed how communication involves political relations and therefore inequality between those communicating.

In the definition of globalisation earlier, it was suggested that cultural difference was represented in the ideas of the 'local' and the 'regional'. It was also suggested that such local differences could form the basis for challenging and resisting the homogenising and assimilating spread of global values. However, it is clear that the regional and the local are not always guaranteed to be successful in challenging the attempt to communicate 'global' values. In many cases, it may be argued that what difference they do represent is appropriated by global corporations in the interests of greater profits. For example, Belk (2000: 68) argues that, so successfully has McDonald's 'insinuated' itself into the local culture that Japanese boy scouts visiting North America have been surprised at finding what they believed to be a Japanese product so readily available. He explains this as the product of the boy scouts' 'unawareness' of McDonald's' American 'origins'. This is not so much an argument about the failure of local culture to resist the imposition of foreign values as a story about one group of people being unaware or ignorant of their own cultural background. The values and beliefs of local and regional cultures are hardly going to form the basis of any resistance to globalising corporations if the local people do not know what those values are. However, this is just one anecdotal example and because they are not always successful does not mean that they are not the source of difference. Indeed, were the local and the regional not sources of different values, the multinational globalising corporations would not find it necessary to adapt their advertising, packaging and image to local conditions.

The next example of graphic design's relation to globalisation concerns the world wide web. As much of the world's population remains illiterate and without access to print media (Williams 1961: 11), so it seems likely that much of the world's population will remain offline and without access to electronic and digital media. However, the internet is often presented as the best example of global communication in that it enables almost instantaneous contact between (certain classes of) people anywhere in the world. Texts and images speed across the web twenty-four hours a day, every day. In a 2002 seminar at London's South Bank University, Aaron Marcus, of Aaron Marcus and Associates Inc., suggested that the web makes possible the 'global distribution of goods and services'. He was interested in what he called 'cross-cultural user-interface design', which he implied had been profoundly affected by globalisation (see http://cise.sbu.ac.uk/hci2002/cross.html, April 2004). Basically, Marcus's position is that websites and browsers are looked at and used by people from many different cultures and these cultures have different 'needs, wants, preferences and expectations'. These different values, he says, have an 'impact' on the understanding of 'web-based communications' and his question, which he addressed in the seminar, concerns how the designers of websites, browsers and information graphics are to take account of those different values. In order to illustrate some of these problems, Marcus discusses the different ways in which the sacred is signified in different cultures. In Judaeo-Christian traditions, he says, the sacred is signified by the colours red, white, blue and gold: in Buddhism, saffron yellow is used and Islamic cultures use green. The implication is that a secular website that uses green to sell products in an Islamic culture is going to be in trouble. Marcus's solution to these problems is to 'pay attention' to the differences between cultures, to learn a culture's values, preferences and expectations. He also suggests examining one's own 'cultural orientation', presumably in order to highlight any cultural predispositions towards the choice of shapes and colours. Both of these things will enable designers to 'achieve . . . global solutions' to the problems of communicating with members of other cultures.

Now, these 'global' problems and their solutions do not sound so different from the problems and solutions discussed in previous chapters. The 'elderly' market for *The People's Friend* and the 'teenaged male metal fan' who read *Metal Maniacs* were discussed above in precisely these terms. In order to communicate with the 'elderly' readers of *The People's Friend*, certain typestyles and layouts, for example, were chosen; *Metal Maniacs* used metallic gold letterforms and lurid colours in order to communicate with teenaged males. The graphic designers and art directors responsible for each magazine had to understand the values of the cultural and subcultural groups forming the audience, in order to construct a visual style for the magazine that would communicate with them. That this situation is no different in kind, or quality, from what Marcus is describing as a problem that is specific to globalisation may be illustrated by looking at two websites, http://www.hsbc.com and http://www.nike.com.

The former is the website of HSBC, a London-based bank which has 9,500 offices in 79 countries and territories in Europe, the Asia-Pacific region, the Americas, the Middle East and Africa; it boasts an international network linked by advanced technology, including a rapidly growing e-commerce capability and surely represents the globalising, multinational capitalist corporation, par excellence. HSBC's home page makes few concessions to its global status. All text is in English, for example, and where there are icons and pictorial symbols, the text that appears when the mouse is run over them is also in English. The colours used are predominantly white and red. The red may reflect HSBC's nineteenth-century origins as the Hong Kong and Shanghai Banking Corporation, as this colour signifies good luck in Chinese culture. HSBC is keen to stress its social responsibility and boasts about the fact that it spent US$ 3.45 million on the environmental, educational and community projects that it sponsors; see www.hsbc.com/hsbc/society/living-our-values. This compares to pre-tax operating profits for 2003 of US$ 12.8 billion (source http://a248.e.akamai. net/7/248/3622/b384ee4ed985d3/www.img.ghq.hsbc.com/public/groupsite/ assets/investor/hsbc2003ara4.pdf, April 2004). These projects are illustrated with photographs and described in English. The photographs feature local people benefiting from HSBC's largesse. So, while there are attempts to present the bank as community-minded, locally responsible and environmentally sound, the site remains unconvincing and any claims to global communication must be questioned. This is because local values and beliefs are not represented at all strongly in the site: there is little attempt explicitly to include local customs and practices, or local cultures, in HSBC's activities. As it says, the people they are ostensibly helping are 'living our [HSBC's] values'.

Nike's website, in contrast, is largely pictorial and Flash animated. While it ignores the Middle East entirely, there are links to Pacific Asia and Latin America, as well as to Europe and North America. The Asian and Latin American sites employ images of western sports stars (such as the soccer player Thierry Henry and the tennis player Venus Williams) but are partly written in local languages. The sites to which one is directed when one clicks on Japan, or Latin America – Portuguese, for example, are basic sites with local variations. Although the Japanese football (soccer) site opens with a photograph of Thierry Henry in his Arsenal shirt, it does feature Daisuke Nasu, the Japanese Under-23 defender, along with other European stars. Similarly, while the Portuguese language site includes downloads involving European players, Figo and Ronaldo feature heavily and a Nike ad in which the Portugal and Brazil sides play like gods in the tunnel may be downloaded. Although it is hardly a textbook example of how to communicate globally, Nike's website makes much more of an effort to include references to the local cultures than HSBC's does.

This is not to say that there are not serious problems involved in the design of websites, internet browsers and information graphics. Because the users of these products are members of many different cultures, one might reasonably expect the graphic design of the 'interfaces' to be different. If the icons on a web browser are too culturally specific, that is, too iconic or too motivated, then they will not be recognised or understood by people who are not members of that culture. If the icons are too unspecific, too abstract, symbolic or unmotivated, then they will need to be learned by most people. For example, in one of the antique internet browsers that I use, 'home' is signified by a square building, with a tiled roof and a chimney; in another, 'home' is signified by a circular building with a conical roof. Members of cultures in which square buildings with chimneys are unknown will have to learn what this icon means in order for it to communicate meaningfully with them. Most westerners do not live in homes that are circular buildings with cone-shaped roofs; they have to learn that this means 'home'. In Explorer, 'source' is signified by a pictogram of a sun, with 'rays' emanating from a central circle: the connection between an html address and the sun is far from natural and must be learned. The 'search' function is signified in different browsers by a variety of icons; a little man running, a hieroglyphic eye and a magnifying glass, for example, may all be found. The arbitrary nature of the sign is well illustrated by these different images and the point that the signifiers will have different meanings in different cultures is made quite clearly. Again, however, these problems are encountered with all signs and communication; they are not specifically postmodern or global problems.

The final example in this section concerns Naomi Klein's (2000) argument with corporate globalisation, and by implication with graphic designers, in her *No Logo*. She begins her argument with the observation that the 'astronomical growth in the wealth and cultural significance of multinational corporations' can be linked to a single idea, that corporations produce and sell 'brands' rather than products or things (Klein 2000: 3). Branding is different from advertising because branding is the 'image' or 'core meaning' of the corporation and advertising is the 'vehicle used to convey that meaning to the world'. The role of advertising, and thus graphic design, here is to 'build' those images and meanings (Klein 2000: 5, 6) and 'convey' them to the world. Global corporations, such as Nike, Gap, Starbucks, McDonald's and Coca-Cola, for example, see themselves as 'meaning brokers', rather than producers of products and those people who construct brands are described as 'meaning seeking' (Klein 2000: 21, 36). Meaning, as the product of the interaction between the values of a cultural group and the brand, is a cultural phenomenon here and Klein says that branding becomes 'troubling' when a brand 'strips' a culture of its 'inherent value' and treats it as a 'promotional tool' (Klein 2000: 39). Her case here is essentially the same as that explored above with regard to McDonald's. It may be expressed as a syllogism:

- brands are now global
- brands are culture (meanings)
- therefore culture is global.

The role of graphic design in this argument is to construct the meanings or images of brands and to produce the advertisements which 'convey' that meaning or image to the world. Graphic designers are therefore part of the process in which local cultures are 'stripped' of their values and beliefs on behalf of globalising corporations. As Klein's argument here is the same as the one explored previously, it admits of the same refutation as the one above: meaning and communication do not work in the ways that her argument presupposes. The idea that meaning is something that can be 'conveyed' in a 'vehicle' from one place to another was shown to be inaccurate in Chapter 2 and need not be rehearsed in detail here. Suffice it to say that meaning is constructed in the interaction between a person's values and beliefs and the texts and images: it is the set of values and beliefs that generates the meaning and produces the person as a member of a cultural group.

Indeed, the arguments concerning globalisation considered so far admit of the same objection, that they are true in parts but ultimately fallacious. The fallacy they commit is known in logic as 'Illicit Process of the Minor Term'. In such arguments, the conclusion makes an assertion about the 'minor term' (in this case, cultural meanings) that is not contained in the premises. Klein's argument, which is essentially that used against McDonald's earlier, was expressed syllogistically, as:

- brands are now global
- brands are culture (meanings)
- therefore culture is global.

This is the same form of argument as the following, in which the fallacy may be clearly seen:

- all cheese is made from milk
- all cheese is fattening
- therefore everything fattening is made from milk.

The problem here is that although brands may now be found all over the world, and although brands are meanings and therefore cultural constructions, it is not the case that culture is now global, that the same meanings or cultural constructions are found all over the globe. Because there are different cultures, holding different values, beliefs and so on, each culture will have a slightly different take on the meaning of an advertisement or a brand. It is the values that generate the connotational meaning of the advertisements and brands, and if the values are different, then the meaning constructed will be different. This problem applies to the argument against McDonald's and to Klein's arguments concerning globalisation in general.

CONCLUSION

The conclusion that globalisation is to postmodernity as internationalism is to modernity is neat and therefore an attractive one. After all, postmodern, global graphic design and modern, international graphic design are both forms of communication, both rely on cultural values in order to construct and communicate meanings and both produce and reproduce political relations. Where modernist graphic design was, in the Bauhaus's case, explicitly and avowedly internationalist, globalising tendencies have been proposed as a particularly postmodern aspect of graphic design. Such a conclusion is to suggest that there is in this respect a difference of quantity, rather than of quality, between modern graphics and postmodern graphics. The question remains as to when the point at which a quantitative difference turns into a qualitative one. One possibility is that that point has not been reached yet: the modernist International Typographic Style has not, so far, been replaced by a postmodernist Global Typographic Style (but see http://www.typotheque.com/articles/benzin.html for a discussion of the place of 'Swiss' graphic design in postmodernity).

The idea that postmodernist globalisation does not represent a difference of kind or quality from modernist internationalism, and that the position and role of graphic design is much the same in both, has been supported by considering the nature of communication. As the construction of meaning in the interaction between people's cultural values and graphic designs (rather than the conveying of a pre-formed message between already constituted subjects), the nature of communication demands that globalisation cannot be the imposition of a dominant culture's 'global' values on local, and different, cultures. While not denying that graphic communication is one of the ways in which political relations are constructed and reproduced, neither politics nor communication is about the simple one-sided domination of the powerless by the powerful. This may be seen to an extent in the 2004 UK television advertisements for the HSBC bank. In these ads, western business people and travellers visit remote locations to find that their values, and therefore the meanings that they give to signs, are not those of the local culture. One young man causes offence and courts

160

violence by using the western hand-sign for 'OK' in Brazil, where it means something very rude; Japanese and western business people find themselves unsure whether to bow or shake hands. Despite the fact that these are ads, produced on behalf of a powerful globalising corporation, it is still interesting to see that either each party has to learn about the other, or the westerner gets into trouble: the local culture is a source of puzzlement and potential resistance, rather than something to be dominated and assimilated.

Having explained the similarities of, and differences between, modernist and postmodernist graphic design, and having explained both as communication, the next chapter will examine the question whether graphic design is, or can be considered to be, art.

FURTHER READING

- **Derrida's textual strategies** are explored in Ellen Lupton and J. Abbott Miller's excellent essay 'Deconstruction and Graphic Design', in their (1999) *Design, Writing, Research: Writing on Graphic Design*, London: Phaidon. They are also explored in postmodern, illustrated, collaged and thoroughly deconstructive fashion by Jeff Collins and Bill Mayblin (1996) in their *Derrida For Beginners*, Cambridge: Icon.
- A much fuller account of **postmodernism** in graphic design will be found in Rick Poynor's (2003) intelligent and trustworthy *No More Rules: Graphic Design and Postmodernism*, London: Lawrence King. Dick Hebdige's (1988) *Hiding in the Light*, London: Comedia/Routledge, analyses and explains 'Biff' cartoons and *The Face* magazine as examples of postmodern graphic design.
- The website at http://www.rmit.edu.au/adc/appliedcommunication/smm/emery (April 2004) contains an mpeg of a lecture given by Australian designer Garry Emery in September 2002 on **postcolonialism, globalism and regionalism** from an Australian perspective. For an entirely uncritical view of these topics, see http://www.hsbc.com (the 'global home of the world's local bank') for more globalising graphic design. The 'HSBC in Society' button takes you to the HSBC's 'values' and its position on local communities, social responsibility and environmental matters.

8

GRAPHIC DESIGN
AND ART

INTRODUCTION

Chapter 8 will consider the relation between art and graphic design and, even if it is the case that only graphic design students worry about this question (see Wild 1997: 92), the question addressed here will be whether graphic design is art or not. The answer proposed will be that graphic design and art are different from each other, but not in the ways that they are popularly or commonly thought to be. Although the chapter is toward the end of the book, the issues it raises are in fact central to all that has gone before: it will touch on issues surrounding the very identity of graphic design, the nature of communication and the character of the activities that graphic designers undertake. It must also question the nature of art. For, as Benjamin (1992: 220) says, while nineteenth-century thinkers devoted much 'futile thought' to the question whether photography, a form of mechanical image reproduction, was or could be art; the 'primary question' was, rather, whether mechanical reproduction had not 'transformed the very nature of art'.

The chapter will effectively be investigating what has been described as the tension between culture, or art, and commerce. Where Milton Glaser argues that, in the battle between culture and commerce, commerce has already won and graphic designers have long been 'transformed into industrial workers' (Glaser 1997a: 255), this chapter will side with Engels, who argues that people in every occupation, including artists and graphic designers, have been turned into wage-labourers (Marx and Engels 1968: 70; 1985: 82). Traditional, or popular, notions of art and the artist will be explained and compared to those of graphic design and the designer. The ways in which the definitions and practices of graphic designers have approached and diverged from those of artists will be explained. Concepts of individuality, expression and creativity which are happily applied to 'art' will be examined in order to determine whether, and to what extent, they may be used to explain and understand the practice of graphic design. The ways in which design, and graphic design in particular, has been presented and understood in popular understanding as 'functional' will be charted here. Benjamin's (1992) work on 'aura' will then be explained and will be used to provide a genuine difference between two types of what he calls 'works of art', those possessing 'aura' and those not possessing 'aura'.

All except the last of the following sections will examine various arguments which suggest that graphic design is different from art. They will show how these arguments are false or invalid. The last section, on aura, will investigate a genuine distinction between graphic design and art.

ART, GRAPHIC DESIGN AND MEANING

The first and probably the weakest argument in support of the idea that art is different from graphic design concerns meaning. The argument is that, because the meaning of a piece of graphic design is obvious or easily understood and because the meaning of a work of art is not obvious or easily understood, the two are different kinds of thing. Jonathan Jones (2004) proposes a version of this argument when, writing about Marc Quinn's sculpture *Alison Lapper Pregnant*, he says that 'this is an object so forthright, so plain, that it falls short of being art'. The idea can only be that, if something communicates in a 'forthright' and 'plain' fashion, then it cannot be art. Graphic design, which many people would say is in the business of forthright, plain communication, cannot be art on this account. Jones (2004) expands his case by saying that 'poetry, ambiguity and difficulty are necessary constituents of art'. Again, the idea must be that, as much of graphic design exists to communicate unambiguously and easily, it cannot be art. Or, it might be thought that, as some postmodernist graphic design is calculatedly difficult to understand, it counts as art, but modernist graphic design, functional and legible, does not. One of the weaknesses of Jones' argument can be seen if one considers a sign, in a park in Tokyo, saying 'Keep off the grass'. Because it is not easily understood by people who do not read Japanese, because it is neither forthright nor plain to people who do not read Japanese, it must be art on Jones' account. Because the sign is ambiguous and difficult it counts as art on Jones' account. Another weakness can be seen if one considers any of the paintings that Jones discusses in his weekly column for the *Guardian*. In this column, he explains the meaning and background of a painting. The meaning of the painting is perfectly clear to him (if it were not, how could he explain it?), and cannot, therefore, count as art on his account. The problem here is that his argument takes no account of cultural, class, national, gender, age, ethnic or indeed any other differences. Those differences ensure that some examples of visual culture are easy for the members of one group to understand, but difficult for other, different, group to understand. Art cannot be distinguished from graphic design by arguing that meaning in art is ambiguous and difficult but easy and plain in graphic design. As this book has shown, meaning is a product of cultural and social values and what is easily understood by one group need not be easily understood by another.

THE ARTIST AND THE DESIGNER

This section considers the argument that graphic design and art are different from each other because the nature of the activities peculiar to each are different. Walker (1983: 20) suggests that mass media products, such as those of graphic design, are 'the work of groups of specialists operating as teams in response to briefs, commissions or specifications laid down by employers or clients'. The 'specialists' Walker refers to include picture editors, researchers, photographers, animators, graphic designers and set designers and one might add typographers and typesetters to his list. While 'scope for individual creativity and imagination' exists within graphic design, Walker suggests that fine artists 'enjoy' much more 'artistic freedom and independence'. Indeed, as Walker says, fine art is 'regarded as a highly experimental and risky area of work where the emphasis is on creativity and self-fulfilment' (Walker 1983: 21, 17). To the notions of creativity and freedom, the graphic designer Leo Lionni (1997: 182) adds the idea of expression. 'When you paint', he says, you often look at the paintings to 'see . . . how well they express you', but when you design, 'self-expression lies so deep . . . that it is virtually irretrievable'.

Some of the problems involved in this account of 'art' or 'design' activities may be illustrated by Michael Baxandall's (1972) *Painting and Experience in Fifteenth Century Italy*. Baxandall studies the work and social context of people like Piero della Francesca, Botticelli, Fra Angelico and Mantegna. These people are routinely and unproblematically thought of as artists. To say that Botticelli was a Renaissance artist is not to court controversy. However, many aspects of these artists' practices fall under Walker's definition of the designer. Walker says that designers work in a team, where artists are independent. Baxandall (1972: 19–20) describes how Fra Angelico went from town to town with his 'team', which included senior and junior members who were paid accordingly. Walker says that designers work to briefs and specifications laid down by clients where artists enjoy 'artistic freedom'. Baxandall reproduces contracts agreed between these 'artists' and their clients in which the 'artist' has very little scope for imagination or free expression. One such contract, between Domenico Ghirlandaio and Father Bernardo regarding the *Adoration of the Magi* in Florence, demands that Ghirlandaio submit, 'in every particular according to what I, Fra Bernardo, think best' (Baxandall 1972: 6). It goes on to specify the subject matter of the image, the size and exact location of the image, the colours (and the grades of colours) to be used and the date the image was to be completed by, along with penalty clauses in case it was late.

164

Father Bernado seems determined to limit Ghirlandaio's experimental activities and creative freedoms as much as he possibly can here.

Now, clearly, this is an extreme case and it has been chosen especially to support the argument that not all those whom one might want to call artists are experimental risk-taking loners who revel in their creative freedom; some are and have been bound by strict contractual obligations to produce exactly what they are told to produce. There can be no doubt that examples could be produced of people whom one might want to call artists who enjoyed rather more 'freedom' than Ghirlandaio. Modern artists, such as Gauguin, Van Gogh, Picasso or even Tracey Emin or Damien Hirst could be adduced as examples of artists who are or were singularly free to express themselves creatively. Did not Gauguin abandon France for Tahiti? Is Van Gogh not almost synonymous with the very idea of expressive individuality? Where is the evidence for Picasso the team player? What is Tracey Emin's work if it is not experimental? And how could you describe Damien Hirst's work without using the words 'risky' or 'imaginative'? However persuasive these questions, and their already understood answers, it is the case, as the art critic Clement Greenberg (1986: 10) said, that 'no culture can develop . . . without a source of income'. Did Gauguin's friends not warn him against returning to France because what 'meagre market' there was for his work was for the 'exoticism' of the island paintings (Mackintosh 1990: 74)? Are Van Gogh's letters to his brother Theo not full of requests for more money? Was Picasso not commissioned by advertising agencies to provide illustrations for the town of Nice and De Beers Consolidated Mines Ltd (Bogart 1995: 157–9)? Tracey Emin and Damien Hirst's work is so risky and experimental that at the time of writing the former is considering legal action against some school children concerning the ownership and retail price of a piece of collaborative work, and the latter's work is sold before the gallery doors open. The issue here is that there is some point at which the 'artist's' freedom and expressivity is inevitably compromised by economics: what is produced has, eventually, to be marketable in order for the 'artist' to be able to live. Even in the limit cases, there is something like a client and the 'artist' is constrained to produce something that 'end-user' will want to buy.

CULTURAL SIGNIFICANCE

The argument to be considered here is that fine art and graphic design are different from each other because art is culturally more significant than graphic design. Where art is perceived to be of lasting value, graphic design is said to be 'ephemeral' (Cronan 2000: 216). Items such as oil paintings, sculptures and architecture are said to be art and to possess a sense of permanence while the products of graphic design, such as labels, posters, books and magazines are seen as impermanent and transitory. These observations are linked to the cultural significance of the products; because art production is long-lasting it is seen as more culturally important and because graphic production is not long-lasting it is seen as culturally insignificant. Connected with these ideas is the perception that art has more to say about a culture than graphic design. Architecture or oil painting is commonly thought of as being more expressive of an age or a culture than packaging or town signage. This section will show that this argument is false and that graphic design can be every bit as significant as fine art.

There are two counter-arguments to consider here. The first is made by Heller and Pomeroy (1997) in their *Design Literacy*. They argue that graphic production has been 'undervalued' and suggest that some graphic production is not as 'ephemeral as the paper it is printed on' (Heller and Pomeroy 1997: ix). They are saying that some graphics is art because it can and does 'endure' and it can possess a sense of permanence. They assert that 'certain advertisements, posters, packages, logos, books and magazines endure as signposts of artistic . . . achievement'. Many examples of graphic design, they say, are 'preserved and studied', just as art is preserved and studied, and it may therefore be considered as being as culturally significant as art. Indeed, they go further, to argue that some graphic design products can be more artistic than art in some respects. In particular, graphic production can be more artistic than art because it 'speak[s] more about particular epochs . . . than fine art' (Heller and Pomeroy 1997: ix). So, posters, packaging and logos on this account can be more expressive of an age or a culture than oil paintings and sculptures.

The second counter-argument may be found in Berger's (1972) *Ways of Seeing*. Berger is concerned with advertising graphics, or 'publicity' as he calls it, and he wants to show what the graphic design found in advertising has in common with art. To show this would have the effect of minimising the differences between art and graphic design. So he asks 'does the language of publicity have anything in common with that of oil painting?' (Berger 1972: 134). This is a question about the rhetorical techniques used by advertising and oil painting: how things and people are portrayed and what the images are trying to do. Berger says that there is a 'direct continuity' between the traditions of western oil painting and advertising graphics. Advertising graphics has inherited or taken over the rhetorical techniques of western painting to use them regularly in 'publicity'. So, on Berger's account, the graphic design that is found in advertising is no different from art in so far as both use the same illustrative and persuasive techniques. The reason why this lack of difference between art and design has gone unrecognised is what Berger (1972: 134) calls 'cultural prestige'. The higher cultural status afforded art in western culture has 'obscured' one of the aspects it shares with graphic design, so that it has been possible to argue, mistakenly in Berger's view, that graphics is different from art.

So, it is difficult to maintain the position that art and graphic design are different from each other because one of them is more culturally important, or more culturally expressive than the other. The American Institute of Graphic Arts asserts that graphic design is a 'cultural force' (Cronan 2001: 217) and a persuasive case can be made for graphic design being at least as culturally significant and eloquent as art.

EXPRESSION AND INDIVIDUALITY

The argument to be considered here is that graphic design is different from fine art because fine art is about self-expression and individuality while graphic design is not. This section will show that neither art nor design is about self-expression and individuality and that therefore they are not different from each other in these ways. It will show that what appears and is experienced as expression and individuality in both art and design depends upon the existence of structures, systems of conventions, which make communication possible.

The idea that art is to do with free expression, individuality and creativity while graphic design is not was touched on above in the paragraph on the artist and the designer. Here it was pointed out that many people consider graphic design to be working to someone else's brief while under commercial constraints and communicating someone else's pre-existing message. The potential for self-expression and individuality was seen as being much lower than it is in art practices. Gareth Williams, who is curator of architecture and design at the V&A Museum, voices this view when he says that 'art is about self-expression. It is a manifestation of an internalised world-view. Design . . . has been created with an end user in mind . . . it is ultimately destined for a market' (quoted in Kirwan-Taylor 2004: 51). It is as though something is going on inside the artist's head, which needs to be got out or expressed, but that this is not the case for the designer. Richard Hollis (1994: 8) says that the meaning of graphic images 'has little to do with those who made or chose them. The designer's message serves the . . . needs of the client who is paying for it'. That is, meaning in graphics is not a matter of, or derived from, the individual graphic designer's intentions. And the graphic designer Leo Lionni explicitly compares art and design on the matter of expression. 'When you paint', he says, you often look at the paintings to 'see . . . how well they express you', but when you design, 'self-expression lies so deep . . . that it is virtually irretrievable' (Lionni 1997: 182). The consistent argument here is that the designer's work is not about self expression or individuality, but that the artist's work is.

In his essay 'Expression and Communication', Ernst Gombrich (1963) contends that the idea of expression is not the simple equivalence of an individual's intention with external form. Moods, feelings, thoughts, ideas, emotions and other 'internal' phenomena are not simply or naturally equivalent to visible shapes, lines colours and textures. He argues that what appears and is commonly understood as expression makes no sense without a theory of the 'structural conditions of communication' (Gombrich 1963: 62). He uses various examples from art and design to make his point:

> The artist who wants to express or convey an emotion does not simply find its God-given natural equivalent in terms of tones or shapes. Rather . . . he will select from his palette the pigment from among those available that to his mind is most like the emotion he wishes to represent.
>
> (Gombrich 1963: 63)

It is not the case that red, for example, is naturally expressive of an upbeat mood. The colour may also be associated with prostitution, danger, blood, Manchester United, the Boston Red Sox or an amplifier having been left on. A blue canvas does not express melancholy if we know that blue was the only colour the artist had not run out of that day. It is not the case, then, that the use of the colour simply and unproblematically expresses what is in the artist's mind. What we need to know, according to Gombrich, is the structure from which artists make their choice. In this case, the structure is the available pigments. Paint applied with a palette knife does not naturally mean high emotion: the knife may have been all the artist had. But a section of paint applied with a palette knife next to a section constructed with delicate dabs of paint carries a recognisable charge (Gombrich 1963: 64). It is the structure, the system of differences, that generates the meaning here, not the inherent, naturally expressive qualities of the colour or technique.

Gombrich includes two examples from design. He uses the example of black printer's ink. If black were naturally expressive of mourning, gloom and failure, one might expect all book printers to be permanently despondent and despairing. This book is printed in black ink, but neither I nor the printers are at all despondent. The use of black ink is, as Gombrich (1963: 61) says 'of no expressive significance'. Frascara supports Gombrich here, arguing that the notion of self-expression is a 'romantic' conception and the idea that graphic design is about self-expression is 'one of the distorting conceptions of the profession' (Frascara 1988: 29). Where black is used as a sign for grief, in western funeral practices, for example, it is because a choice has been made from a structure consisting of all the other colours that could be used. It is conventional in western funerals to wear black rather than red or white, for example, both of which are routinely used in the funeral practices of other cultures. It is the knowledge of the structure, the choice made from the structure and the conventionalisation of that choice that generates meaning here, not the expression of some inner state.

The second example is from typography. Gombrich (1963: 65) introduces two words, 'ping' and 'pong', and suggests that if typefaces were naturally expressive, then it would be 'obvious' that 'ping' should be printed in a light typeface, while 'pong' should be printed in **bold**. However, the effects generated by a bold '**ping**' or by a light 'pong' are not so 'obvious', they are not so easy to explain in terms of expression. Only if one knows the structure (**bold** or light) and thus the choices that had been made, can one understand the subtle and unusual boldness of the bold '**ping**' or the peculiar delicacy of the light 'pong'. Similarly, an *italic* face is naturally expressive of nothing in particular: this entire book could have been printed in italic and while it might *look* odd, it would not mean that I wanted to emphasise the entire book. In the book printed entirely in italics, emphasis would have to be indicated by a non-italic, or plain, type. It is the *difference* between the plain type and the italic type, not the natural expressiveness of the italic, that generates the meaning that this particular word is to be stressed, and the difference between the two types forms a simple structure. Only the understanding of the structure (*italic* or not-italic), the choice of one face rather than another and conventionalisation of that choice would communicate the meaning that *this* word rather than that one is to emphasised.

So, if all communication is made possible, not by some equivalence between an individual's thoughts and emotions and the shapes, lines and colours that they use, but by structures from which choices are made and combined into text and image, then it cannot be argued that art is to do with self-expression and that graphic design is not. Neither art nor design is about expression in the sense claimed and they are not different from each other in the ways suggested by popular understanding. And, if meaning is not simply the product of individual intention (but rather the result of those syntagmatic combinations of choices from paradigmatic sets), then it cannot be argued that art is to do with individual intention and that graphic design is not. Neither art nor design is about intention in this sense and they are not different from each other in the ways suggested.

CREATIVITY AND PROBLEM-SOLVING

The prevalent conception and accompanying argument here is that graphic design and art are different from each other because graphic design can be characterised as 'problem-solving', while art is 'creative'. This section will argue that creativity is more appropriately thought of as cultural production and that both graphic design and art are examples of cultural production. They are not, therefore, different from each other in the ways that the prevalent conception of art and design suggests. The ideas surrounding expression and individuality are very closely related to the idea of creativity. Indeed, is it not uncommon to find each of these words used to define and explain the others. The preceding section and the one on The Artist and the Designer provide evidence for the seemingly inextricable relations between these ideas. If the situation were not complicated enough, Raymond Williams (1961: 19) points out, 'no word carries a more consistently positive reference than "creative"'. It is thereby also affected by the matter of cultural prestige (discussed earlier), and institutional significance (to be discussed later). Finally, while there is a sense in which arguments against certain conceptions of expression and individuality are at the same time arguments against certain conceptions of creativity, this section will attempt to keep the idea of creativity separate from those of expression and individuality as they were discussed in the previous section and deal only with creativity.

As already noted, then, it has become almost a commonplace in design writing to refer to graphic design as 'problem-solving'. The briefs, commissions and specifications with which the designer deals are often understood as problems. Meggs (1992: viii), for example, suggests that 'most designers speak of their activities as a problem-solving process because designers seek solutions to public communications problems'. Wild (1997: 94) points out that 'even the most self-indulgent designers refer to themselves as "problem-solvers"'. She does not explain 'self-indulgent', but the reference to 'self' unavoidably connotes the 'self' in 'self-expression' and may be taken to mean that even the most 'artistic' designer considers her- or himself a problem-solver. By contrast, art is said to offer more scope for creativity than graphic design. Indeed, as Walker (1983: 17) says, fine art is 'regarded as a highly experimental and risky area of work where the emphasis is on creativity'.

There are various arguments against the idea that graphic design is different from art because art is creative but design is problem-solving. One argument would be to say that problem-solving is itself a creative activity, that finding a solution to a communication problem is itself an example of creative activity. If this is the case, then it can be claimed that graphic design is not different from art in that both are creative. Such reasoning, however, is lazy and unphilosophical and it merely pushes the problem back a stage. We are still operating with an unexamined notion of creativity and we are likely to be stuck with the uncritical and mystifying conception of creativity that got us into difficulties in the first place. Pierre Macherey, for example, makes the point that if creativity is conceived as expression or 'the release of what is already there', then explanation is impossible because 'nothing has happened', what was inside is now outside (quoted in Wolff 1981: 138). If it is conceived as as 'irruption', the manifestation or bursting in of a vision (see Williams 1961), then explanation is impossible because what has happened is by definition 'inexplicable' (Wolff 1981: 138). Where explanation is impossible, mystification prevails. An alternative conception of creativity must be found.

For Macherey, the alternative may be found in the idea of 'production'. And it is as production, or cultural production, that Janet Wolff (1981) and

Raymond Williams (1961) also begin the explanation of 'creativity'. The following paragraphs will consider Williams' (1961) explanation of creativity as it is described in his *The Long Revolution*. Williams' account begins with perception and he says, uncontroversially enough, that perception is not simply the passive reception of material. Rather, it is active. There is, he says,

> no reality of familiar shapes . . . [and] colours . . . to which we merely open our eyes. The information that we receive through our senses from the material world around us has to be interpreted, according to certain human rules before what we ordinarily call 'reality' forms.
>
> (Williams 1961: 33)

The active part of perception is the interpretation of sense information according to 'human rules'. These 'rules' are the ways in which different cultures interpret sense information so as to form what is experienced in those cultures as 'reality'. Perception and our ordinary experience are human creations, then, and their sources are the brain and the interpretations produced by different cultures. Seeing the world is explained by Williams as learning to describe (Williams 1961: 34, 39) and, as different cultures have different experiences of the world, they see the world differently, so they describe the world differently.

Description is explained as communication (Williams 1961: 39–40). Description is 'putting the experience into a communicable form' (1961: 40). There is, literally, no sense in an experience that cannot be communicated and description is the way in which experience is made into something that can be communicated to others. As Derrida (1981: 30) says, 'all experience is the experience of meaning' and meaning is nothing if it is not communicable. The activity of description is performed by artists, and by scientists and philosophers, says Williams (1961: 40), 'but also, and necessarily, by everyone'. This is a crucial move in Williams' argument as it means that the creative production of the everyday experience of reality is something that everyone necessarily does. Art and design may now both be explained as parts of a general human creativity. It may be that art, and 'the arts' are an 'intense' form of general communication (Williams 1961: 41, 44), but they are not different in kind from everyday life and everyday life is no less the result of creative interpretation.

It is the erroneous separation of art from everyday life that, for Williams, leads to the privileging of the creativity found in art over that found in everyday life in the production and communication of everyday experience. All subsequent theories of creativity have simply been the reformulation of 'the same error' (Williams 1961: 54). It is this error that is reformulated in the claim, for example, that art is 'creative' but graphic design is 'problem-solving'. The idea that art is somehow apart from everyday life leads to the mystifying conceptions of creativity as either a bursting out or a bursting in of a personal vision, for example, and encourages the view that art is a different kind of activity from graphic design.

To summarise, then: Williams explains culture as communication. Culture depends on communication. Communication is explained as creativity. And creativity is said to be the interpretation and description of sense information that 'produces' what we experience as 'reality':

> Everything we see and do, the whole structure of our relationships and institutions, depends, finally, on an effort of learning, description and communication. We create our human world as we have thought of art being created.
>
> (Williams 1961: 54)

The first consequence of Williams' account for the arguments considered in this section is the idea that both graphic design and art are creative in the sense that they are two of the ways in which experience is made meaningful and communicated. This means that graphic design is not different from art because art is creative and graphics is not. The second consequence is the idea that neither graphic design nor art is creative, in the mystified senses of irruption or expression that were discussed above. This means that one cannot argue that problem-solving is itself a creative activity in the sense that 'creativity' has hitherto been understood, as irruptive or expressive. On Williams' account of creativity, both graphic design and art are different institutional examples of the same form of cultural production. They are different institutions, different organisations, having different members and existing for different purposes, practising the same form of creativity. Both graphic design and art are ways in which experience is visually produced, described and communicated. This is an important addition to the understanding of graphic design as communication that is being pursued by this book.

FUNCTION

The popular conception and underlying argument here is that graphic design is different from art because design is functional and art is not. The argument is that graphic design is there to perform various jobs or functions, but that art has no function. It was noted in Chapter 2 that graphic design performed various functions – informing, persuading and so on. The popular account of art has it that art is not functional, it just is. Art is not there to sell frozen peas or inform one of the emergency exits and therefore graphic design and art are different from one another. This section will show that this argument is false. It will argue that, like graphic design, art has a number of functions, but that those functions are denied or ignored.

In *ArtReview* for February 2004, for example, Helen Kirwan-Taylor (2004: 51) argues that art and design have been 'traditionally separated by one word: function'. Traditionally, art has been said not to be functional. Design, including graphic design, 'is supposed to do something' (Kirwan-Taylor 2004: 51). Gareth Williams expands on this traditional distinction by suggesting that art has been thought of as a 'contemplative' practice, the expressing of an 'internalised world view' (quoted in Kirwan-Taylor 2004: 51). Art, then, is to do with contemplation, or 'the aesthetic'; design is to do with function, or 'selling' (Rand and Rand 1999: 140). However, as Kirwan-Taylor (2004: 51) points out, these traditional boundaries have 'now become so blurred that what is art could easily be interpreted as design and vice versa'. It is probably the case that the boundaries have been 'blurred' for a long time; Paul and Ann Rand were writing about 'the advertising artist' and 'the commercial artist' in the 1960s. But, whatever the history of the debate has been, it has now reached the stage where 'artists' such as Donald Judd are mentioned in the same breath as the 'designer' James Dyson and where a piece of furniture can be said to become a piece of art.

In a round table discussion entitled 'What's the Use of Art?', Ossian Ward (2004: 66), the editor of *ArtReview*, commented that if a piece of furniture 'isn't functional, then it can become a bit of art'. While this may be begging the question (if a piece of furniture has no function, it could equally be argued that it is not a piece of furniture in the first place), Ward's comment shows that he thinks it is possible for art to 'become' design. Louisa Guinness, an art and design dealer, replied, 'Isn't that the big difference? A work of art won't have a function built into it during the creative process' (quoted in Ward 2004). Quite how a function is to be 'built into' a work of art is not clear, but that Guinness thinks there is, or wants there to be, a 'big difference' is clear. Ron Arad, Head of Design Products at the Royal College of Art and quite possibly losing patience at this point, reminded them of Oscar Wilde's 'comment' on this debate; he took a Rembrandt painting and used it as an ironing board (quoted in Ward 2004). Arad's position is surely correct; there is no essential difference between art and design that can be explained in terms of the function or lack of function an item 'possesses'. It is the use of the item and the (institutional) context it is a part of that determine whether it is considered art or design.

Taking a slightly different tack, Andrew Cracknell (then Creative Director at BSB Dorland) said in 1993 that the functionality of advertising was no bar to its appearing in art galleries (quoted in Bell 1993: 29). This is to freely acknowledge that design has a function, but to argue that its function does not prevent it being called art. After all, he said, art galleries already contain functional items, including pieces of design and architecture. He is correct; an advertisement for British Airways appeared in

New York's Museum of Modern Art in the 1990s and Tony Kaye has long argued that his advertising work for Dunlop should be in the Tate Gallery in London (quoted in Bell 1993: 29). Tony Cox (then Creative Director at BMP DDB Needham) turns Cracknell's case around, to present it from the opposite direction. 'Putting advertising in art galleries robs it of its purpose', he says (quoted in Bell 1993: 29). Where Cracknell says that function is no impediment to the inclusion of advertisements in art galleries, Cox says that putting advertisements in galleries strips them of that purpose. Again, there is no 'essence' of 'art' or 'design'; something that can be added or taken away depending on whether it appears on a printed page or in an art gallery cannot be 'essential'. And again, it is the use, and the institutional context, that determines whether the item is considered art or design.

A more philosophical contribution to the debate is made by Carroll (1999: 146–7). He is searching for a limit case, the most extreme example of a work of art that has no function. If he can find one, then he can argue that artworks are those items with no function. If he cannot, then it is not possible to say that there are artworks with no function. He asks, what about artworks that are just about form? Some artworks are said to be only about form. Their use of shape, line, colour, texture and visual organisation is what they are about, nothing else. Possessing no purpose, 'the artwork is just its form'. Carroll (1999: 147) argues that saying the artwork is only about form is 'shorthand for saying that the the function of the artwork is to bring form to our attention, so that we may contemplate it'. The very same 'contemplation' that is used by Williams (1961) to characterise art's functionlessness is used here by Carroll to denote a function of art. The function of the work that is supposedly only about form is to make the viewer think about the work's use of form, 'perhaps to reflect on the way in which they mold our experience of them'. Where an artwork lacks even this reflexive function, where the work is said to be only about beauty, Carroll says that 'the artwork is still functional'; it functions to arrest or enrapture the viewer (Carroll 1999: 147). Carroll is clear that his philosophical investigations of function show that there is no functionless artwork. There is thus no essential difference between artworks that are called art and those that are called design. As with the previous two arguments, only the institutional contexts and the uses to which they are put distinguish 'art' from 'design'.

It is precisely these contexts and the uses to which items are put that interest Walker (1983) in his *Art in the Age of Mass Media*. Walker begins from the distinction between fine arts and the applied arts, or mass media (by which he means photography, press, advertising, magazines, books, comics and so on (Walker 1983: 18)). Like the participants in the 'What's the Use of Art?' debate, he says that this distinction is commonly explained in terms of function, the 'utilitarian/non-utilitarian opposition' as he puts it.

However, he says that the fine arts/mass media distinction does not map onto non-utilitarian/utilitarian opposition; 'the idea that the fine arts are exclusively concerned with aesthetic pleasure and have no practical function is a dubious one' (Walker 1983: 16). Like Carroll, then, he is not happy with the idea of a 'functionless art'. But, unlike Carroll, Walker wants to argue that fine art, like the mass media, performs various functions. The problem is that fine art, unlike graphic design, is usually 'detached from' its religious and secular social functions. As Benjamin (1992: 218) says, the nineteenth-century doctrine of *l'art pour l'art*, or art for art's sake, denied the social function of art. Institutions such as public museums and private galleries (along with certain people who work in them, such as museum staff and art historians) have promoted the impression that art is 'autonomous, growing . . . out of earlier art rather than out of any external social demand' (Walker 1983: 16). Where the social and cultural 'demands' are easy to discern and understand in graphic design, they are denied or hidden by the institutions surrounding art with the consequence that eventually, they are said not to exist.

AURA

This section will investigate an area in which the debate leads to a genuine discontinuity between graphic design and art. The area is that surrounding the term 'aura', proposed by Walter Benjamin in his 1936 essay 'The Work of Art in the Age of Mechanical Reproduction' (in Benjamin 1992). The definition of graphic design that was suggested in Chapter 2 depends upon the notion of the reproducibility of image and text. It was said there that graphic design exists, at least potentially, in multiple copies and that fine art does not. Hollis (1994: 8), for example, said that 'unlike the artist, the designer plans for multiple production'. It is this idea of reproducibility that is at the heart of Benjamin's notion of the loss of 'aura'. For the first time in history, he says, the work of art 'becomes the work of art designed for reproducibility' (Benjamin 1992: 218). Although Benjamin is mainly interested in photography, what he says applies also to graphic design and although he is concerned with mechanical reproduction, his arguments are also relevant to electronic and digital reproduction.

Benjamin's argument is essentially that some works of art possess 'aura' and that others, mechanically reproduced works (such as graphic designs), do not. Aura is the sense of uniqueness and authenticity that is felt before a work of art. Uniqueness, the sense that there is a single work of art, is 'inseparable' from that work of art's place in a tradition and authenticity is grounded in the ritual or cultic function of art (Benjamin 1992: 214, 217). The reproduction of text and image, whether mechanical (woodcut, for example) or process (such as lithography and photography), destroys aura in two ways (Benjamin 1992: 212, 213). First, by enabling a plurality of copies, the reproduction of an image precludes the possibility of a unique, one-off or original image. It makes as little sense to ask for an 'original' or 'authentic' photographic or lithographic print as it does to ask for the 'original' of a jpeg (1992: 218). Second, the existence of the image in many copies detaches the reproduced object from a context in a tradition, thus enabling it to 'meet the beholder' in their own 'particular situation' (1992: 215). Prints and digital images may exist anywhere, at any time, without losing anything (unlike an oil painting, which can be in only one place at any one time), and are thus available to any and all 'situations' (1992: 214).

Aura, then, is generated by the artwork's imbeddedness in the 'fabric of tradition' (1992: 217). This 'contextual integration' was originally found in cult, or ritual practices, where the authenticity and uniqueness of the work is essential for the work to perform its function (cf. Aumont's (1997) account of the functions of images in Chapter 2). Mechanical reproduction, however, separates or emancipates art from its place in cult, ritual and tradition and permits the reception of the image in terms of its 'exhibition value' (Benjamin 1992: 218). The age of mechanical reproduction is one in which the image is designed or planned with reproduction and exhibition in mind (cf. Hollis 1994: 8). Today, Benjamin (1992: 219) says, the emphasis on the exhibition value of the work has become absolute and the reproduced image has taken on 'entirely new functions'. These functions are political, rather than ritual and the 'reaction' of the masses towards the image has been 'changed' by mechanical reproduction. The viewer of prints and photographs is now 'challenged', captions in picture magazines are now 'directives', which may be right or wrong and photographs are now 'evidence for historical occurrences', with 'political significance' (Benjamin 1992: 218, 227, 220).

One of the consequences of these ideas for graphic design and communication is that, with the move from ritual to exhibition, from aura to reproduction, it has become possible for the consumption of the image to become active rather than passive, progressive rather than reactionary (1992: 227). Meaning is no longer tied to or derived from tradition, but may now be encountered and contested by the viewer in their own 'situation'. So, not only is graphic design emphatically not art (in the sense of a unique, authoritative and tradition-bound work) on this account, but also as mechanical reproduction, it radically alters the way our perception is 'organised': Benjamin (1992: 216) says that a 'new kind of perception' is generated by the possibility of the mechanical reproduction of images and the 'decay' of aura that it implies. Moreover, these changes in the economy of perception, along with the decay of aura they imply, may be explained by showing their 'social causes'.

This debate leads, as did the previous one, to Walker's (1983) *Art in the Age of Mass Media*. Walker's book may be read as developing these themes in so far as he is concerned to investigate the social causes of the changes described by Benjamin. In this book, Walker argues that:

> it is not the technology in itself which produces the distinctions between fine art . . . and mass culture, but rather the way in which materials and tools are habitually used (the different formal conventions) and the social institutions within which works are produced, distributed, consumed and categorised.
>
> (Walker 1983: 16)

It is the social conventions surrounding images, along with the social institutions within which images are produced and consumed that distinguish fine art from graphic design. Walker's account of the differences between art and design relates to Williams' (1961) account of creativity. Following Williams' argument, graphic design and art were said to be different institutional examples of the same kind of creativity. If Walker's conclusions are followed, then it is the different institutions and conventions that determine whether something is called 'art' or 'design'. His example of Richard Hamilton's 1958 work entitled $he is instructive. The work contains, or quotes, fragments of a number of advertisements for domestic appliances and uses some of the media and techniques used by graphic designers (Walker 1983: 30–1). However, as Walker (1983: 32) says, it is not enough for an artist to incorporate popular imagery, and graphic techniques and media in order for their work to become a piece of design. Hamilton's work is to be found in the Tate Britain Gallery, in London, it is not mass produced, its purpose is not in fact to sell irons and vacuum cleaners and its 'values of handwork and painterliness run counter to those of machine-made images' (Walker 1983: 32). Walker shows that the conventions (painterliness, for example), and the institutional setting, which possesses its own conventions of practice and expectation, prevent the work from being understood as a piece of design.

In her *Artists, Advertising and The Borders of Art*, Michele Bogart (1995) continues the investigation of the ways in which the social institutions and cultural conventions surrounding the production and consumption of visual material provide, or fail to provide, an answer to the question as to whether an image is 'art' or 'design'. One example will have to suffice to show the immensely complex relationships between art, advertising, business, education and entertainment that need to be disentangled here. Bogart recounts the story of the US television programme, *You Are an Artist*, which ran weekly on NBC between 1946 and 1971 (Bogart 1995: 295ff.). The show was sponsored by Gulf Oil and presented by Jon Gnagy, a former advertising art director. Gnagy, 'goateed and plaid-shirted', encouraged viewers to 'express' themselves and to learn to reduce what they saw to 'ball, cone, cube and cylinder'. Despite the show's attracting criticism from the 'art educators' at the Museum of Modern Art, who claimed that Gnagy 'stifled creativity', Andy Warhol later testified that 'Gnagy taught me how to draw' (Bogart 1995). Institutions such as education (in the form of the Museum of Modern Art), entertainment (NBC), and the oil industry (Gulf Oil) are either allied or opposed here, arguing about whether what the people following the show are producing is 'art' or not. Conventions of dress and 'artistic demeanour' and of 'artistic production' (the cone, cube and cylinder) conflict with conventions of art education (learning art production from the television?). And the 'artist' who exhibited silkscreen prints of Campbell's soup-cans and Coca-Cola bottles in art galleries claims to have been taught to draw by a graphic designer. The striking complexity of these relationships is clear, but, in the absence of an essence for either art of design, they are where the differences, as Bogart describes them, are to be found.

CONCLUSION

This chapter has explored the relation between graphic design and art. It considered four areas in which it has been suggested that graphic design and art are different, but where those differences turned out to be specious. And it considered one area in which a genuine difference was found. Both sets of arguments led to the conclusion that the most productive way of discussing and investigating what differences there may be between graphic design and art is to look at the institutional locations and social and cultural conventions surrounding them.

FURTHER READING

- Michelle Henning (1995) develops Benjamin's ideas on **aura** in her 'Digital Encounters: Mythical Pasts and Electronic Presence', in Lister, M. (ed.) *The Photographic Image in Digital Culture*, London: Routledge. She investigates the power of digital imagery to disrupt and shock. Some of the implications of Benjamin's ideas for **cultural studies** generally are briefly outlined in John Storey's (1993) *An Introductory Guide to Cultural Theory and Popular Culture*, Hemel Hempstead: Harvester Wheatsheaf, pp. 108ff.
- On the use of **'art' in advertising**, see Judith Williamson's (1986) ' . . . But I know What I Like', in her *Consuming Passions: The Dynamics of Popular Culture*, London: Marion Boyars.
- Chapter 2 of Noël Carroll's (1999) *Philosophy of Art*, London: Routledge, is as thorough an account of **art and expression** as anyone is likely to need at this point.
- Rick Poynor (1998) presents an interesting discussion on whether graphic design is or can be **art** in his 'Design without Boundaries', in his *Design without Boundaries: Visual Communication in Transition*, London: Booth Clibborn.

9

CONCLUSION

This book has tried to explain graphic design as a form of visual communication. In order to do this, it has been necessary first to explain what communication is and then to present examples of graphic design as communication. Of the two basic models of communication investigated, those found in communication theory and semiological theory, the latter was shown to be more useful and productive for describing, analysing and explaining graphic communication. Where communication theory proposed the sending and receiving of already constituted messages between already existing subjects, semiology proposed that membership of cultural formations was produced and either challenged and reproduced in the active construction of meanings. Communication in graphic design was explained as the interaction of the beliefs and values held by members of cultural groups and the formal elements of graphic design (such as shapes, lines, colours, imagery, text and layout, for example). Rather than existing, naturally and prefabricated, in graphic designs, meaning was explained as being constructed in the activity of communication itself. As such, graphic design is not the innocent, or even the guilty, conveyor of messages but the constructor of (other people's) identities. The notion of the arbitrary nature of the sign, and the following emphasis on difference – as what Derrida (1973: 141) calls the non-full, non-simple 'origin' of meaning – was seen to be fundamental to this conception of communication, as Saussure (1974: 68) rightly pointed out at the beginning of the twentieth century. Semiological theory was then used to explain the variety of different types of signs and the ways in which signs could be constructed as meaningful. The types of signs were explained as icon, index and symbol; denotation and connotation were explained as analytic distinctions between two types of meaning; layout was presented as a way of constructing meaning and the role of words and texts in relation to images was explained as anchorage and relay.

It was then argued that what are commonly presented as the contexts of, or backdrops to, graphic design (society, culture and economy) are more usefully thought of as being produced by graphic design. The ways in which graphic design contributes to the formation of social and cultural identities and to either the reproduction or the contesting of those identities was explained in Chapter 4. Graphic design's place and role in capitalist economy was illustrated in terms of consumption which, straddling social and cultural concerns, is central to both the reproduction and the contestation of that economy. Some of the implications of the model of communication that is adopted by this book were also investigated in terms of what are usually referred to as the target markets, or audiences, of graphic design. Identities involving ethnicity/race, age and gender were explained as being not so much targets to be aimed at as different people to communicate with through the medium of graphic design. The role of graphic designers in culture, society and economy is therefore one of considerable responsibility. Again, communication as the interaction of cultural beliefs and values with formal graphic elements in the construction of meaning was proposed as a more accurate way of accounting for the differences between examples of graphic design.

An apparently more historical approach was adopted in Chapters 6 and 7, which studied graphic communication in relation to modernism and post-modernism. These chapters outlined the beliefs and values of modernism and postmodernism and explained the ways in which graphic designers selected from and incorporated those values into their work. These chapters were 'apparently' more historical because modernist and post-modernist graphic design were treated as communicating the beliefs and values that were selected. European graphic designers chose to produce and reproduce a subtly different selection of beliefs and values from those selected by American designers, for example. Globalisation was defined and illustrated and the ways in which graphic designers communicated the values of dominant globalising corporations were described. It was argued that globalisation itself was not a different kind of thing and did not operate in different ways from any of the other examples of communication that had been studied in this book. Consequently, the role and responsibilities of graphic designers were no different in globalising postmodernity than they were in internationalist modernity. Finally, some old problems concerning whether graphic design was, or could sometimes be considered to be, art were discussed. Five arguments in which some people try to show that graphic design is art were shown to be invalid and one way in which graphic design is demonstrated not to be art was seen to be valid.

So much for the brief summary of the things this book said it would try to do. There is one thing that it said it would not do which stands in need of further comment. It was pointed out in Chapter 1 that this is not a 'How to Do It' book; it would contain no intentional advice on how to produce more effective websites and was never intended as a guide to producing better advertisements. And Chapter 5 was described as not being interested in carrying out market research for capitalism. Markets and audiences were not approached there as exploitable or more or less affluent consumers from whom advertising and product packaging design could help commercial companies extort money. When I first started teaching the history and theory of graphic design (when design studios at college contained drawing boards and magic markers, and when students would arrive for tutorials with printer's ink under their fingernails), a colleague told me that his motivation for teaching history and theory was to stop students doing graphic design. I took this to mean that students would be so busy pondering the nature of the sign, syntagms and the relation between connotation and ideology that they would have no time to produce sexist advertising and sleek capitalist corporate identities. The problem, or paradox, is that understanding how communication works will not stop students, or anyone else, doing graphic design and it may even, ironically enough, help them to produce more persuasive advertisements, more effective websites and even sleeker corporate identities.

The understanding that communication involves the viewer's beliefs and values and that, in order to communicate with people, graphic designers have also to understand their beliefs and values can only aid communication. To that extent, this is a 'How to Do It' book and my intentions and those of my colleague are neither here nor there. However, the 'other side' of this sword is that (because there is no communication that does not produce and reproduce social, cultural and economic values and identities) the social, cultural and economic responsibilities of graphic designers have to be taken seriously. As Andrew Howard (1997: 195) says, there is such a thing as society (and culture and capitalist economy), and graphic design is one of the ways in which it is (and they are) produced and reproduced. The version of communication explored in this book contains both of these ideas and makes no sense if either is absent. Consequently, the answer to Michael Rock's question, 'Can design be socially responsible?' (1994: 191) is that it always already is responsible. It is already, and always was, the production and reproduction of society and as such is partly responsible for society being the way it is. Such an argument may not stop people doing graphic design, either, but this author hopes that it will make them think about it a little more, and a little more intelligently, than Rock's question implies they do.

The form in which Rock's question is posed presupposes that graphic designers have any choice about whether to be 'socially responsible' or not. 'Can X be Y?' suggests that X either may or may not be Y. It also implies that graphic design is not necessarily always socially responsible. If graphic design were already socially responsible all or some of the time, then there would be no need to ask the question. This book has argued that, because of the nature of communication, graphic design has no choice as to whether it is socially responsible or not and that it always is responsible for the production and reproduction of social, cultural end economic identities and relations. It is because communication is the construction and reproduction of social, cultural and economic identities in the interaction between beliefs and values and the formal elements of graphic design that the latter is 'responsible' for that social, cultural and economic production and reproduction. Because of the nature of communication, there is no choice here and Rock's question is misplaced.

Finally, and briefly, another problem that was raised in Chapter 1 and which has not been mentioned since concerns the blind spot that western culture seems to have regarding graphic design. This problem can be expressed as two questions, neither of which will be answered in any convincing fashion here. The first is, how can graphic design pass unnoticed, when it stares people in the face all day and every day? In response to a recent brief, BA(Hons) Graphic Design students at the University of Derby asked shoppers in the city centre 'What is graphic design?' The answers they received were interesting, ranging from 'something to do with architecture?', 'the drawings for fashion design', 'it's labels and packaging', to 'art, done more neatly'. Clearly, this is anecdote and not evidence, again. But equally clearly, graphic design is not well understood by these people. Yet more people see and are affected by more examples of graphic design in a day than they see art in a year. From the moment they look at the numbers on their alarm clock in the morning, read the paper or watch morning television, catch the logo- and advertisement-covered bus, or check the car speedometer on the way to work, to the moment they see the time on the clock, put down their bedtime reading and go to sleep, people are surrounded by graphic design. Graphic design has more effect on people than art ever does. It tells them where the football match or the airport is, what's in their food; it persuades them what to buy; it decorates their living rooms and workplaces and it reminds them of their past, of their relatives, and their loved ones. How is it that the majority of people do not know what graphic design is, let alone how to analyse and explain it?

The second question is, given the centrality of graphic design to people's lives, how is it that there is no discipline in the history and theory of graphic design that even remotely compares to the history and theory of art? Where is the history of graphic design? A quick visit to Google brings 300 UK references to 'BA(Hons) History of Art' in a fraction of a second, but none to either 'BA(Hons) History of Graphic Design' or 'BA(Hons) Graphic Design History'. Every graphic design degree has a Contextual Studies or a Complementary Studies component but institutionally, it seems, the history and theory of graphic design is buried so deep in those contexts that even Google cannot find it. Where is the history of graphic design's Heinrich Wolfflin, Otto Werckmeister, Erwin Panofsky, Ernst Gombrich, Clement Greenberg, Roger Fry, Tim Clark or even Sister Wendy? The ideas discussed in Chapter 8 concerning the relative social and cultural significance of fine art and graphic design may give some idea of the beginning of an answer. W. J. T. Mitchell's (1995a, 1995b) analysis and proposal concerning the definition and study of visual culture in general may further an answer by investigating the status and history of the study of visual culture, rather than 'fine art'. But it is evident that, socially, culturally economically and institutionally, the historical and theoretical study of graphic design has a long way to go.

BIBLIOGRAPHY

Appadurai, A. (1990) 'Disjuncture and Difference in the Global Cultural Economy', in
Featherstone, M. (ed.) *Global Culture: Nationalism, Globalization and Modernity*,
London: Sage.

Arisman, M. (2000) 'Is There a Fine Art to Illustration?', in Heller, S. and Arisman, M. (eds)
The Education of an Illustrator, New York: Allworth Press.

Arnason, J. P. (1990) 'Nationalism, Globalization and Modernity', in Featherstone, M. (ed.)
Global Culture: Nationalism, Globalization and Modernity, London: Sage.

Ashwin, C. (ed.) (1983) *History of Graphic Design and Communication: A Sourcebook*,
London: Pembridge Press.

—— (1989) 'Drawing, Design and Semiotics', in Margolin, V. (ed.) *Design Discourse:
History/Theory/Criticism*, Chicago, Ill.: University of Chicago Press.

Aumont, J. (1997) *The Image*, trans. C. Pajackowska, London: BFI Publishing.

Aynsley, J. (1987) 'Graphic Design', in Conway, H. (ed.) *Design History: A Student's
Handbook*, London: Routledge.

Back, L. (1998) 'Local/Global', in Jenks, C. (ed.) *Core Sociological Dichotomies*, London:
Sage.

Back, L. and Quaade, V. (1993) 'Dream Utopias, Nightmare Realities: Imagining Race and
Culture within the World of Benetton Advertising', *Third Text*, 22: 65–80.

Baker, S. (1985) 'The Hell of Connotation', *Word and Image*, 1(2): 164–75.

Barnard, M. (1995) 'Advertising: The Rhetorical Imperative', in Jenks, C. (ed.) *Visual
Culture*, London: Routledge.

—— (1998) *Art, Design and Visual Culture*, Basingstoke: Palgrave.

—— (2001) *Approaches to Understanding Visual Culture*, Basingstoke: Palgrave.

—— (2002) *Fashion as Communication*, 2nd edn, London: Routledge.

Barthes, R. (1972) *Mythologies*, London: Paladin.

—— (1977a) 'Rhetoric of the Image', in Barthes, R., *Image, Music, Text*, Glasgow: Fontana/
Collins.

—— (1977b) 'The Photographic Message', in Barthes, R., *Image, Music, Text*, Glasgow:
Fontana/Collins.

Bätschmann, O. (1988) 'Text and Image: Some General Problems of Art', *Word and Image*,
4(1): 11–24.

Bauman, Z. (1992) *Intimations of Postmodernity*, London: Routledge.

Baxandall, M. (1972) *Painting and Experience in Fifteenth Century Italy*, Oxford: Clarendon
Press.

Bayer, H. (1999) 'Towards a Universal Type', in Bierut, M., Helfland, J., Heller, S. and
Poyner, R. (eds) (1999) *Looking Closer 3: Classic Writings on Graphic Design*, New
York: Allworth Press.

Belk, R. W. (2000) 'Wolf Brands in Sheep's Clothing', in Pavitt, J. (ed.) *Brand.New*, London:
V&A Publications.

Bell, E. (1993) 'Is Hanging Too Good for Them?', *Observer*, 20 June.

Bell, S. (1999) *Bell's Eye: Twenty Years of Drawing Blood*, London: Methuen.

Belloc, H. (2002) *Cautionary Tales for Children*, illustrated by E. Gorey, New York: Harcourt Brace.

Benjamin, W. (1992) *Illuminations*, ed. H. Arendt, trans. H. Zohn, London: Fontana.

Berger, J. (1972) *Ways of Seeing*, London: BBC/Penguin.

Berman, M. (1983) *All that is Solid Melts into Air: The Experience of Modernity*, London: Verso.

Bielenberg, J. (1997) 'Thinking about Communication', in Bierut, M., Drenttel, W., Heller, S. and Holland, D. K. (eds) *Looking Closer 2: Critical Writings on Graphic Design*, New York: Allworth Press.

Bierut, M., Drenttel, W., Heller, S. and Holland, D. K. (eds) (1994) *Looking Closer: Critical Writings on Graphic Design*, New York: Allworth Press.

—— (eds) (1997) *Looking Closer 2: Critical Writings on Graphic Design*, New York: Allworth Press.

Bierut, M., Helfland, J., Heller, S. and Poyner, R. (eds) (1999) *Looking Closer 3: Classic Writings on Graphic Design*, New York: Allworth Press.

Bierut, M., Drenttel, W. and Heller, S. (eds) (2002) *Looking Closer 4: Critical Writings on Graphic Design*, New York: Allworth Press.

Blackwell, L. (1995) *The End of Print: The Graphic Design of David Carson*, London: Laurence King.

Bland, D. (1962) *The Illustration of Books*, London: Faber & Faber.

Bogart, M. H. (1995) *Artists, Advertising and the Borders of Art*, Chicago, Ill.: University of Chicago Press.

Booth-Clibborn, E. and Baroni, D. (1979) *The Language of Graphic Design*, New York: Harry N. Abrams.

Boyne, R. and Rattansi, A. (1990) *Postmodernism and Society*, London: Macmillan.

Bracewell, M. (2004) 'Happy Days', *Guardian* Weekend, 28 February: 28–31.

Britt, D. (ed.) (1990) *Modern Art*, London: Thames & Hudson.

Buckley, C. (1989) 'Made in Patriarchy: Toward a Feminist Analysis of Women and Design', in Margolin, V. (ed.) *Design Discourse: History/Theory/Criticism*, Chicago, Ill.: University of Chicago Press.

Byrne, C. and Witte, M. (1994) 'A Brave New World: Understanding Deconstruction', in Bierut, M., Drenttel, W., Heller, S. and Holland, D. K. (eds) *Looking Closer: Critical Writings on Graphic Design*, New York: Allworth Press.

Carey, J. W. (1992) *Communication as Culture*, London: Routledge.

Carroll, N. (1999) *Philosophy of Art: A Contemporary Introduction*, London: Routledge.

Carson, D. (2004) *Trek*, Corte Madera, Calif.: Gingko Press.

Chermayeff, I. (1994) 'Some Thoughts on Modernism: Past, Present and Future', in Bierut, M., Drenttel, W., Heller, S. and Holland, D. K. (eds) *Looking Closer: Critical Writings on Graphic Design*, New York: Allworth Press.

Cherry, C. (1966) *On Human Communication*, Cambridge, Mass.: MIT Press.

Cobley, P. (ed.) (1996) *The Communication Theory Reader*, London: Routledge.

Collins, J. and Mayblin, B. (1996) *Derrida for Beginners*, Cambridge: Icon.

Conway, H. (ed.) (1987) *Design History: A Student's Handbook*, London: Routledge.

Corner, J. and Hawthorn, J. (eds) *Communication Studies: An Introductory Reader*, London: Edward Arnold.

Cortese, A (1999) *Provocateur: Images of Women and Minorities in Advertising*, Lanham, Md: Rowman & Littlefield.

Crafton-Smith, M. (1994) 'Culture is the Limit: Pushing the Boundaries of Graphic Design Criticism and Practice', *Visible Language*, 28(4): 297–315.

Cronan, M. (2001) 'None of my Business', in Holland, D. K. (ed.) *Design: How Graphic Design Informs Society*, New York: Allworth Press.

BIBLIOGRAPHY

Crow, D. (2003) *Visible Signs*, Crans-Près-Céligny, Switzerland: AVA Publishing SA.

Curran, J. (1982) 'Communications, Power and Social Order', in Gurevitch, M., Bennett, T., Curran, J. and Woollacott, J. (eds) *Culture, Society and the Media*, London: Methuen.

de Harak, R. (1997) 'Some Thoughts on Modernism: Past, Present and Future', in Heller, S. and Finamore, M. (eds) *Design Culture: An Anthology of Writing from the AIGA Journal of Graphic Design*, New York: Allworth Press.

Derrida, J. (1973) *Speech and Phenomena*, Evanston, Ill.: Northwestern University Press.

—— (1976) *Of Grammatology*, Baltimore, Md: Johns Hopkins University Press.

—— (1977) 'Limited Inc', in *Glyph II*, pp. 162–254.

—— (1978a) 'The *Retrait* of Metaphor', *Enclitic*, 2(11): 5–33.

—— (1978b) *Writing and Difference*, Chicago, Ill.: University of Chicago Press.

—— (1979) *Spurs/Eperons*, Chicago, Ill.: University of Chicago Press.

—— (1981) *Positions*, London: Athlone Press.

—— (1982a) *Margins of Philosophy*, Hemel Hempstead: Harvester Wheatsheaf.

—— (1982b) 'Sending: On Representation', *Social Research*, 49(2): 294–327.

—— (1986) *Glas*, Lincoln, Nebr.: University of Nebraska Press.

Dodd, N. (1999) *Social Theory and Modernity*, London: Polity Press.

Doy, G. (1998) *Materialising Art History*, Oxford: Berg.

Drucker, J. (1999) 'Who's Afraid of Visual Culture?', *Art Journal*, 58(4): 37–47.

Dyer, G. (1982) *Advertising as Communication*, London: Methuen.

Falk, P. (1997) 'The Benetton–Toscani Effect', in Nava, M., Blake, A., MacRury, I. and Richards, B. (eds) *Buy This Book: Studies in Advertising and Consumption*, London: Routledge.

Featherstone, M. (ed.) (1990) *Global Culture: Nationalism, Globalization and Modernity*, London: Sage.

Featherstone, M. and Wernick, A. (eds) (1995) *Images of Aging: Cultural Representations of Later Life*, London: Routledge.

Fiske, J. (1990) *Introduction to Communication Studies*, London: Routledge.

Fleming, N. (2002) 'Keep Us Posted', *Guardian* G2, 1 May: 12–13.

Foucault, M. (1983) *This is Not a Pipe*, Berkeley, Calif.: University of California Press.

Fox-Genovese, E. (1987) 'The Empress's New Clothes', *Socialist Review*, 17(1): 7–30.

Frascara, J. (1988) 'Graphic Design: Fine Art or Social Science?', *Design Issues*, 5(1): 18–29.

Frascina, F. and Harrison, C. (eds) (1982) *Modern Art and Modernism*, London: Paul Chapman.

Gauntlett, D. (2002) *Media, Gender and Identity: An Introduction*, London: Routledge.

Giddens, A. (1990) *The Consequences of Modernity*, Cambridge: Polity Press.

Giroux, H. (1994) 'Consuming Social Change: The United Colors of Benetton', in Giroux, H., *Disturbing Pleasures: Learning Popular Culture*, London: Routledge.

Glaser, M. (1997a) 'Design and Business: The War is Over', in Heller, S. and Finamore, M. (eds) *Design Culture: An Anthology of Writing from the AIGA Journal of Graphic Design*, New York: Allworth Press.

—— (1997b) 'Some Thoughts on Modernism: Past, Present and Future', in Heller, S. and Finamore, M. (eds) *Design Culture: An Anthology of Writing from the AIGA Journal of Graphic Design*, New York: Allworth Press.

Gombrich, E. (1963) 'Expression and Communication', in Gombrich, E., *Meditations on a Hobby Horse and Other Essays on the Theory of Art*, London: Phaidon.

Gorey, E. (1997) *The Haunted Tea-Cosy*, London: Bloomsbury Press.

—— (1998) *The Gashleycrumb Tinies*, London: Bloomsbury Press.

Green, H. (1997) 'Burgers Make a Breakthrough', *Guardian* G2, 4 May: 21.

Greenberg, C. (1982) 'Collage', in Frascina, F. and Harrison, C. (eds) *Modern Art and Modernism*, London: Paul Chapman.

BIBLIOGRAPHY

—— (1986) 'Avant-Garde and Kitsch', in *Clement Greenberg: The Collected Essays and Criticism Volume 1 – Perceptions and Judgements 1939–1944*, ed. J. O'Brien, Chicago, Ill.: University of Chicago Press.

—— (1993) 'Modernist Painting', in *Clement Greenberg: The Collected Essays and Criticism Volume 4 – Modernism with a Vengeance 1957–1969*, ed. J. O'Brien, Chicago, Ill.: University of Chicago Press.

Gurevitch, M., Bennett, T., Curran, J. and Woollacott, J. (eds) (1982) *Culture, Society and the Media*, London: Methuen.

Hall, S. (ed.) (1997) *Representation: Cultural Representations and Signifying Practices*, London: Sage.

Hall, S. and Jefferson, T. (eds) (1976) *Resistance through Rituals: Youth Subcultures in Post-War Britain*, London: Routledge.

Hebdige, D. (1979) *Subculture: The Meaning of Style*, London: Routledge.

—— (1988) *Hiding in the Light*, London: Comedia/Routledge.

Heidegger, M. (1958) *The Question of Being*, New Haven, Conn.: College and University Press.

Heller, S. (2001) 'Fortunato Depero: Cheering up the Universe', in Heller, S. and Ballance, G. (eds) *Graphic Design History*, New York: Allworth Press.

Heller, S. and Arisman, M. (eds) (2000) *The Education of an Illustrator*, New York: Allworth Press.

Heller, S. and Ballance, G. (eds) (2001) *Graphic Design History*, New York: Allworth Press.

Heller, S. and Finamore, M. (eds) (1997) *Design Culture: An Anthology of Writing from the AIGA Journal of Graphic Design*, New York: Allworth Press.

Heller, S. and Pomeroy, K. (1997) *Design Literacy: Understanding Graphic Design*, New York: Allworth Press.

Henning, M. (1995) 'Digital Encounters: Mythical Pasts and Electronic Presence', in Lister, M. (ed.) *The Photographic Image in Digital Culture*, London: Routledge.

Heskett, J. (2002) *Toothpicks and Logos*, Oxford: Oxford University Press.

Hillis Miller, J. (1992) *Illustration*, London: Reaktion.

Hine, T. (1995) *The Total Package*, Boston, Mass.: Little, Brown.

Hoffmann, H. (2000) *Strewwelpeter*, London: Belitha Press.

Holland, D. K. (ed.) (2001) *Design Issues: How Graphic Design Informs Society*, New York: Allworth Press.

Hollis, R. (1994) *Graphic Design: A Concise History*, London: Thames & Hudson.

hooks, b. (1992) *Black Looks: Race and Representation*, Boston, Mass.: South End Press.

Howard, A. (1997) 'There is Such a Thing as Society', in Bierut, M., Drenttel, W., Heller, S. and Holland, D. K. (eds) *Looking Closer 2: Critical Writings on Graphic Design*, New York: Allworth Press.

Ivinski, P. A. (1997) 'Women Who Turn the Gaze Around', in Bierut, M., Drenttel, W., Heller, S. and Holland, D. K. (eds) *Looking Closer 2: Critical Writings on Graphic Design*, New York: Allworth Press.

Jameson, F. (1971) *Marxism and Form*, Princeton, NJ: Princeton University Press.

—— (1984) 'Postmodernism, or the Cultural Logic of Late Capitalism', *New Left Review*, 146: 53–92.

—— (1991) *Postmodernism, or, The Cultural Logic of Late Capitalism*, London: Verso.

Jenks, C. (ed.) (1995) *Visual Culture*, London: Routledge.

—— (ed.) (1998) *Core Sociological Dichotomies*, London: Sage.

Jhally, S. (1990) *The Codes of Advertising*, London: Routledge.

Jobling, P. and Crowley, D. (1996) *Graphic Design: Reproduction and Representation since 1800*, Manchester: Manchester University Press.

Jones, J. (2004) 'Bold, Graphic, Subversive – But Bad Art', *Guardian*, 16 March: 3.

Kalman, T. (1991) 'Good History Bad History', *Design Review*, 1(1): 48–57.

BIBLIOGRAPHY

—— (1997) 'Photography, Morality and Benetton', in Bierut, M., Drenttel, W., Heller, S. and Holland, D. K. (eds) *Looking Closer 2: Critical Writings on Graphic Design*, New York: Allworth Press.

Kalman, T., Miller, J. A. and Jakobs, K. (1994) 'Good History/Bad History', in Bierut, M., Drenttel, W., Heller, S. and Holland, D. K. (eds) *Looking Closer: Critical Writings on Graphic Design*, New York: Allworth Press.

Kinross, R. (1989) 'The Rhetoric of Neutrality', in Margolin, V. (ed.) *Design Discourse: History/Theory/Criticism*, Chicago, Ill.: University of Chicago Press.

—— (1997) 'Fellow Readers: Notes on Multiplied Language', in Bierut, M., Drenttel, W., Heller, S. and Holland, D. K. (eds) *Looking Closer 2: Critical Writings on Graphic Design*, New York: Allworth Press.

—— (1998) 'Introduction to the English Language Edition', in Tschichold, J. (1998) *The New Typography*, Berkeley, Calif.: University of California Press.

Kirwan-Taylor, H. (2004) 'Art by Design', *ArtReview*, 55(February): 48–53.

Klein, N. (2000) *No Logo*, London: Flamingo.

Kress, G. and van Leeuwen, T. (1996) *Reading Images: The Grammar of Visual Design*, London: Routledge.

Kruger, B. (1983) *We Won't Play Nature to your Culture*, London: ICA Publications.

Lavin, I. (ed.) (1995) *Meaning in the Visual Arts: A View from the Outside*, Princeton, NJ: Institute for Advanced Study.

Lavin, M. (2001) *Clean New World: Culture, Politics and Graphic Design*, Cambridge, Mass.: MIT Press.

Leach, E. (1970) *Lévi-Strauss*, London: Fontana.

Leiss, W., Kline, S. and Jhally, S. (1990) *Social Communication in Advertising*, London: Routledge.

Lionni, L. (1997) 'The Experience of Seeing', in Heller, S. and Finamore, M. (eds) *Design Culture: An Anthology of Writing from the AIGA Journal of Graphic Design*, New York: Allworth Press.

Lister, M. (ed.) (1995) *The Photographic Image in Digital Culture*, London: Routledge.

Livingston, A. and Livingston, I. (2003) *The Thames & Hudson Dictionary of Graphic Design and Designers*, London: Thames & Hudson.

Loos, A. (1997) *Ornament and Crime: Selected Essays*, Riverside, Calif.: Ariadne Press.

Lunn, E. (1985) *Marxism and Modernism*, London: Verso.

Lupton, E. (1989) 'Reading Isotype', in Margolin, V. (ed.) *Design Discourse: History/Theory/Criticism*, Chicago, Ill.: University of Chicago Press.

Lupton, E. and Miller, J. A. (1997) 'Critical Way Finding', in Bierut, M., Drenttel, W., Heller, S. and Holland, D. K. (eds) *Looking Closer 2: Critical Writings on Graphic Design*, New York: Allworth Press.

—— (1999) *Design Writing Research: Writing on Graphic Design*, London: Phaidon.

McCarron, C. (2001) 'First Things First: A Second Look', in Holland, D. K. (ed.) *Design Issues: How Graphic Design Informs Society*, New York: Allworth Press.

McCoy, K. (1988) 'Graphic Design: Sources of Meaning in Word and Image', *Word and Image*, 4(1): 116–20.

—— (1994) 'Rethinking Modernism, Revising Functionalism', in Bierut, M., Drenttel, W., Heller, S. and Holland, D. K. (eds) *Looking Closer: Critical Writings on Graphic Design*, New York: Allworth Press.

—— (1997) 'Countering the Tradition of the Apolitical Designer', in Bierut, M., Drenttel, W., Heller, S. and Holland, D. K. (eds) *Looking Closer 2: Critical Writings on Graphic Design*, New York: Allworth Press.

—— (2001) 'American Graphic Design Expression: The Evolution of American Typography', in Heller, S. and Ballance, G. (eds) *Graphic Design History*, New York: Allworth Press.

BIBLIOGRAPHY

McDermott, C. (1992) *Essential Design*, London: Bloomsbury Press.

MacDonald, M. (1995) *Representing Women: Myths of Femininity in the Popular Media*, London: Hodder Arnold.

Mackintosh, A. (1990) 'Symbolism and Art Nouveau', in Britt, D. (ed.) *Modern Art*, London: Thames & Hudson.

McLoughlin, L. (2000) *The Language of Magazines*, London: Routledge.

McLuhan, M. and Fiore, Q. (2001) *War and Peace in the Global Village*, Corte Madera, Calif.: Ginko Press.

McRobbie, A. (1998) *British Fashion Design*, London: Routledge.

Margolin, V. (ed.) (1989) *Design Discourse: History/Theory/Criticism*, Chicago, Ill.: University of Chicago Press.

—— (1994) 'Narrative Problems of Graphic Design History', *Visible Language*, 28(3): 233–43.

—— (2001) 'Construction Work', in Heller, S. and Ballance, G. (eds) *Graphic Design History*, New York: Allworth Press.

Margolin, V. and Buchanan, R. (1995) *The Idea of Design*, Cambridge, Mass.: MIT Press.

Marx, K. (1973) *Grundrisse*, Harmondsworth: Penguin.

Marx, K. and Engels, F. (1968) *Selected Works in One Volume*, London: Lawrence & Wishart.

—— (1970) *The German Ideology*, ed. and introd. C. J. Arthur, London: Lawrence & Wishart.

—— (1985) *The Communist Manifesto*, London: Penguin Classics.

Meggs, P. B. (1983) *A History of Graphic Design*, New York: Viking.

—— (1992) *Type and Image: The Language of Graphic Design*, New York: John Wiley.

—— (1997a) 'Saul Bass on Corporate Identity; Interview by Philip B. Meggs', in Heller, S. and Finamore, M. (eds) *Design Culture: An Anthology of Writing from the AIGA Journal of Graphic Design*, New York: Allworth Press.

—— (1997b) 'Mondrian as a Marketing Tool', in Heller, S. and Finamore, M. (eds) *Design Culture: An Anthology of Writing from the AIGA Journal of Graphic Design*, New York: Allworth Press.

—— (2001a) 'For the Voice', in Heller, S. and Ballance, G. (eds) *Graphic Design History*, New York: Allworth Press.

—— (2001b) 'The Rise and Fall of Design at a Great Corporation', in Heller, S. and Ballance, G. (eds) *Graphic Design History*, New York: Allworth Press.

Miller, J. A. and Lupton, E. (1994) 'A Natural History of Typography', in Bierut, M., Drenttel, W., Heller, S. and Holland, D. K. (eds) *Looking Closer: Critical Writings on Graphic Design*, New York: Allworth Press.

Mills, M. (1994) 'The (Layered) Vision Thing', in Bierut, M., Drenttel, W., Heller, S. and Holland, D. K. (eds) *Looking Closer: Critical Writings on Graphic Design*, New York: Allworth Press.

Mitchell, W. J. T. (1986) *Iconology*, Chicago, Ill.: University of Chicago Press.

—— (1994) *Picture Theory*, Chicago, Ill.: University of Chicago Press.

—— (1995a) 'Interdisciplinarity and Visual Culture', *Art Bulletin*, 77(4): 540–4.

—— (1995b) 'What is Visual Culture?', in Lavin, I. (ed.) *Meaning in the Visual Arts: A View from the Outside*, Princeton, NJ: Institute for Advanced Study.

Modleski, T. (ed.) (1986) *Studies in Entertainment: Critical Approaches to Mass Culture*, Bloomington, Ind.: Indiana University Press.

Morgan, J. and Welton, P. (1986) *See What I Mean: An Introduction to Visual Communication*, London: Edward Arnold.

O'Sullivan, T., Hartley, J., Saunders, D., Montgomery, M. and Fiske, J. (1994) *Key Concepts in Communication and Cultural Studies*, London: Routledge.

Panofsky, E. (1955) *Meaning in the Visual Arts*, London: Penguin.

BIBLIOGRAPHY

Pavitt, J. (ed.) (2000a) *Brand.New*, London: V&A Publications.

—— (2000b) 'In Goods We Trust?', in Pavitt, J. (ed.) *Brand.New*, London: V&A Publications.

Peirce, C. S. (1955) *Philosophical Writings of Peirce*, New York: Dover.

Popeau, J. (1998) 'Race/Ethnicity', in Jenks, C. (ed.) *Core Sociological Dichotomies*, London: Sage.

Poynor, R. (1994) 'Type and Deconstruction in the Digital Era', in Bierut, M., Drenttel, W., Heller, S. and Holland, D. K. (eds) *Looking Closer: Critical Writings on Graphic Design*, New York: Allworth Press.

—— (1998) *Design without Boundaries: Visual Communication in Transition*, London: Booth Clibborn.

—— (2003) *No More Rules: Graphic Design and Postmodernism*, London: Lawrence King.

Rand, P. and Rand, A. (1999) 'Advertisement: Ad Vivum or Ad Hominem?', in Bierut, M., Helfland, J., Heller, S. and Poyner, R. (eds) *Looking Closer 3: Classic Writings on Graphic Design*, New York: Allworth Press.

Robertson, R. (1990) 'Mapping the Global Condition: Globalisation as the Central Concept', in Featherstone, M. (ed.) *Global Culture: Nationalism, Globalization and Modernity*, London: Sage.

Rock, M. (1994) 'Can Design be Socially Responsible?', in Bierut, M., Drenttel, W., Heller, S. and Holland, D. K. (eds) *Looking Closer: Critical Writings on Graphic Design*, New York: Allworth Press.

Rockwell, T. (ed.) (1988) *The Best of Norman Rockwell*, Philadelphia, Pa: Courage.

Roque, G. (2001) 'The Advertising of Magritte / The Magritte in Advertising', in Heller, S. and Ballance, G. (eds) *Graphic Design History*, New York: Allworth Press.

Saussure, F. de (1974) *Course in General Linguistics*, Glasgow: Fontana/Collins.

Schroeder, J. (2002) *Visual Consumption*, London: Routledge.

Shannon, C. and Weaver, W. (1949) *The Mathematical Theory of Communication*, Champaign, Ill.: University of Illinois Press.

Sontag, S. (1970) 'Posters: Advertisement, Art, Political Artifact, Commodity', in Bierut, M., Helfland, J., Heller, S. and Poyner, R. (eds) (1999) *Looking Closer 3: Classic Writings on Graphic Design*, New York: Allworth Press.

Storey, J. (1993) *An Introductory Guide to Cultural Theory and Popular Culture*, Hemel Hempstead: Harvester Wheatsheaf.

Thomas, H. and Walsh, D. F. (1998) 'Modernity/Postmodernity', in Jenks, C. (ed.) *Core Sociological Dichotomies*, London: Sage.

Thomson, P. (1972) *The Grotesque*, London: Methuen.

Timmers, M. (ed.) (1998) *The Power of the Poster*, London: V&A Publishing.

Tschichold, J. (1998) *The New Typography*, Berkeley, Calif.: University of California Press.

Van den Berghe, P. L. (1981) *The Ethnic Phenomenon*, New York: Elsevier.

Vignelli, M. (1994) 'Long Live Modernism', in Bierut, M., Drenttel, W., Heller, S. and Holland, D. K. (eds) *Looking Closer: Critical Writings on Graphic Design*, New York: Allworth Press.

Walker, J. A. (1983) *Art in the Age of Mass Media*, London: Pluto Press.

—— (1989) *Design History and the History of Design*, London: Pluto Press.

Ward, O. (2004) 'What's the Use of Art?', *ArtReview*, 55(February): 61–5.

Washington, M. Y. (2001) 'Souls on Fire', in Heller, S. and Ballance, G. (eds) *Graphic Design History*, New York: Allworth Press.

Wells, M. (2001) 'Channel 4's "Go on, jump" Advert Rapped', *Guardian*, 21 February.

Wernick, A. (1994) *Promotional Culture: Advertising, Ideology and Symbolic Expression*, London: Sage.

Wheeler, A. (1997) 'If It's Not in the Dictionary, It's Not a Real Word', in Heller, S. and Finamore, M. (eds) *Design Culture: An Anthology of Writing from the AIGA Journal of Graphic Design*, New York: Allworth Press.

BIBLIOGRAPHY

Wild, L. (1997) 'Art and Design: Lovers or Just Good Friends?', in Heller, S. and Finamore, M. (eds) *Design Culture: An Anthology of Writing from the AIGA Journal of Graphic Design*, New York: Allworth Press.

Wildbur, P. and Burke, M. (1998) *Information Graphics*, London: Thames & Hudson.

Willans, G. and Searle, R. (1999) *Molesworth*, Harmondsworth: Penguin.

Williams, R. (1961) *The Long Revolution*, Harmondsworth: Penguin.

—— (1980) *Problems in Materialism and Culture*, London: Verso.

—— (1981) *Culture*, London: Fontana.

Williamson, J. (1986) '. . . But I Know What I Like', in Williamson, J., *Consuming Passions: The Dynamics of Popular Culture*, London: Marion Boyars.

Winkler, D. (1994) 'Morality and Myth: The Bauhaus Reassessed', in Bierut, M., Drenttel, W., Heller, S. and Holland, D. K. (eds) *Looking Closer: Critical Writings on Graphic Design*, New York: Allworth Press.

Wolff, J. (1981) *The Social Production of Art*, London: Macmillan.

Wozencroft, J. (1988) *The Graphic Language of Neville Brody*, New York: Rizzoli.

—— (1994) *The Graphic Language of Neville Brody 2*, New York: Rizzoli.

Wright, M. I. (2003) *You Back the Attack! We'll Bomb Who We Want!*, New York: Seven Stories Press.

INDEX

Numbers in *italic* indicate an illustration.

and graphic design 81
and modernist graphic design 132–3
Carson, David 4, 74, 143
cartoons 64–5, 81
Cassandre, A. M. 131
Cheret, Jules 114
childhood 68–71
children's magazines 102–4
christianity 61
Clark, Kenneth 66
client 170
code/s 26–8
  cultural 27, 82
  encoder/decoder 21
  highway 27, 34
  postmodern 146
Colors magazine 89
comics
  Find Out! 102–4, *103*
  2000AD 46, *47*
commerce, graphic design and 162
communication 7, 67, 85
  as cultural production 170–2
  and culture 67, 170–2
  defined 18
  failure 24
  and globalisation 156
  neutrality of 19
  and postmodernism 155
  semiological model 9, 24–8
  sender/receiver model 9, 18–25
  and signifying system 67
  as social production 61, 67
  theory 18–24
  visual 11
connotation 35–8, 70
  and communication 37
  and construction of identity 36
consumption 7, 75ff., 80
  and globalisation 153ff.
  and politics 76ff.
  see also anti-consumption
contextual studies 58
corporate identity 75, 130–4, 136
Cranbrook Academy 148, *149*
Crumb, Robert 64
cultural function 68ff.
cultural identity
  constructed by graphic design 36ff.,
    82ff., 87
culture
  art and design as 165–7
  as communication 67, 171–2

and connotation 36ff.
as 'context' of graphic design 66–8
and creativity 171–2
defined 66–7
global 151–60
jamming 79–80, 81
multilinear conception of 67–8
as signifying system 67, 75, 90
unilinear conception of 66–7
cut and paste 116

deconstruction 147–50, *149*, 161
decoration 15
  see also ornament
Depero, Fortunato 124, 136
Derrida, Jacques 19, 25, 140–2, 161
design
  and function 173
  and individual expression 164–5,
    167–9, 178
designer 164
Deutsche Werkbund 124
Diesel clothing 74
Dwiggins, William Addison 2–3
Dysphasia typeface 144, *145*

Earls, Elliott 144, *145*
economics 12, 75
  as 'context' of graphic design 75ff.
education
  design 75
Einstein, Albert 121, 143
ekphrasis 56
ethnicity/race 82, 85–92, 109
  and advertising 88ff.
  defined 85–6
  and illustration 86ff.
  and meaning 25

fashion 84, 88–9
femininity *see* gender
Find Out! comic 102–4
'First Things First 2000' 79
Fiske, John 20ff.
form/function 114, 136, 174
Foucault, Michel 49ff.
Fougasse (Bird, C. K.) 64
Fraktur typeface 127, *128*, 140
framing 44
function 22, 126
  aesthetic 13
  cultural 66–71
  decorative 15

s are to be ret..ned on or b...